A DIVA IS THE CEO OF HER LIFE
AND SHE'S NOT ABOUT TO LET IT BECOME
A NONPROFIT ORGANIZATION!

Have you lost your moxie or your courage? Is all that's left in your life an emptiness that becomes filled with the daily "must-do" routine? Well c'mon, you gorgeous Diva, rip off those control-top stockings, leave those excuses by the wayside, and jump into the sparkling bubble bath of life—it feels great!

• FIND YOUR DIVA ROOTS: Gauge your current stage of Divadom by checking where you are along the Diva Contentment Continuum. Are you already Divalicious? A Diva-in-waiting? A Diva Wanna-Be? Or a dire Diva Emergency?

• DISCOVER THE FIVE CORE ELEMENTS OF DIVA STYLE: The Power Diva, The Glamour Diva, The Fun Diva, The Rock Star Diva, and The Sexy Diva.

• GET A SCRUMPTIOUS DIVA REALITY CHECK: Create a Diva Pie Chart—using a real pie, of course—to find out what matters in your world, both inside and out.

• EXPAND YOUR CAPACITY TO LOVE: Learn how a Diva forgives her mistakes and others' because she loves herself and those around her.

I AM DIVA! will help you see what's possible and ignite the fury of your passion for life, love, laughter, and happiness. It's all yours for the taking, Diva. So go out and charm the world!

I AM DIVA!

Every Woman's Guide to Outrageous Living

ELENA BATES

MAUREEN O'CREAN

MOLLY THOMPSON

CARILYN VAILE

ILLUSTRATIONS BY BRENDA DELA CERNA

WARNER BOOKS

An AOL Time Warner Company

Warner Books, Inc., 1271 Avenue of the Americas, New York, NY 10020

Visit our Web site at www.twbookmark.com.

An AOL Time Warner Company

Printed in the United States of America

First Printing: April 2003

10   9   8   7   6   5   4   3   2   1

Library of Congress Cataloging-in-Publication Data

I am diva! : every woman's guide to outrageous living / Elena Bates ... [et al.].
        p. cm.
    Includes bibliographical references.
    ISBN 0-446-67955-0
        1. Women — Psychology. 2. Women — Conduct of life. 3. Self-realization. I. Bates,
    Elena
HQ1206.I5 2003
305.42—dc21   2002033126

Book Design by Mada Design, Inc./NYC

Cover design by Jon Valk

To the women we know and those we don't. We're all gorgeous, fabulous, inspirational, scintillating babes who have the possibility of achieving our wildest dreams. Enjoy your journey to being totally, outrageously self-expressed!

– The Four Divas

Acknowledgments

$\mathcal{W}$hile we may never know where we will end up at the beginning of a journey, one thing is certain: We will never ever undertake it alone. We are so grateful for the kindness, generosity, patience, and talent of those who aided us in the manifestation of this book. We applaud our fabulous Diva Editrix Extraordinaire, Caryn Karmatz Rudy, who believed in us from the very beginning. Thank you Caryn for all your inspiration and guidance along this fabulous and educational road to Divadom. Your name may not be on the cover, but you are certainly felt throughout this book. Thank you so much for sharing our vision and for challenging us to see the even bigger one. You took our diamond in the rough and polished it to a brilliant shine.

To Diva Sarah Ban Breathnach for your wild enthusiasm, vivacious giggles, gigantic vision, gracious and generous words. You are our source of amazing support and inspiration. Thank you for believing in us. To our Divo agent, Jonathan Diamond, you know diamonds are definitely a Diva's best friend. Thank you so much for making our dream possible, for your dry wit, attention to detail, and level head in the midst of six Divas (Caryn and Sandy included)!

To Jake Morrissey, for your request for depth, substance, and research, which shaped today's book. To Brenda Dela Cerna for your beautiful and heartfelt illustrations that brighten the entire book. Thank you, Molly Chehak, for your Diva-style organization and fabulous attention to detail. Thank you Laura Jorstad and Penina Sacks for your marvelous care of our manuscript. You make us look so good in print. To the talented art team of Brigid Pearson and Jackie Meyer, thanks for putting us in the "pink." And to our fabulous Warner sales team, thanks for believing in us and bringing our fun to the women of the world—our tiaras are tipped to you. To Kevin Cornwall for capturing our original visions in art form and Jack Walser of Walser's in Torrance, California, for his creative computer prowess and for guiding and assisting us from the very beginning. Our original proposal would have never looked so good if it weren't for him. To Mike Williams, thank you for creating a Web site that captures our true Diva essence on the Worl Wide Web. To our dear friends, the Diva Speed Readers for their honest feedback and reducing a year of reading to four weeks; we are forever in your debt. To Landmark Education and the Communication Program, for the structure and belief that life is a game to be played. Our book is the result of one such game. And, finally, being Divas ruled by spontaneity, we tend to run quite close to our deadlines, so The Four Divas thank FedEx for giving us our world on time!

• • •

I want to acknowledge my loving husband, Hal, for his endless support, patience, and understanding throughout this long process. A special thanks for all the nights I came home and you had dinner waiting for me. You are the best! To my son, Jason, and daughter-in-law, Erlynn, who never faltered in their enthusiasm, my special cheering section. To my granddaughters, Anne Janelle and Remy Taelyn, for always reminding me to play and have fun and take pleasure in the smallest of things. To my brother, Gary, and son-in-law, Kevin, for their loving encouragement. To my friends who were sometimes neglected while I was writing, but loved me anyway. To Brenda and Kristi, for keeping things running smoothly in the office while I was at meetings and rewrites. And FrancisRyan, who came in to help them so the apparel business could grow. Most important, to my daughter and business partner, Carilyn, a gigantic thank-you for your inspiration, and for holding the vision for this book and pushing us along to completion. It means so much that you include me in your outrageous projects. Thanks, also, for your sense of style and fun and for keeping me "cool."

— *Elena*

• • •

To the Divas and Divos in my life who lovingly took such great care of me, in total Diva style over the last three years. I am so grateful, especially to my sons, Patrick Munger, for your unwavering belief in my ability to do anything in the world under any circumstances and Alex Crean, for a belief in me so strong and grounded that you never question my ability to do anything. To my lifeline, Maria Del Cid, I do not know what I would do without you. I love you so much. To my Divos Jonathan Vakneen and Steven Griffith, thank you for teaching me that my dream counts too. To my dear new friends Patty Ellis, Michelle Goodlett, Sandy Heeley, and Loni Dietz for all the pickups, car pools, and deadline sleepovers and to my dear old friends for the late-night phone calls of support. To my sister, Sarah Ban Breathnach, thank you for your belief and support. I couldn't have done it without you. To my brother Sean Crean, thanks for staying so close to me that Maine seems like it is just next door. To my brother Patrick Crean, who never ceases to believe in me, no matter what, thank you will never cut it.

But most of all, I must acknowledge that Carilyn Vaile is the true reason that you hold this book. Unbeknownst to her, Carilyn, with her passion, insistence, persistence, charm, and dream to be a spokesperson for Rolex, beguiled me into revoking a lifelong vow never to be in the public eye. This vow, cast in stone on that fateful eve of my debut as a performance soloist in Westbury, New York, when all thirty pearl buttons went flying off the bodice of my dress as I inhaled to hit the high note of "Exodus." Before a crowd of hundreds at the ripe old age of thirteen, I decided never to risk in public again. Thank God for Carilyn—may all her dreams and yours come true.

— *Maureen*

• • •

To Scott, my Sweetie, thank you for challenging me to dig deeper and aim higher, and for nurturing, loving, and supporting me to pursue my dreams; you make me feel like the Queen of the Universe every single day! To Jeffrey, my medium Sweetie, thank you for being the amazing kid you are and for teaching me the ropes of being a parent. And to my two littlest Sweeties, Avery and Jack, you have added an entirely new and truly joyous dimension to my world that I never even knew was possible; thank you for becoming part of this journey and for teaching me to slow down and enjoy the ride. I can't wait to discover the universe with both of you!

I would not be where I am today without the strong values and importance of family bonding my parents instilled in me all those years ago. My deepest gratitude and appreciation go to my biggest fan club, my parents, Susan and Frazier Reams, who always believed in me and knew I was a Diva long before I did! And to my favorite brothers, Eddy, David, and John, and their families, especially Kara and my nieces, Christy, Catherine, Meryl, and Hanna. Without all of your love, support, and occasional teasing, I would not have had the courage to follow my own little star! To my aunt Sandy and cousin Lisa, as well as the rest of my Diva/Divo universe in the Reams/Rodawig clans—there is no one more enthusiastic, fabulous, and outrageous than all of you! And thank you to Jan Bock for her love, generosity, and support; it doesn't go unnoticed.

To all my Divalicious friends around the globe who love my quirks and Mollyisms, thank you for the never-ending support and encouragement that keep me lit up and inspired to have fun every day. Special Diva love to Cyndi, Gina, Erica, Kirste, the Margarets, Corinne, Charlie, Sabrina, JJ, Heidi, and all my other Sweet Petunias, Cupcakes, and Buttercups whom I love and adore. For any others I haven't named, please know that you also make an ongoing difference in my life.

And finally, thank you to Carilyn, Elena, and Maureen for constantly loving, laughing, crying, and growing with me; this has been such a fabulous ride and I am so grateful that we took it together!

— Molly

. . .

To my beautiful daughter, Remy, for always making me stop and smell the flowers and for constantly showing me the ways of a Diva. For me this book is dedicated to you, my little baby bear. Thank you for being in my life and for reminding me what life is really about. I love you, you rascal. To my husband, Kevin, for conquering his rational, left-brained mentality and giving me the freedom to find and live this wild Diva dream. Thank you for loving me, for making me laugh, for believing in me, and for your commitment to us. I love you.

Thanks, Mom, for raising me to be the woman I am today. Thank you for believing in me, for encouraging me to try new things, and for always being there for me when I did. Thanks, Dad, for always looking out for me, encouraging my creativity, and teaching me to dream big. To my bro, Jason, thank you for your sense of humor and your impeccable timing with it. You are the best "big" brother. To my sister-in-law, Erlynn, thank you for sharing yourself with me and for hopping on the Diva train with us. To my niece, Anne Janelle, thank you for brightening my days with your unconditional love and unending enthusiasm. To my cousin Sharon, who introduced me at a tender young age to the fabulous world of outrageousness, thank you! Long live purple hair and GPPs! Thank you so much, Hal Bates, for making my dreams possible with your contributions and for encouraging Mom to go after her dreams. Thank you, Uncle Gary, for sharing your creative spirit with me. To Ginger, for opening my eyes when I couldn't see my greatness. To Michelle, thank you for your openness, your insight, and for always being up for anything!

Thank you from the bottom of my heart to Kristi Beisel and Brenda Dela Cerna for always being one step ahead of me and for "T. C. B.'ing," ASAP, 24/7. You are my angels. Thank you for keeping me sane! To Elvia Rivera, thank you for taking such good, loving care of my baby bear. You are awesome. I could never have done this without you! To all my Diva Posse of family and friends, thank you for recognizing, encouraging, and often joining in my need to be outrageous!

— Carilyn

...

To my brother Pat—the apple never falls far from the tree. Thank you for teaching me the power of believing.

— *Maureen*

Contents

CONTENTS

CONTENTS

CONTENTS

The Legend of Diva

Once upon a time in a land not so far away two sisters were born: Cinderella and Divarella. Although most of us have heard Cindy's story, Diva's story has remained a mystery . . . until now.

From the very beginning both girls were taught how to be "proper" ladies, how to act, what was expected of them. They learned how to be good and appropriate, how to be patient and let the world come to them. There was pressure to conform and not to rock the boat. Day after day, once the chores were finished, Diva watched as Cindy would retreat into her fantasy world. Cindy was happy pretending to dance with her prince, and spent hours talking to the birds and mice about her dream man, telling them, "Someday, he will come." Diva tried to pretend, too, but instead of making her happy, it made her anxious. Where Cindy was singing, Diva was screaming.

Over the years Cindy seemed to relinquish herself more and more fully to her make-believe world, letting the real one simply pass her by. Diva tried to get Cindy to explore the outside world, beyond the gates of their small town, but Cindy refused. She was happy waiting for things to get better, dreaming about her prince sweeping her off her feet and out of her hellish existence. It was not that way for Diva, who felt her discontent growing slowly over time. One day their stepsister burst into the tiny room Diva and Cindy shared and demanded that one of them iron her dress immediately. Cindy jumped up and snatched the dress out of her hands, always eager to please. Diva, however, stayed right where she was. She had had enough.

Something inside Divarella began to stir. She felt as if she didn't belong to the destiny to which she seemed predetermined. She felt lost. It had been deeply ingrained in her to "do the right thing," but she began to wonder if that was truly her heart's desire. *Sure, Cindy will get the hunky man and the beautiful glass slipper*, Diva thought to herself, *but there's got to be so much more out there*. She longed to experience life, not dream about it. Diva sensed that the life that had been planned for her would be fine but somehow, "fine" didn't cut it anymore. Predictability didn't appeal to her, nor did settling, and certainly not being at the beck and call of anyone, especially those who were mean to her. Diva wanted to learn more about herself and discover—or better yet, create—who *Diva* really was. As she slowly took her hair down from her tight bun, she also felt herself unwind. She was no longer willing to wait around and to live her life by others' expectations. While she was tempted by promises of safety, security, and a "good" (read *predictable, boring*) life, Diva couldn't ignore the little voice in her head that started as a whisper and steadily grew louder until it sounded to her like a choir of the purest voices singing, "I am sensuous, succulent, passionate; I am outrageous, electrifying, fabulous; *I Am Diva!*"

Diva felt the surge of emotions in her body. She began to dance a wild and freeing dance of sensuality. Cindy was shocked as Diva swayed her hips back and forth to the music that only she could hear. Diva stripped off her torn and tattered dress and examined her body in the mirror for the very first time. She liked what she saw. Cindy was speechless and covered her head with a blanket. "Cindy, could a life of stellar proportions be possible?" Diva exclaimed as she strutted back and forth across the room in her imaginary high heels. She didn't know the answer, and Cindy was too paralyzed with fear to speak. Diva decided that taking the risk to find out who she was was worth the adventure.

And with that thought, she shook her hair free and did the unthinkable: She took scissors to her flowing locks. Her mother had always told her she must keep her hair long, because that's how men liked it, but what a nuisance it was now. As she threw the first cut of her hair to the floor, she felt her power surge through her body, her Diva power. Halfway through the process of cutting her hair she looked in the mirror and got a glimpse of a woman with chic tousled hair—a welcome change from that straitlaced bun, no matter what her mother or anyone else thought.

Now she was ready to begin her quest to start creating her own destiny based on her own rules and definitions of what pleased her. She saw a glimmer of what was possible in the mirror, and it ignited into a fury of passion for life, love, laughter, and happiness. What had seemed a distant, blurry, and unattainable fantasy suddenly came into sharp focus. For the first time it seemed not only possible, but probable; Diva had stumbled onto the greatest untapped natural resource anybody had ever seen: her inner self, her Diva self! "This is *it!*" she exclaimed. No more would her self-expression be squashed by the rules of society or her creativity suppressed by the naysayers; from here on out she would live by her own rules of outrageous self-expression and unlimited possibilities. She would live the delicious, juicy, over-the-top, off-the-charts, spectacular life she had previously only dreamed of. She would never be bored again.

But in the midst of her epiphany, a glimmer of self-doubt set in. Scrutinizing her reflection in the mirror, she became horrified. Just look at the mess she'd made! Her hair was a fright—half long, half short. The "Anti-Diva" within her showed her ugly face for the first (but not necessarily the last) time as she shouted, "What have I done?" Diva quickly decided that she needed help, and turned to her beloved—if somewhat repressed—sister. Cindy heard the urgency in Diva's voice and rushed over to finish the job. "You gorgeous thing you!" Cindy cried as she set eyes on her sister. "Two more snips and you'll be a knockout."

Diva jumped up and hugged Cindy. "Cindy, I want you to know how wonderful this feels," said Diva. And although Cindy declined to cut her own hair, Diva enthusiastically set out on a mission to share her "treasures" with gal pals and support them in their mission and commitment to living spectacular, stellar, joyous lives.

Like a sponge she soaked up qualities she admired in others, gaining momentum along the way. She learned something from every experience, from every encounter with a friend or stranger. Diva learned how to tap into her inner resources, her inner fire, passion, zest for life, love, and pursuit of happiness. She found that no matter where she was, she felt energized. For the first time in her life she was truly, deeply gratified, and that deep satisfaction quickly spread to others.

"I've unlocked the secrets to pleasure, fun, freedom, and passion!" she would rejoice. "Let me show you the way to Divadom!" Women everywhere followed her like the Pied Piper. Together they formed a village, which would later turn into a nation, a planet, and ultimately a universe of empowering, outrageous, fully expressed, joyous Divas!

Now it's your turn. For in this book we will share the secrets Divarella has taught us on our own quest to Divadom. So go ahead, turn the page, and let's begin!

The Divalution: Our Evolution to Diva

The future belongs to those who believe in the beauty of their dreams.
— ELEANOR ROOSEVELT

We all grow up wanting to be Cindy, to have that secure lifestyle, only to realize one day that there's something more to life out there. You get the promotion you were hoping for and then you realize it looks like more work with a new title, or you meet the man of your dreams and in three months you still feel unfulfilled. No matter when or where the feeling hits you, listen to it. That is Diva starting to stir. What is a Diva? She is the woman in you who wants to feel the joy of life down to her bones. Who wants to be the very best woman she can be, and to know the very fabric of her soul, so she's no longer indecisive or prone to living her life only to please others. She's balanced, giving and taking in equal proportions, for she knows that life is a flow of energy. Diva removes the blocks to receiving that we set in place so long ago, we probably don't even remember them. As women, we were designed to be cherished, to be adored, and to receive. Somehow, though, our generosity to others skewed the balance and we forgot that we needed to give to ourselves first, in order to have something left to give to others. Divas restore this balance. And what is *I Am Diva?* Why, nothing less than the quest to have it all: more fun, more passion, more happiness and fulfillment at every moment.

Our own quest for Diva began with Maureen—at fifty, a successful business consultant and president of her own corporation—starting her life over again in California. A divorced, single parent of two sons, she was overwhelmed by all her responsibilities and woke up with a start one day realizing the fun had somehow been sucked out of her life. Fueled with the desire to get it back, she committed herself to play a game she called I Am Diva: she would find ways to tap into the Diva she knew existed inside herself! She asked Carilyn, her role model for fun, to help her define, play, and win this game of creating the Diva. Carilyn, thirty-four, had a husband who loved her, a thriving fashion design and manufacturing business, many friends, and a close family, and yet she also felt unfulfilled; her passion for life had been lost. The spark that was ignited that dazzling Diva day with Maureen was a wake-up call for Carilyn, revealing the importance of friends and the difference they can make in our lives. Maureen and Carilyn were not alone.

Molly, thirty-seven, had recently left friends and family in the Midwest and moved to California, gotten married to Scott, become a parent to her husband's son, Jeffrey, changed careers, and longed to expand her family by having children of her own. She was searching for an avenue to fully express her humor, passion, and energy. Inspired by Maureen's and Carilyn's contagious self-expression and commitment to fun, she saw an opportunity to ramp up her life and joined these Diva sisters in their quest.

The trio also realized that there was a world of wisdom that was only available through life experience and that a guide through these areas of life's passages would be helpful to themselves and other women. So Elena, sixty—Carilyn's ever-encouraging and -supportive mother and business partner—was invited to join the quest. Excited by the opportunity for another adventure with her daughter, Elena joined in, bringing with her the wisdom, thoughts, and successes of being a mom, wife, grandmother, businesswoman, mother-in-law, and friend. She had experienced much of what life has to offer; she was at a perfect place in her journey, enjoying the fruits of her labor over the years, and became an invaluable resource for the group. The four charter Divas assembled, the group was complete, and together we embarked upon the journey that would provide the foundation for this book.

As we looked at what Diva meant to us, explored the qualities Divas possessed, and identified Divas in the world, we realized this enlightening information had to be shared beyond the confines of a game for one woman, or four. All women deserved this knowledge and deserved to play the Diva game. Spreading the word of Diva was a mission we passionately accepted; our fantasy was of women everywhere knowing and experiencing their beauty and magnificence—expressing it freely and outrageously! We began to imagine an entire world of Divas—a Divadom—and set out to make it happen.

We knew there would be challenges having four women collaborate, but we discovered that the rewards of friendship, accomplishment, and sharing of ourselves were fun, exciting, and enlightening. We learned how to be vulnerable with ourselves and each other, how to love our imperfections, how to support each other, and how to trust, deeply and powerfully, as we navigated the swirling waters of true intimacy. Along our journey together we experienced the thrill of being Diva, as well as the agony of her nemesis, "Anti-Diva"—the woman in all of us who stands in the way of our having everything we've always wanted. The Anti-Diva holds no room for possibility, fun, or confidence. Fortunately, through our experiences, The Four Divas have learned what triggers her as well as the tools to conquer her when she arrives.

This book is structured around fifty-two weeks, organized into thirteen sections designed to Unleash Your Diva! Some of the Diva lessons will fit you and your lifestyle, some won't. Some will be hidden messages for your soul that will be revealed to you when the time comes, some will remind you of the lessons that you have learned and your desire to pass your wisdom on to the next generation of Divas in your life.

The greatest lesson that we learned on this journey together is that we are all kindred spirits and, just like you, we run the gamut—single and married, thin and full figured, with children and without—so somewhere within our teachings we feel confident that you'll discover secrets to keep with you at all times and, we hope, trigger the Diva within you. We hope to inspire you to live a better life. Our fondest wish is for you to have fun now, always, and forever! That's it, no deep awakening (although it may happen), no quest for anything but your place of joy in who you are and what you're doing.

Divadom is accessible to anyone, and it's yours for the taking. So c'mon, you gorgeous Diva creatures, leave the excuses behind; it's time to rip off the panty hose and climb way out onto the skinny branches of life! We know the way and we can't wait to show it to you!

—The Four Divas: *Elena, Maureen, Molly, Carilyn*

I

DUSTING OFF THE DIVA

In order to change directions, you must first know where you are.
The time has come to rip off those control-top stockings
and jump on in; the water's warm!

The Journey to Divaness

You are an extraordinary woman, how can you expect to live an ordinary life?
—Louisa May Alcott

When I was a little girl, I believed I was special. I didn't know exactly what that meant other than a certainty that I had a precious gift to give the world. As I grew older, though, I didn't feel special anymore; I only felt different. I never seemed to belong, and like Cindy, I wanted more than anything not to be different anymore. In my thirties I worked endlessly to blend in with everyone else. It never worked. I don't know why I wasted all that time silencing my true self. I am different, I am special, and so are you.

How do you know? Well, have you ever reached a point in your life where you just wanted to slap yourself silly and scream, "*Wake up, girl!* Smell the coffee *and* the roses, read the writing on the wall, do anything, but please, please, please, not one more boring minute of life"? I know I have. I've spent years denying who I am, to the point that on many days I truly didn't know who I was anymore. Sometimes enough is just enough, and we wake up to find our life speeding past us as if it were on a turbo train.

I had one of those wake-up calls a few years ago when, in a swirl of emotions, fear, and excitement, my life landed in sunny California, like Dorothy's house in the Land of Oz. Full of expectations that life would be just grand now, thank you very much, I was astonished to find my new "Technicolor life" was still as dull as black and white—again. Really, how many times do we have to do the same things over and over again and get the same results? I had become a master of disguise. If things looked different, I convinced myself they were different. *Ooh*, here it is: a new man, a new job, a new diet, on and on and on. That is, until the day—which, by the way, *always* comes—when I recognized that it was my same old patterns returning. Apparently I had to repeat the past almost to infinity before I could discover my Diva roots.

I'd love to spare you some of that endless repetition. Maybe you're coming to this book late in the game and, like me, have done it wrong millions of times already. Maybe you're just starting out and want to avoid the pitfalls of doldrums living. No matter what your current status, you can make a turnaround now. How? First gauge your stage by checking where you are along the Diva Contentment Continuum. Answer the following questions, and yes, honesty is the best policy:

1. If you were to take your clothes off right now, the world would see:

    a. Your favorite matching bra and panties. You go, girl!

    b. Beautiful separate pieces, just not in the same color palette.

    c. Acceptable, clean white underwear with no noticeable holes.

    d. Stretched elastic in the panties, holes on the left cheek, and the wire out of the rim on one side of your bra.

2. Your girlfriend calls you on the spur of the moment and invites you out for dinner. You answer:

    a. "Great," whip a fabulous outfit together, and meet her in thirty minutes.

    b. "Can't, have to work late, can we reschedule?"

    c. "I'd love to but my hair's not done."

    d. "Sorry, I'm busy. I can't miss *Dawson's Creek* again!"

3. You've just met the most fabulous man at the coffee shop and he wants to walk you back to your office. Your first thought is:

    a. This is perfect; he'll get to see my favorite colors and flowers for future reference.

    b. I wish I'd tidied up my desk and put the nail polish away.

    c. I hope my boss isn't there to remind me about the report that's late.

    d. I don't want him to see my office: "Let's go to your office instead."

4. You're meeting some new friends for lunch. It's a very expensive restaurant, and you were expecting to go to the diner. When the menu comes, you think:

    a. No problem, I'll put the meal on my credit card, because I pay the balance off every month.

    b. I'll just have an appetizer; I think I have twenty bucks on me.

    c. I'll say I'm on a diet and have a salad.

    d. I'll use my debit card and hope I don't bounce another check.

5. You've been working at a feverish pace for the past few weeks. You finally have a day off, so you're going to:

    a. Go to the spa, get your nails done, and see an old friend.

    b. Sleep in and read a trashy romance novel.

    c. Run errands and get caught up on your mail.

    d. Make a few meals for the week and get caught up on the laundry.

Answer key for the Diva Contentment Continuum: Give yourself 20 points for each a, 15 points for each b, 10 points for each c, and 5 points for each d answer.

    100: Divalicious! Congratulations. You're on the right path. The Diva journey will simply enhance your pizzazz.

 80–99: Diva-in-Waiting. You have some great things going for you; all you need is a little polish on this Diamond in the Rough. The Diva journey will bring out your shine.

 70–89: Diva-Wanna-be. Your priorities are stretched to the max and you long to have fun. This book will put the zest back into your life.

  0–70: Diva Emergency. You give and you give and this is what you get? A life with too much stress and too little fun. Stay with us and by the end of the year you won't recognize yourself.

AND NOW, BACK TO ME!

My score on the Diva Contentment Continuum was a 25, so I decided it was time to start living as if this life weren't a practice session. I'd always believed that I was destined for more, but how could I break through all the obligations I'd accumulated? My time was overcommitted: to the Parent-Teacher Organization, and the church, and community service projects, and work, and Little League. It seemed like the same six women showed up for every project in town, and I was one of the six. Like Divarella, I longed for a strong voice to say, "No. Thank you very much, but No." I believe that all of us are special. Within each one of us is a tiny bud set to bloom, at a time that is uniquely ours. I don't know the exact moment of awakening for you, or for myself for that matter, but we're assured by the Legend of Diva that we will indeed blossom. We're also assured that we can't grow too old to bloom, thank God, for the spirit of our Diva is more resilient than our ovaries.

Over time, we begin to feel the stirring of our Diva. We become quietly disheartened with our trophies and gadgets and more in tune with seeking our own individual voices. It might come as quietly as the urge to take dancing lessons at the local high school, or change our hair color, or try a new style of clothing. It doesn't really matter how the bud begins to stir. It only matters that we nurture ourselves and give ourselves permission to burst with life.

One day, full of discontent, I thought, *What would a Diva do?* and my journey began. I began to seek out evidence of Divas. Whenever I felt powerless or helpless, I would imagine what Audrey Hepburn, or Madonna, or Oprah would do in the same situations. Sometimes it was Michael Jordan (representing my male energy, I'm sure). I made a collage of my "Divas and Divos" to inspire me to be more than I was being in that moment. I would actually visualize Audrey Hepburn, head held high, back straight, shoulders erect, and my demeanor would automatically shift. It worked every time.

As I started this journey filled with excitement, guess what showed up? Every area of my life where I was not living up to my full Diva potential. I would look at Madonna dressed in a fabulous outfit and ask myself, *Why did I listen to play-it-safe rules?* When I looked in the mirror, sure enough, I was dressed in my standard black outfit, which bored me to tears. Where was my self-expression and style? My clothing might have made me look thinner but it sure didn't lift my spirits—and that glumness in my reflection added more weight than any black pantsuit could hide. It was time for a change, a drastic change in my life. And my journey began, just like yours will today.

My greatest inspiration of all time comes from the movie *The Wizard of Oz*. At one point Dorothy says to Glinda, the Good Witch of the North, "How do I start?" The all-knowing Glinda lovingly gazes in the eyes of the distraught Dorothy and says, "It's best to start at the beginning."

You are off on the adventure of your lifetime. Enjoy!

— Maureen

To get you started on your journey, you'll want some basic supplies to record your fabulous transformation. We urge you to record your journey so that you will remember how far you've come. Buy a big, blank sketchpad or scrapbook—make sure it's acid-free paper so your diary will last. If you like, decorate it Diva-style, with glitter, velvet, or a boa trim. The purpose of the decorations is for you to be excited every time you pick it up. My Diva Diary is trimmed with a light pink marabou boa and it's delightful.

You'll also want to create a Diva Supply Box to help, so here's our suggested list of Diva supplies: glitter, glitter pens with feathers in your favorite colors, scissors, glue sticks (we like the ones that go on purple and turn invisible), sequins, invisible tape, highlighter pens in at least three colors, stickers for a job well done, and any little Diva specialties that you create.

*D*IVA DO'S FOR THE WEEK:

Every week we will list some Diva Do's to help you play—and win—the Diva game. This week's Do's help lay the foundation for your journey.

1. Make your own inspirational Diva collage. Identify your role models of Divine qualities. Look for love, passion, beauty, strength, power, vision, persistence, loyalty, grace, gentleness, courage, integrity, charisma, style, and authenticity. Find pictures in magazines of people who inspire you to cut out and put in your Diva Diary. Label each one with the quality you want, so you'll always remember why you chose this person.

2. Pick one quality you admire to focus on. Don't be discouraged; when you start this process, a cruel trick of fate is to show you every time you fall short of this quality. Take fifteen minutes each day to reflect on what will be present in your life if you have, for example, more grace.

3. Create a new action to integrate this quality into your life. When I practice gentleness, I speak softly and move slowly. When I first started I could only do it for a little while. Like muscles, we grow stronger with practice.

4. Before you go to bed at night, look at your collage to help you dream about what you desire. Keep a pen and paper handy to record your dreams when you wake up. You can transfer any special dreams into your Diva Diary later.

Most of all, enjoy your practices. If you stress, take the Diva Default—take a bubble bath instead.

*F*RIVOLOUS DIVA DO:

TRANSFORM YOURSELF—EVEN IF IT'S ONLY TEMPORARY. *Buy yourself some water transfer tattoos and put them in all your favorite risqué places. I put a red heart on my breast and felt truly "bad."*

Escaping the Dungeon

If it isn't fun, it won't get done.
— CYNTHIA ROWLEY

*A*s you look at your life right now, is your vantage point from atop the Diva's castle balcony basking in the sun with a babe-licious tan and a juicy cocktail, enjoying uninhibited fun and festivity? Or do you feel trapped way down in the dungeon, with loads of work to do, no time to do it, and not a peep of possibility for escape? . . . the dungeon? Surprise, surprise . . . Not to worry, ladies, the Divas have the magic key!

It seems before we realize our true Diva nature, we're condemned to waste our precious time on detrimental needs to please others, impress others, and live up to others' expectations. The more we do this, the more the pleasure in our lives slides its merry way down the toilet. All that's left is an emptiness that becomes filled with the daily "must-do" routine. The desire for individuality, excitement, and fun is lost and we are derailed off the life path our hearts intended to live. Now, don't fret, my pretties, the Diva knows what to do. *And,* if Divarella has taught us anything it's that the time is *now* to get back on track to fulfilling the life of our dreams, insert fun and adventure, and unleash the Diva within!

The first step is to commit yourself. No, not to the mental institution, which I know may seem more relevant, but instead to Diva—to *you.* A Diva is clear what she's committed to, and to her commitments she is faithful. You may feel like you are already committed to many things, but let's take a closer look. Are they commitments or obligations? There is a difference. A commitment is an expression of who you are—a representation of your individuality. It makes you feel good about yourself. An obligation, on the other hand, is something you do in order to please someone else, or to look good in someone else's eyes (your own eyes included). Obligations get in the way of the fun and dream fulfillment our commitments bring us.

Sometimes we need to break out of our everyday lives in order to truly prioritize our commitments. Many moons ago, just after college, my stepsister, Michelle, and I decided to drive across the country from California to get to the free condo that awaited us in Florida. It was simply a way to save on airfare; little did I know this trip would give me the experience of life's true potential. We stopped anywhere we wanted to with only a single mission: to eat at every Taco Bell we could find along the way. We experienced the lifestyles of different towns and states. In Oklahoma we almost had rifles pulled on us for videotaping three men sitting in front of their shack. We barely escaped jail for stealing gas when our little brown hatchback Honda, "Henri" (pronounced *en-REE—bien sur!*), was mistaken for the actual perpetrator's car. In Arkansas we bought housedresses circa 1950 for ninety-nine cents and drove to Texas videotaping ourselves the entire way. The video camera, squeezed between my legs, was running when we rode the largest roller coaster at Six Flags over Texas. To this day the tape of our screaming faces makes me laugh hysterically. We saw June bugs piled two feet high in a supermarket parking lot. We washed our dirty feet in toilets. We slept overnight in a Las Vegas hotel parking lot to save cash. We laughed and laughed and laughed. "Anything-goes" was the game and "Silliness" was its name!

When I returned home to my usual routine, my view of life had been altered. This "reality check" gave me the gift of recognizing the importance of fun and outrageousness in my life and granted me a resource to call on when I felt it slipping. A Diva's life and key to reaching the castle's balcony is her commitment to fun.

I began to use the memories of that fabulous, uninhibited adventure as what we Divas call a "fun-o-meter": a check-and-balance system for the fun factor in life. When life feels mundane I can remember that trip and am reminded of ways to insert fun back in. The importance of letting go of a tight schedule and fabricated demands and replacing or enhancing them with a few matters of insignificance and silliness becomes clear again. As long as my fun-o-meter stays high, so do my spirits!

We all have done something at one time or another that gave us an amazing feeling of freedom and self-expression. What was it? How did you feel? Use it as your own fun-o-meter, or create a new fun-o-meter measure. And as you build your life by trying new things, experimenting and exploring, remember to take stock. If your fun-o-meter is at zero it's time to sprinkle in some fun and wackiness. Of course, having fun doesn't mean a person doesn't go to work or have responsibilities; a true Diva knows how to bring fun to every area of her life, including the work and responsibilities she has chosen.

It's important on your Diva journey that you take this stand for *you* and the Diva's commitment to *fun!* You deserve to be happy in life and enjoy your every move. Give yourself permission. If you're not ready to give it to yourself yet, no problem, The Four Divas will do it for you! Fill out the slip, gals, 'cause we're giving you permission *right now* to have some wild fun, already! Place it where you will see it often; color it in if you want to—you deserve it, Diva!

—Carilyn

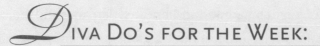

DIVA DO'S FOR THE WEEK:

1. It's time for your Diva Reality Check . . . create a Diva Pie Chart. What's a Diva Pie Chart? Because we are The Four Divas, it's against our beliefs to work with something as conventional as a normal pie chart. So Maureen came up with this Diva spin on pie charts—a real pie! Choose your favorite-flavored pie, one you've either baked or purchased. You're going to cut it into representative sections of your life. To get a true glimpse of how to slice the pie, take a look at where your time and energy are spent over the next couple of days. Are they going to obligations you feel from others, or to commitments that you're passionate about and that honor the Diva? Keep in mind that every pie is different, even if the categories are basically the same. For example, work may be obligation for some of us but a passionate commitment to others. For me, showering is sometimes an obligation (yes, I still do it), but for my husband it's part of nurturing the Diva (or "Divo," as we like to call our male counterparts). Then cut the pie into slices representing all the roles you play: Diva, mom, wife, lover, career woman, friend, daughter, housekeeper, et cetera. Eat the "Diva" section. Is that the smallest section? What a crime! Perhaps now you have some motivation to put yourself first, honor yourself and have some fun! The Diva's goal? To eat the whole pie, of course!

2. Make a sign that says ARE WE HAVING FUN YET? and place it on the fridge or in your daily calendar—wherever you will see it most—as a reminder of your commitment to fun.

3. Create your own fun-o-meter! Purchase fun and fanciful stickers and draw a thermometer-type shape in your Diva Diary. Label it with the five different levels of excitement, giving yourself the appropriate stickers in your calendar for each time you allow yourself some fun:

Sizzling	Steamy	Hot	Warm	Cool
5 stickers	4 stickers	3 stickers	2 stickers	1 sticker

Form a "fun habit": Every week that you give yourself twenty stickers, treat yourself to an extra-special reward (a Diva always rewards herself!). Mine? I get to indulge in my favorite pastime, shoe buying.

4. Have your friend take a Polaroid picture of you (or take one of each other). Sign and date it. This should prove to be quite a conversation piece and great for giggles in the fifty-one weeks to come as the Diva transformation unfolds!

ℱRIVOLOUS DIVA DO:

FOR A QUICK SHOT OF FUN AND SILLINESS, *perfect to escape any moment of monotony, jump up and down on your bed like you did when you were six.*

Defining the Diva in You

Far better it is to dare mighty things, to win glorious triumphs, even though checkered by failure . . .
than to take rank with those poor spirits who neither enjoy much nor suffer much,
because they live in a gray twilight that knows not victory nor defeat.
—THEODORE ROOSEVELT

Do you see the Diva in you? Look in the mirror, and look carefully. She's there in the reflection of the way we laugh; in the color we paint our nails; how our favorite outfit makes us feel; how our relationships are going; a secret that our best friend just told us. She's a delicate flower, a force to be reckoned with, a quiet, subtle presence—here to guide us through all the twists and turns and peaks and valleys. She's all of these things, and she's in all of us. And from time to time we need to stop and check in with her to see how our lives are going. Are we satisfied with our careers? Our images? How about our finances and our hair? Wherever you are on the Diva Contentment Continuum, breathe . . . deep breath in, and exhale. Now that you feel your blood pumping again, it's time to examine the Diva and her world to assess how well we're taking care of ourselves. For the sake of practicality, let's break it down into two divisions:

The Diva	The Diva's World
Self-esteem and confidence	Relationships (kids, parents, spouse, siblings)
Health and body	Career
Grooming (hair, skin, nails, and so on)	Finances
Image and presence	Surroundings (home)
Emotion	Community

Now that we've laid out these categories, keep in mind that all aspects of our lives are interrelated. The inside and the outside work hand in hand; if an area of one category is out of whack, others probably are, too. For example, if something isn't working within you—like your self-esteem or your body—then your world will not run smoothly. Is there a particular area that isn't working for you? Let's take a look; now is the golden opportunity to examine it and determine how you would like to have it enhanced or developed. Be brave, Diva.

When I first tried this exercise, I made a list of how I wanted my life to look when I turned forty (in just a few short years) and compared that to where I am now. In doing so, I started taking an inventory of myself to see how my Inner Diva (self-esteem, health, image, and so on) matched what was going on in my world (relationships, finances, career, what have you). When I looked in the mirror, I saw the lines on my face as a gentle reminder of how much I love to laugh; my body reflected my new commitment to health—not perfect, but headed in the right direction. Then I couldn't help but notice something shocking—my roots. I was almost three months past my due date to become a "natural blonde" again. Coincidence? I think not. I made the excuse that I was too busy to drive an hour just for my hair (even though I regularly drive that far for other reasons) or that I had decided to grow out my real color (not a good idea, as anyone who's seen it can attest), but in reality I knew that something else was off kilter. I have a commitment to taking care of myself; when I feel good about myself, other people notice. But lately it had become less of a priority.

When I brought up this topic with my sister Divas, it became a major Diva discussion; everybody had something to say. For example, Maureen pointed out that her hair was a direct reflection of her self-esteem, so she'd recently rescheduled an opportunity to meet with a potentially major client until she could get her hair done to cover up the two inches of gray that had grown in. We couldn't stop talking about how we felt each time we had our hair cut, colored, or highlighted, or it received whatever magic our hairstylists worked on us. My friend Lisa Oliver is my hairstylist extraordinaire who gives me a fabulous look every time I see her. The caveat about having her do my hair is not the distance I have to drive, but the fact that she happens to work at the "in" salon John Frieda in Hollywood where the prices are a reflection of the many A-list celebrities who also go there. But I have come to realize that for me, it's important to work her visits into my budget; I'll do what it takes to make this happen. I always know that my hair looks great—and that makes me feel great. Another friend, Lowell, once told me, "I've noticed that when my women friends want to make a major lifestyle change, they cut their hair." Here's a pointer. Pay attention when you get the impulse to change your hair—it just may mean that something else in your life needs changing.

Now is the perfect time to try Carilyn's "pie" exercise in Week 2 from another point of view. In addition to seeing how big your slices of pie are, notice what flavor the pie is. What I realized is that in certain areas of my life, like my career, I had a huge slice of pie, but it was mincemeat pie. I don't even like mincemeat; my favorite is rhubarb. All this time, I was eating the wrong pie. And it doesn't matter how big your slice is if you don't like the flavor. As a true Diva, don't settle for anything other than your favorite pie. How can you sweeten each slice? Think about what really matters in your world, both inside and out. Examine your commitments and priorities. Don't put it off—start right here, today.

— Molly

$\mathcal{D}$IVA DO'S FOR THE WEEK:

Get out the Diva Diary . . . by this point, you might as well keep it with you at all times along your journey!

1. Take a look at the areas of the inventory we've just discussed, and rate yourself in each category. For example, I would rate my relationship as *S* for "stellar"; my health and body would get an *OFD* for "opportunity for development"; and my home gets a *Y* for "Yikes!" Use a rating scale that empowers you and that takes the emotional attachment out of any areas you plan on repackaging/developing/expanding. Remember, the best part of this entire journey is that there are no right or wrong, good or bad answers. This is the opportunity for you to simply reflect on any areas that are missing, unbalanced, or in need of a fine-tuning. No need to beat yourself up for any one thing—we've all done enough of that, my Diva dears! For those areas in which you aren't right on the mark (or even if you are), begin your own self-examination. Are you getting a big enough slice of the pie that you love?

2. The Four Divas created a power tool to use individually and as a group. We call it the Diva Declaration, and it's a phrase or sentence spoken in the present tense *(I am, I have, I believe, I trust,* and so forth*)* that the Diva says to herself either silently or aloud that sparks her inner fire. Here are some examples: *I am loved; I am powerful; I am a sex kitten.* Once you get going, create Diva Declarations that inspire you, that ignite your inner fire, that spark the embers of fun and passion in your life: *I am spontaneous, free, and totally self-expressed. I release myself from lack and limitation in my life. I now commit my life to celebrating me—to unleashing my Inner Diva!* Write them down and keep them handy. Repeat them as often as possible. Notice that the more you say them, the better you feel, the more inspired you get; notice what starts to happen around you . . .

3. Should you decide to go for a radical Diva makeover and cut ten inches or more off your mane, consider donating your tresses to an organization called Locks of Love, a charity that provides real hair from men, women, and children to

financially disadvantaged boys and girls under the age of eighteen who suffer from medical hair loss. To find out more, check out their Web site, www.locksoflove.org.

FRIVOLOUS DIVA DO:

CREATE A FUN DIVA DECLARATION *that you will say to yourself every day this week; share it with others. Mine is:* I deserve to be a natural blonde every day!

Acknowledge the Goddess Within

She changes everything She touches and everything She touches, changes.
— STARHAWK

Every smart traveler on a journey has a guide, and the Diva is no exception. The Goddess is the core of the Diva's inner power. And as women, we are *all* Goddesses and we deserve our due! The Great Goddess was once revered around the world, and it's time to bring her back to her place of honor in you. From 30,000 to 3000 BCE women and the Goddess were honored as creators of life, priestesses, primary providers of food, healers, artisans, builders, and leaders. To our ancestors, birth was a great mystery. A woman could grow a baby inside her. She could re-create herself by delivering a girl or create an even bigger miracle by creating her opposite—a boy. Add to this amazing power the fact that she alone could sustain their life by nursing them. Our ancestors were in awe of these abilities and concluded that *all* things—plants, mountains, rivers, everything—came from the "Great Mother," a Goddess, a "mother of all things." She is also called "Grandmother." Get it? "The Grand Mother."

As the Grandmother Diva, I love the fact that these two words are synonymous and that grandmothers were once revered. In today's society, older women are hardly noticed. But in actuality we are fountains of wisdom, and as an older woman I can tell you, in my head I'm the same person I was at thirty-three. My skin may have some wrinkles but I still feel young and plan to accomplish, see, and do many more things.

Besides my role as mother I have had four different careers (a nurse, a sales Diva of direct marketing, presently an owner of a women's apparel manufacturing company, and now a writer), but the one I am proudest of, and find the most rewarding, is mother. I felt so fortunate that both my daughter-in-law and daughter invited me to be in the delivery room with them and their husbands. To witness the birth of my granddaughters was a miracle and one of the highlights of my life. I can understand why our ancestors were awed by women creating and sustaining life. Yet today's women just fit it into their busy schedules.

As I enter my seventh decade, I feel free to do whatever I want. I have a peacefulness I never had before, and I'm comfortable with myself. With my parents now gone, I'm the matriarch of the family, which is a pleasing and challenging place to be. As the Grandmother Diva, I possess wisdom to pass on to my children and to you emerging Divas. I look down two generations and see my web: my son and daughter and granddaughters. I am a Goddess!

Now Divas, before you say "I'm no Goddess" as you stare at your reflection in the mirror, let me tell you Goddesses come in all shapes and sizes. Not just thin, blond, and tall like the Norse gods of old. The Romans chose images of shorter, dark-haired, full-figured women as their Goddesses. Beauty is all in the eye of the beholder, and a Diva sees beauty in everything and everyone, including herself. Besides their physical attributes, Goddesses embody many qualities, good and bad, not just those we consider "feminine." Along with love and nurturing, compassion, sensuality, and peacemaking, there is power, honesty, death, and rebirth. She can be a warrior and she can celebrate life and creativity, just like us.

The Goddess I identify with is Spider the Creatrix (North America, circa 1300 CE). Spider is the symbol of the universe—Earth Mother or Goddess from which all things come. In Native American myths Spider Grandmother created the sun as represented in her web's design. She is also known as the weaver since she spins life out of her own body. And she is the protector and guide for humanity, our spiritual leader. Besides her nurturing of us, she is the mother of all creativity—works of art, livelihood, relationships. We are all connected to her web and she is inside all of us. She is connected to us with threads of silk from the tops of our heads. She fills us with wisdom and love. We need to keep this connection open, so we don't lose our way. We do this by chanting or praying to Spider Woman. What are your Goddess's qualities? This week it's your turn to find your Goddess Guide.

In order to pick the Goddess whom you'd like to be your guide and source of power on your journey, you'll need to do some research. Here is a list to start you off, but to learn more, try the Internet or visit your local library.

- Athena: Greek Goddess of Wisdom and Justice, patroness of artistry in all crafts. Presided over battle strategy in wartime and domestic arts in peacetime. Practical, rational thinker, and protector. Roman name—Minerva.
- Artemis: Greek Goddess of the Hunt and the Moon. Skilled as a huntress to feed all people. Cycles of the moon influence all growing things. Independent, sets goals and reaches them. Enjoys friendships with women. Roman name—Diana.
- Demeter: Greek Goddess of Grain and Agriculture. Earth Mother. Maternal and nurturing of others; generous. Roman name—Ceres.
- Freyja: Norse Goddess of Beauty and Love. Guardian of fertility. Has magical powers.
- Hathor: Egyptian Goddess of Bodily Pleasures. Likes music, dance, song, the arts, and all sensual pleasures of the body.
- Hekate: Greek Moon Goddess of Darkness and Magic. Associated with the uncanny and mysterious. Goddess of the Crossroads of Life—the convergence of three roads where one path ends and new choices must be made. She teaches that when the old dies, new growth occurs, and we must move forward into the new.
- Hera: Greek Goddess of Marriage, protector of women. She personifies the role of wife—commitment and fidelity. Roman name—Juno.
- Kwan Yin: Chinese Goddess of Compassion and Mercy, guardian angel of humans. If anyone is in pain, she will help.

- Lakshmi: Hindu Goddess of Prosperity and Good Fortune. She is everywhere—in jewels, even in cows. Hence the Hindu reverence for cows.
- Sarasvati: Hindu Goddess of Knowledge, River or Water Goddess. Inventor of all the arts and sciences, including writing and music.

Today the Goddess is emerging again as a whole entity. There is a growing need to connect with our spiritual self, our creative self, and take back our womanly power! As we look at the creation aspect, we must consider how we create the various aspects of our lives. With the Diva Goddess in each of us we have the power of transformation. We can change ourselves. We can change the world! We can live fully and creatively right now! A Diva knows she has the powerful forces of her Goddess to call on at will and guide her to full outrageousness!

— *Elena*

*D*IVA DO'S FOR THE WEEK:

1. Design your own Goddess—draw her, mold her from clay, cut out a picture of her—and name her! Keep her with you. If you're coming up blank, declare yourself the Goddess of Charm, Passion, or Self-Expression. Give yourself the secret powers or qualities that you want to develop and practice them.

2. Create a Goddess ritual. Write a meditation or prayer to call to her to help you with something in particular.

3. If you'd like to read about different Goddesses, here are several titles:
   The Heart of the Goddess by Hallie Iglehart Austen
   The New Book of Goddesses and Heroines by Patricia Monaghan
   The Book of Goddesses by Kris Waldherr (juvenile section)

*F*RIVOLOUS DIVA DO:

DEEM YOURSELF THE GODDESS OF FUN. *Sprinkle glitter in your hair and that of others you meet this week, and declare for them "More Fun in Your Lives!"*

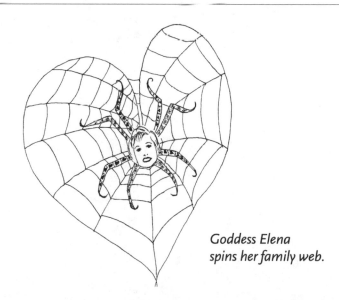

*Goddess Elena
spins her family web.*

II

$\mathcal{T}$HE HEART OF THE DIVA

SECRETS TO LOVE, INSPIRATION, AND FUN!

The essence of the Diva is the space she holds for herself and others to
forgive mistakes, celebrate victories, and love the humanity in herself
and those around her. In this section we will explore avenues to expand
our capacity to love.

Week 5

Generosity

Kind words can be short and easy to speak, but their echoes are truly endless.
—MOTHER TERESA

Have you ever noticed how other women light up when you compliment them? Armed with such abilities, why do we hold back? Instead of being the caterpillar locked in her cocoon, the Diva lives life like the butterfly—looking beautiful, feeling confident, flying wherever she wants, and spreading pollen (or love drops) far and wide.

While some women believe building up others detracts from themselves, a Diva knows that there is no finite amount of praise, so spreading it lavishly is what she does and all benefit. The dreaded Anti-Diva makes us stingy with our compliments, but the true Diva knows that whatever you give away generously comes back severalfold.

But generosity is about more than just bestowing praise on others. In conversation, it's how we listen and share. Do we need to be right or have the last word? Are we thinking about what we want to say next to top the speaker? Can we instead listen without judgment and learn something we never knew about other people, or give them that glorious final word? If knowledge is power, then listening is the key to having it. Do this exercise when listening: In your mind consciously decide to indulge Divarella instead of the Anti-Diva and pretend there's a hidden treasure in what they're saying. Your job is to listen until you find what their gift to you is. This makes a win–win ending: You gain an insight and they feel valued.

Another way of expressing generosity is sharing of ourselves. A Diva tells those close to her of their importance. She acknowledges their magnificence. A Diva allows herself to be vulnerable, overcoming her fears. If ever the Diva is in error, she does not hesitate to apologize. Saying, "I'm wrong. I'm sorry," takes great courage, but has the power to mend a relationship. And we Divas know that saving relationships means saving our support systems.

Generosity includes giving of your time to help others, and it is satisfying to your soul. As you know, I have two granddaughters, and I'll baby-sit an evening, a day, a weekend to give their parents some time together. Sure, I'm donating the precious commodity of time, but I reap the even more valuable benefit of my granddaughters' unconditional love and their desire to spend time with their "Nonni." They are forever teaching me as I rediscover the world through their eyes. They're so curious and so excited about everything. And they're both so affectionate; their hugs and kisses are a wonderful gift. Also, they share their food and toys. We can all learn a lot from these mini Divas.

Contrary to the popular myth that Divas are rude and self-absorbed, kindness and good manners are essential Diva attributes because we can see how easily small gestures can alter our own or another's mood. I notice that when I smile and say "Hi!" to people, they smile back—and I feel good and more relaxed. When I lose my patience and get annoyed at standing in line or being in traffic, everything looks terrible. And then more terrible things happen. It's that old saying, "What goes around, comes around." Remembering to say "Thank you" to people for little things, like holding the door open, or you holding the door open for someone else could, in turn, open doors for you! People love to be acknowledged and are more willing to help again if they feel appreciated.

Gift giving is another fun and generous Diva indulgence. I get so excited when I find something just right for a friend or family member, I can't wait to give it to them. I have a girlfriend who has seven—yes, seven—cats. One day while I was shopping I happened upon a brocade purse with cats on it. My friend is one of those people who has everything and is difficult to buy for so I bought it on the spot. She loved it and uses it all the time. That was a rewarding gift for me to give.

I also love receiving gifts (what Diva doesn't!). Another girlfriend of mine spends a lot of time picking out just the right card. Also, because she knows I like butterflies, she might find a butterfly gift bag or top a package with a butterfly. Knowing someone took that time for me is very gratifying, and when I look at the gift, I am instantly reminded of the giver, and all the love she put into her present. It's very comforting. Are you feeling all warm and fuzzy? A Diva knows there's a ripple effect to giving, just as when you throw a pebble in the water and ripples go out from it forever. So pass it on!

Now for Grandmother Diva's first rule: Be generous to yourself. Ask for hugs. Buy yourself treats. I was craving something for the house in leopard, so I went out and bought a pillow. It was a small purchase, but it feels so luxurious. I love it and now I'm going to accessorize my home office in leopard!

The generous Diva includes in her life sincere listening and sharing; the giving of time, money, and gifts; and kindnesses to others as well as herself. She gives generously and receives graciously. What comes back to her is an abundance of love and the knowledge that she has made a difference in the world!

– Elena

𝒟IVA DO'S FOR THE WEEK:

Each day this week:

1. Do something to make someone else happy: Smile, send a card, give a hug, put a quarter in the parking meter, give recognition, listen with your heart, leave a big tip.

2. Do something to make yourself happy: Have a hot fudge sundae, buy yourself fresh flowers, read a new book, have a manicure.

3. Be thankful for something.

4. This week give someone a gift for no reason, choose a charitable deed to do, or make a donation.

𝒻RIVOLOUS DIVA DO:

BUY YOURSELF A GIFT AT A STORE *that wraps and ships gifts. Have them wrap and send your gift to you and delight in the surprise of its arrival!*

𝒟IVA TRIVIA:

- Dolly Parton, through her Dollywood Foundation and Imagination Library, sends a book to every child in the county around her hometown—Locust Ridge, Tennessee—to encourage reading.

- Rosie O'Donnell, through her For All Kids Foundation, has donated millions of dollars to children's charities.

Acceptance—Sweet Surrender

How prone are we to blame others, when we ourselves only are in fault.
—MARGUERITE BLESSINGTON

At one time my life was a pendulum, swinging back and forth between the high of praise for myself and the lows of self-criticism and judgment of others. What the Diva in me strives for today is the pendulum at rest—peace and no major extremes in either direction. It isn't what happens in life that kills us, it's the drama we create before, during, and after the experience that leaks our power. We waste our life energy if we spend our time driven by the judgments of others or—sometimes even more destructively—our own. Living under the binding constraints of judgment helps no one and hinders our own personal growth. Mastering the voices in our heads brings us the gift of sweet surrender—acceptance.

I first started to examine the role of judgment in my life while I was reading *The Courage to Be Rich*, by Suze Orman. Her words stunned me: "May every thought that you think be etched in fire in the sky for the whole world to see, for in fact it is." I actually envisioned my hideous thoughts and judgments blazing across the sky. Oh my God! How could I think such mean, nasty thoughts about my friends and family? How could I be so mean to myself? I had no idea how I'd been undermining my own power with these judgments.

In that moment I really became conscious of my thoughts and made a decision to clean them up. It will take some work, but I'm happy to tell you that it can be done. A life free of the endless criticism you've been living with may be a struggle to achieve, but when you get there, aahh, the peace is wonderful.

When I was in my early twenties I considered myself a very well-informed, dynamic woman with strong opinions. I was the one at parties engaged in lively, spirited conversation with the person who was wrong. What I realize today is that opinions are really judgments of others masquerading as our "truths." How did I move from judgment to acceptance? It is surprisingly quite simple.

The first step I took was to pay closer attention to my thoughts. I discovered the "All About Them" show had been playing continuously in my head. "They" were mean or too fat or lazy or indifferent or weird or too thin or their hair was funny. My goodness, it was an endless tirade of totally insignificant crap. My spiritual teacher, Paul Movessian, taught me a technique years ago designed to help us capture our thoughts. I decided to try it. In this basic technique—simple in concept yet difficult in practice—you force yourself to be present by recognizing where you are and repeating it to yourself. For example, if I were to practice self-observation right now, I would repeat, "I'm here, sitting in my home on my blue couch, typing my chapter." By stating exactly what you're doing, you force yourself to be present, or "in the moment." And by staying "in the moment" and repeating exactly what you're doing over and over again, you cultivate a new awareness of your life.

If you can keep this up for sixty seconds, congratulations, you're a master! In the beginning expect to be happy if you can do it for five seconds before your mind takes over and leads you somewhere else—like reminding you that you haven't done the laundry yet or that you need a snack. Interruptions like this are frustrating, but don't give up. This practice of self-observation quiets your mind, and you can actually experience an insight that your intuition has been waiting to tell you or just be present to the splendor of your life. Try it—it's really enlightening.

Once you can slow your mind down, you can begin to hear your thoughts. When my Diva saw that I had something to say about everyone, I had a new place of inquiry. Why did I care to devote so much of my most precious commodity—time—to such trivial matters? So I began my second practice: I decided to see that everyone and everything was a reflection of what I didn't like about myself. Every time I made a judgment about somebody, I checked to see whether I had the same the complaint about myself. What I discovered was truly amazing: I was judging myself on everything. I criticized myself so harshly that I cheated myself out of the joy of life. I could never savor an accomplishment because there must be something wrong with it. I had trained myself as a "something's wrong machine" that operated on autopilot. In addition, no one could be happy around me because all they could see was what was wrong with them. My mental projection of my judgment made my kids and my friends unhappy and kept them from flourishing.

But once I recognized the destructive cycle I was in, I had the power to change it. It was time to abandon that ship, and I decided that swimming in the ocean of the unknown was better than being safe on the Misery cruise line. All of a sudden, right before my eyes, everyone around me started to change. Total strangers, my family, and my friends became prettier and kinder and smarter than I had ever noticed before.

How did I manage to change all those flawed people who were bugging me all the time? It's a little embarrassing to share because it was so simple. I started to cut myself some slack, and the whole world changed overnight. I simply fell in love with my humanity, all the good and all the bad that I bring to the party. Once it was safe for me to be with my flaws, I was able to take actions to change the things I could and accept those things I couldn't. I will always be five feet tall and my vision is that of a giant. But as I began to love and nurture myself, forgive my mistakes, and delight in my success, everyone around me shifted. We all started being happy and accepting of each other. Oh sure, some days my buttons still get pushed, and that's okay. After all, we're only human. But what I want you to know from the bottom of my heart is that you are perfect, just the way you are. This week, you have the Divas' permission to be kind to yourself. Practice the techniques and see the world come alive, for you are awesome, just the way you are. Mother Teresa once said, "Where there is judgment, there is no room for love." Enjoy: You have now entered The Diva's Judgment-Free Zone, where only love can survive.

— *Maureen*

$\mathcal{D}$IVA DO'S FOR THE WEEK:

1. Three times daily take a break to practice self-observation. Place a note on your bathroom mirror, on your dashboard, and on your bed to remind you. Just repeat exactly whatever you happen to be doing. For example, "I'm brushing my teeth, the toothpaste tastes minty, the water is cold, the brush is stiff, I'm going up and down and side to side," and so on. Keep this up as long as possible. By the end of the week you will hear your thoughts.

2. Each evening, write down all the judgments of others you remember during the day. Then look to see if you judge yourself in those areas.

3. Write yourself a letter of forgiveness. It can come from your Higher Self, or from the vantage point of you as a young child. How would you speak to her about the same events you are beating yourself up about? Would you treat her that way?

4. Celebrate your Great Divaness. At the end of the week, treat yourself to something out of the ordinary. Make a gourmet meal for yourself, just to celebrate how awesome you are.

$\mathcal{F}$RIVOLOUS DIVA DO:

BUY YOURSELF A MINI GAVEL *and keep it with you. Bang it every time you feel a judgment coming on. You'll be cured in no time.*

Passion

The most absurd and reckless aspirations have sometimes led to extraordinary success.
—LUC DE CLAPIERS, MARQUIS DE VAUVENARGUES

I'm actually a high-school dropout who had a passion for music. . . .
—NANCY BERRY, VICE CHAIRMAN, VIRGIN MUSIC GROUP WORLDWIDE AND VIRGIN RECORDS AMERICA

*W*hat is the secret of a Diva's zest for life? Passion, pure and simple! Her energy is irresistible, her charm, seductive. Passion is the driving force in a Diva's heart. In *Passion*, one of the most inspiring books I have read, Barbara De Angelis, Ph.D., writes, "The hunger for passion is universal. Something in human nature longs for that experience of complete emotional absorption, that magical moment when we are swept away, finally free from our everyday rules, restraints, and routines." *Complete emotional absorption*—oh yeah!

All of us have that hunger for never-ending energy, breathtaking allure, and the release of our restraints. Take me, for instance. I've always fantasized about being a rock star. I can't sing a tune or play a chord, nor have I taken any action toward achieving my dream, yet I still long for that lifestyle. Usually true passion leads to action, but in this case there was none. What was stopping me from pursuing this lifestyle? I started investigating because something didn't line up. I began by defining what *rock star* meant to me. What did it represent? In two words: *passion* and *freedom!* The freedom to wear whatever I want, no matter how crazy; to *be* however I want, no matter what anybody else thinks; to express myself passionately and globally and inspire others with my creativity. But the true facts were that I was too committed to my family to go on the road for a year and I was way too lazy, impatient, and uninterested to take singing and guitar lessons for ten years. Maybe there was a way to have the qualities I admired in a rock star and still be able to sing off-key and play only the *air* guitar!

As I looked deeper, I realized my life had become dull, monotonous, and predictable but inside I was screaming to have variety and inspiration—the rush and excitement of charting new territory and breaking the molds . . . Mach 2 with my hair on fire . . . so to speak. In that moment I saw what was missing: *complete emotional absorption* . . . my passion.

The desire to have it back was so strong that I vowed to find it no matter what. After wondering *What would a Diva do?* I embarked on a new plan: I looked for energetic people who seemed to possess the qualities I was looking for in the hope of being infected by their enthusiasm. I talked to them and listened to what it was that lit them up and how they got there. I challenged myself to try new things, keeping myself open—not closing any doors in case passion was hiding behind one of them. All these (especially listening) I realized are necessary for the Diva to find her spark.

One of the things I did on this mission was enroll in a seminar on "Living a Life That You Love." That was the weekend I met Maureen. I loved her expansive notions of what we could all accomplish in this life if we put our minds to it, and we quickly became friends. Whenever we got together we would talk about what we were doing in our lives and what our goals were. One day she revealed her desire to be a truly captivating presence, a type of woman she called Diva, and asked if I would help her with her game of becoming one. As we looked at what Diva qualities she would be implementing in her life I noticed a striking resemblance to what I had long called "rock star." Inspired by Maureen's vision, I found the way to make the best of my rock star fantasy come true—by being a Diva: an alluring, powerful, electrifying presence, totally self-expressed! Free to be wild and adventurous yet not have to be on tour, away from my family for years. I had been struck by the lightning of *complete emotional absorption*. I'm sure it's what Clark Kent experiences when he's in the phone booth whirling into Superman. A rush of emotion so strong that you're electrified with the knowledge that nothing can stand in your way. A rush of power filling every cell of your body with sureness that this is what you were born to do!

I became unstoppable, and a vision for my future came clear. All women were already Divas, and my mission would be to make sure they all knew it! A book had to be written . . . a way to let them all know this information. I was born to inspire women to realize their magnificent potential! I committed myself to this newfound passion of inspiring all women to live as Divas, and my life has been changed forever. It quickly encompassed my whole being and spread into other areas of my life such as my fashion design business. My commitment was no longer so much to make money as it was to have women feel beautiful wearing my collection. Out of that, my "work" began to feel more like a hobby, yet its succes became tremendous. Ideas began to pour in everywhere—my energy levels soared—the floodgates had been opened! At home I tossed out the bluish gray bedsheets we'd been sleeping on for a year and replaced them with steamy red ones. I placed fragrant candles on the nightstands. My relationship with my husband began to steam up and spontaneity began to rule again! I also had a new starting point from which to raise my daughter. I want her to always know that she, too, is already a Diva; that her opinions matter, that she can trust herself, to never stop expressing herself or exploring all creative outlets. And now we have so much fun together learning from each other. Life is awesome!

It's not just luck, sisters, it's called *passion* . . . and it's there for you, too! Follow those wild dreams, for *anything* and *everything* is possible! Get out and talk to enthusiastic people. Or at the very least, just get out! Try new things—don't lock yourself up in your house, office, or whatever monotonous confines you find yourself in. When was the last time you were engaged in an activity and time flew by but your energy level increased as you delved further into the activity? . . . that, my darlings, is the presence of the Diva's Passion Playground.

Passion can live in every moment of our lives. Find those big dreams you pushed aside before you realized your Diva status. Big dreams ignite our passion, and our passion fuels us to living these big dreams, overcoming any and all obstacles. When we live passionately nothing feels like a chore, because we're so absorbed by the path we have created for ourselves. This rush of never-ending energy is contagious and will spread to all areas of your life and to others'. It's a magnet for magic and the access to Divadom! *So look out!*

—Carilyn

$\mathcal{D}$IVA DO'S FOR THE WEEK:

1. Daydream. Take some quiet time for yourself. Let your mind wander. What images come up? Don't critique or censor anything. Write in your Diva Diary what you hear and see, as wild or unlikely as it may appear.

2. Take some time creating your ideal life on the page. There are no financial, intellectual, or physical limits in this world. You are unstoppable and totally free to do whatever you can think of. What are you thinking of? What are you envisioning? Re-create each detail in your Diva Diary as if you are living it now.

3. Try one new thing this week. Do something your lover or friend wants to do that you never thought you could or would want to do.

$\mathcal{F}$RIVOLOUS DIVA DO:

PRETEND YOU'RE BARBARA WALTERS. *Interview somebody you know or don't know and really listen to what fuels the passion in his or her life. Dig, Divas, dig!*

Freedom

When you can love the you that has made mistakes, that has failed over and over
to measure up to the ideal, that has been broken again and again for the same stupid reasons,
then you can love others who are dealing with the same struggle, because you know
it is your struggle, too. Life is a self-improvement course, and we are all in the same classroom.
—CHELLIE CAMPBELL, *THE WEALTHY SPIRIT*

*W*hat is the ideal future you created for yourself? Have you lived up to it yet? You haven't? Well, dear Diva, here's a news flash—we have all, in some way or another, failed to live up to the expectations we've created for ourselves. Failed expectations are the shackles that bind us to the idea of living perfect lives; they prevent us from having/doing/being what we want in our lives. I'm not saying that we are all failures; on the contrary, we are all brilliant accomplishment generators, but we resist the journey—and the accomplishments that go with it—to a certain degree. I fully expected to be married at twenty-eight, with three kids by thirty-five. Well, I didn't get married until three weeks before my thirty-fifth birthday, so that expectation went right out the window, putting yet another notch in my list of unfulfilled or thwarted dreams. The rest of my ideal vision of myself included being well educated (I have a degree in French and an MBA); happily married (check!); a mom (I have an awesome stepson, and we're working on our own brood); thin (oops, I'm about fifteen pounds overweight); in great shape (uhhhh . . .); financially secure (oops again; I'm way off on that one)—*uncle!* Stop the bus, I want to get off!

That trapped feeling comes from living a life governed by expectations. To the Diva, freedom is the release of these expectations, both her own and those she has absorbed from others. As she learns to live by her own rules and add fun back to her life, the feeling of freedom fills her world.

I'm in the process of learning the extent to which I've lived my life as a fairy tale, how it was "supposed" to be versus how it really is; the Cinderella version versus the Divarella version. I created my own prison, and I would assert that many of us do. When we're little we create certain "rules" about how our lives will or should turn out. According to these guidelines, we're destined never to make it! The life I was living was completely inconsistent with my childhood ideal—as of course it would be—what eight-year-old knows enough about life to map it all out correctly? So while I have accomplished a great many things, because they didn't match the goals I set more than a quarter century ago, I was constantly left dissatisfied, disappointed, angry . . . Only recently have I become aware of the way I've set myself up for failure. If I had continued living my life in this manner, I would never have been able to live up to the expectations I created. I would have been destined to a life of depression and disappointment, with no chance of parole.

Freedom is a state of mind, and if you can't see and acknowledge your accomplishments, then it's like being in emotional prison, like running around like a horse with blinders on. When your vision is hampered, most of life's possibilities are out of reach. Going down the path of unfulfilled expectations is like always waiting for the other shoe to drop; you have a constant sense of foreboding, a thought that continuously says, *It's never going to work out.* Such thoughts are very dangerous to the Diva—they can become a self-fulfilling prophecy. If you're telling yourself that it's not going to work out (no matter how good your intentions are, even if you're just trying to protect yourself), you're setting yourself up for disaster. Then if, in fact, it doesn't work out, you get to be right—lonely, sad, angry, resentful, and disappointed, but right.

If you, too, have reached this point in your life, it's time to change the rules—it's a whole new ball game, and you are the umpire, catcher, pitcher, and MVD (Most Valuable Diva). You are in charge. This is the moment of truth when you can break free from the chains of expectations and of trying to be perfect, and take on instead being present in your life as it happens. I took on being satisfied with how my life goes—with all its ups and downs. I get to choose how my life turns out. I'm not giving up on my goals; in fact, I'm more committed to them than ever. But I have let go of those goals that I now see were someone else's expectations of me or those that no longer fit my vision of myself, and substituted my own. The real freedom, though, comes not in being driven by the goal, but in being satisfied with everything that happens along the way. The end result may not even ever be achieved—but that's not the point; it's how we live our lives up until then and appreciating the ride along the way. Part of the glory of this is seeing those around us for who they are and who they aren't—and loving and appreciating them either way, flaws and all. I'm also seeing who I am and who I'm not in the various areas of my life and, once I see those flaws, figuring out how—and even if—I should change them. For example, in business and in my relationship, I am an idea generator, a planner—but I'm not strong on follow-up. Still, if I can assign the follow-up tasks to someone reliable, I can plunge full speed ahead, devoting my energies where they are best focused.

Being a Diva isn't about being perfect or being better than anyone else, it's about being able to love yourself in spite of yourself. And it's about giving yourself the freedom to try again after you've fallen on your face; letting go of the restraints and limits you once placed on yourself and trying something new for a change. A Diva learns new things, blazes new trails, and embraces the unlimited opportunities of her unique expression even when she has no idea how everything will turn out. To tell the truth, this may always be a challenge for me, but I'm up to the task. I am willing to take the chance.

In the end, a Diva chooses herself! She is unstoppable, courageous, and inspiring. A Diva knows that life itself is extraordinary, and she celebrates each day!

— Molly

 IVA DO'S FOR THE WEEK:

1. Take a mental snapshot of the areas of your life and start to identify where you're trying to live up to some expectations—yours or someone else's. What price are you paying for trying to be perfect? Write down your observations in your Diva Diary. Until you let yourself off the hook and love yourself for the good, the bad, and the ugly, you won't have any room for others and freedom won't be an option.

2. Take a few minutes to acknowledge your accomplishments. Note all the strides you've made in your quest to live the life you love. Again, write them down, no matter how small or insignificant they may seem to you. This is especially important to have in writing so you can go back and refer to this list when you need a pick-me-up or when you "forget" how good your life is.

3. Play the song "Freedom" by George Michael.

RIVOLOUS DIVA DO:

FREE YOUR MIND COMPLETELY *and give your feet a luxurious massage and a nice, hot soak.*

Step

III

$\mathcal{U}$NLEASHING YOUR FEMININITY

SOURCES OF DIVA GLAMOUR AND POWER

Remember how glamorous you felt when you were a little girl
and you put on your mom's high heels? Well, now it's time to dress up
the Diva for real—real fun, that is! Get ready to assemble
your own Essential Diva Box. Fill it with the Diva's ultimate tools:
a boa, a tiara, perfume, and glitter!

Key to the Kingdom: The Boa!

I can tell you the secret of living a great life. And that . . . is a feather boa and long gloves.
It's all you need. Why, you ask? Because no one can ever be pompous, tragic,
desperate or take themselves seriously if they're wearing a pink feather boa.
You have to loosen up and laugh at yourself and the total absurdity of life. So throw your shoulders
back, sisters. Wrap that boa around your neck, trying not to trail the end in your drink
or thwap it in someone's eyes. Attitude, my children, is everything.

—ANNE STUART

*T*here are some lessons we learn in life that don't have
much meaning for us at the time they're delivered. I've come to
realize that they never disappear; they remain on standby, waiting for the perfect moment
to resonate for us on our Diva journey. Two such lessons altered my destiny on the day I
met Inge, the lady with the boa.

I was at an all-time low in my life while the world thought I was at an all-time high.
I was invited to a black-tie celebrity dinner in Beverly Hills, and I was tipping the scales at
a hundred pounds over my "ideal" (whatever that is) weight. I dreaded the thought of
dressing my bloated body in formal attire, but felt I had to take this opportunity for my
career, so I reluctantly went shopping with my friend Patty Ellis. Patty took one look at my
hangdog expression, grabbed my hand, and led me to her favorite boutique, Inge's
Fashions in Redondo Beach just south of Los Angeles.

At first my experience in the store was typical. I felt fat and ugly, nothing that the
salesperson brought me fit or was flattering, and I felt myself slipping into the black hole
of despair and self-loathing. Suddenly a burst of light swept into the picture. I heard the

voice of an angel as Inge, the store owner, abruptly invaded the sanctity of my dressing room with "Oh no! That is all wrong for you. We need to show your beauty. Don't you worry, Inge's going to take care of you herself." After a brief interrogation about what I needed for the event (in two days), Inge went to work like my own personal Fairy Godmother. Before my disbelieving eyes, she picked and pulled at fabric as she gave me a personal lesson in how to maximize my strengths and minimize my challenges. When she had finished, I was transformed into a vision of beauty that touched the soul of my being. It was then that my first lesson from the past kicked in: The Cabala says for every blade of grass there is an angel who whispers, "Grow, grow." When I first read that saying, I remember thinking, *If God cares that much about a blade of grass, there surely must be an angel assigned to me*. Now, in this precious moment with this beautiful woman, I heard my angel saying, "Grow, grow," and I surrendered to Inge and released all my fear, self-loathing, and judgment.

For the first time in my life I had fun shopping and trying on clothes. Inge drove me to her seamstress, who altered my beautiful silk outfit and beaded jacket in time for the ball. When we were back at the store, I noticed a beautiful ostrich boa, made I'm sure of feathers the ostrich no longer needed and could share with me. Ah, but I was far too plain and old to adorn myself with such an elegant, glamorous, and outrageous item. Inge noticed the longing in my soul to be the woman who could adorn her being with such beauty. She wrapped the boa around her neck and said, "It's quite beautiful, isn't it?" Then she whispered, "I think it's just perfect for you. Would you like to try it on?" In that instant, as she transferred her glamorous way of being to me, I felt like a Diva, and my second lesson trapped in time was made visible to me: the teachable moment.

One of my dearest mentors was a boss I had early in the leadership phase of my career, where he was the vice president of the E.O.C., a school for disadvantaged adults in Troy, New York. I was his assistant director, a novice in managing fifty employees and almost a thousand students a year. His name was Jim Sharp, and he was a no-nonsense bull of a man with the sweetest, most compassionate heart I have ever seen. Our relationship developed into one of mutual respect, and he began to teach me priceless lessons, the most important being the "teachable moment." "It's easy for you to see where another person is making a mistake or can use some advice," Jim explained to me, "but all the knowledge or insight you might have is irrelevant if the person is closed. A person with a closed mind can't hear what you want to say. You must train yourself to read the 'teachable moment,' that unique moment in time when the person is open for help." He added, "If you don't give up on people, a time will come when they present themselves for the lesson that only you are meant to share with them." With this wisdom in hand, I became a sweeter, more patient, and gentler human being.

Now Inge was my teacher, and this was my teachable moment. As Inge wrapped that soft, luscious, warm, sensuous, pure white boa around my neck, I felt glamour and beauty enter every cell of my body. I could almost hear the celestial chorus of angels shouting with delight, "She's got it! Thank God, she's got it!"

I don't know why some items speak to the Diva in our hearts, but I'm sure the boa translates the same message to women around the world. Armed with a boa, we exude confidence, grandeur, and strength. A woman wearing a boa is a woman to be reckoned with, for she knows who she is—a Goddess. My boa is a symbol of the process of acceptance that I have been in since beginning my Diva journey. Recently, armed with my glamour (my boa), I worked up the courage to look at my naked body—and believe me that had been an activity I'd avoided like the plague.

On this day, however, I saw the body of a Goddess, a temple for the heart and the love that I know I am to the world. I'll never be a fashion model, although I know today I'll reach a healthy weight for my body. Even then, my breasts will no longer compete with the firm and perky, be they by nature or human-made; still, I've grown to see that they are the breasts of a Diva. My breasts have produced milk! I, Maureen, have fed and nourished two babies and provided comfort in the dark of night to all the men in my life with my glorious breasts. My boa was the touchstone for all this acceptance. When I see my boa, I see my soul. I live my Divaness.

Begin to experiment with the source of the Goddess and the Diva within you. This week, try on a boa, love your body, and be present to the miracle that you are, right now, just the way you are. Search for your symbols of majesty, grace, and beauty. Remember, your teachable moment is here, and your angel is whispering to you, "Grow, grow."

— *Maureen*

*D*IVA DO FOR THE WEEK:

Buy yourself a boa this week, for no reason at all except you deserve it. It can be the five-and-dime variety or made of gorgeous ostrich feathers. It doesn't matter as long as you buy it. Wear it out and notice the reaction you receive (it is fabulous!) and be a movie star for a day. Imagine the thrill of having people anticipate your arrival.

*F*RIVOLOUS DIVA DO:

GIVE YOURSELF A BEAUTY MARK. *It's easy—use an eyeliner pencil. Dot anywhere you please.*

*D*IVA TRIVIA:

Can you guess for which star costume designer Edith Head created her first boa?
Answer: Mae West

"Tiara" Presence

. . . every woman who is a queen knew she could be one, and everyone else is still pretending she can't.
—MARIANNE WILLIAMSON, *A WOMAN'S WORTH*

Ever since I was a little girl, I've loved tiaras. Tiaras suggest elegance, beauty, and grace, and they personify the fairy-tale (read *perfect*) lives of queens and princesses. I would regularly watch the Miss America pageant and fantasize about the triumphant moment when Bert Parks would place the beloved crown on my head and hand me a huge bouquet of roses; the other women would all gather around and squeal with delight as they all congratulated me on a job well done. I practiced the wave of a queen; who among us hasn't? "As the new Miss America, I'd just like to thank all of my friends and family [sniff, sniff], whose love and support . . ." Long before I discovered tiaras, they were coveted, admired, and worn with pride by some of the most famous and fabulous women in history. There's a great deal of power and meaning in this adornment, and in looking at the historical significance of the tiara, we can start to appreciate why so many women have been drawn to the luster, opulence, and sheer beauty of this fascinating object.

The tiara was once the supreme symbol of honor and imperial authority reserved for royalty and aristocracy. Originally it was used as a sign of respect to crown the heads of royal and noble mummies of ancient Egypt. Over the centuries tiaras have come to hold an important social significance and have been a sign of the times, varying from the heavy "fender"-type models strewn with jewels and opulence typical of the 1800s, to the more subdued, light, and understated styles of the 1920s, each reflecting the splendor, dignity, and self-assurance of the sovereign represented. More often than not, the style of tiara reflected the style of the woman wearing it, as well as the political situation in the land. The popularity of tiaras in the 1800s even led to the pompadour hairstyle. (Yikes.) Happily, that phase passed. During the early to mid-1800s Americans dived headfirst (no pun intended) into the tiara craze, wearing them with ease and grace regardless of whether they were married to diplomats or simply hostesses and guests at formal events in the United States and Europe. They became so popular that people began to mail-order them from London.

In the 1920s and with the influence of trendsetters like *Vogue* magazine, tiaras came back after a brief disappearance. This incarnation brought lighter, more fashionable models to accommodate the new, shorter hairstyles worn by women of the day. When the depression hit in 1929, many jewelers went out of business and new designs were scarce; all displays of luxury came to a screeching halt. Relief came in the mid-1930s, when the Silver Jubilee of George V followed by the coronation of George VI in 1937 caused a stunning revival. A 1935 issue of *Vogue* observed: "Have you noticed lately that tiaras are absolutely the rage? Every woman wears one on the slightest provocation and they always seem to look their best in them." Nowadays it's rare for ladies who have them to don their tiaras, except at special events, and many of the grand stones that once shone in tiaras have now been reset in rings or necklaces.

Tiaras were originally family heirlooms, passed from generation to generation as a way for women of privilege to display their wealth and rank in society. These days, though, the decorative value of the tiara is what matters most. While certain jewelers, including Tiffany's (which has been making head ornaments since the 1870s), are still creating new styles of tiaras, they are now prevalent mostly at events such as debutante balls, weddings, Little Miss pageants, and the occasional drag queen show.

I'm proud to say that I own a tiara. It isn't fancy, but it makes me feel great and I love wearing it! I even bought several extras and gave them to my Diva sisters. It may sound silly, but when I wear it, I feel regal, almost like I have royal presence. I even wear it out occasionally; recently, I wore it to the grocery store—just for fun. As I selected my groceries, I thought to myself, *So this is what it's like when a queen goes shopping*. There's more to wearing this very Diva accessory than meets the eye. *Vogue* had it right—a tiara brings out the best in women. A tiara certainly can help transform your posture. When you put one on, the sheer weight of it (from all those fabulous diamonds and jewels) literally forces you to alter your balance and stand straight. If you've ever seen women wearing tiaras, you've noticed that they move slowly—to keep the tiara in place. If you don't maintain impeccable posture, the tiara will slide off your head and crash on the floor—a definite Diva don't! But a tiara doesn't have to be jewel encrusted to have an effect on your bearing—just knowing it's there can make all the difference. It will do more than just improve your posture. The idea of walking slowly, gracefully, and intentionally is what translates dullsville into Diva.

Before I discovered my Inner Diva, I didn't have the guts to buy and actually wear a tiara. I didn't think I could pull it off. But when my friend Dan found out my fears, he taught me a walking technique that I still practice today, called the "skyhook." Imagine a string that extends up through the middle of your body and out through the top of your head; now imagine that someone is gently pulling the "skyhook" from the top, causing you to walk with your head held high (as if you were wearing a tiara!), almost as if your legs actually began in your ribs. The more I practiced walking with my skyhook, the more confident and self-assured I felt. I stood taller. It actually improves my mood—it's hard to feel sad or upset when you're standing up straight and walking like a queen! I mean, when is the last time you ever saw anyone wearing a tiara and standing all hunched over?

And here's a little psychological tip: When you look up or at least straight ahead, it improves your mood; and having a positive attitude on a daily basis will definitely improve your outlook on life. So if wearing a tiara can improve life's outlook, what are you waiting for? Run and get your tiara right away!

— Molly

𝒟IVA DO'S FOR THE WEEK:

1. Go buy a tiara that suits your own personal style and wear it to a party; it can be fun, funny, eye-catching, or discreet—make it one of your accessories.

2. Add to the collage you created in your Diva Diary from Week 1. This time make your own collage of "presence" by cutting out and compiling photos, sayings, and images that really light you up and represent people with presence—for example, movie stars or business leaders you admire. Start or end your day by flipping through these pages.

3. In your Diva Diary write down not only what you're feeling when you walk using your skyhook, but also what your posture is in any given moment and the mood associated with it. Are you connected to your Diva skyhook?

𝒻RIVOLOUS DIVA DO:

WEAR YOUR TIARA *to the supermarket!*

𝓡EGAL DIVA DO:

RESURRECT A REGAL PRACTICE *from Victorian days. Go to your local printer and have engraved cards made with just your name on them. The recipients will be so intrigued by this air of mystery that it will add to your Diva presence and allure. If you're feeling especially Diva-ish, have it made in a very Diva color. Mine are on opalescent heavy stock paper with hot pink engraving.*

Scents and Scentsabilities

Perfume is like love, you can never get enough of it.
—ESTEE LAUDER

*T*he power of scent is magical. Fragrance can instantly transform us to another time and place. It can fill us with the presence of a familiar person, whether a mother, father, or friend. Most important, especially to the Diva, it helps us become whomever we wish to be—more attractive, sexier, more charming.

Growing up outside of Philadelphia there was an ice skating rink where we went on Friday nights in the winter. When I went inside for hot chocolate I encountered a combination of smells—the rink, the heat, the food—so unique that the few times I've smelled them since, I've been immediately taken back to that long-ago time. We all have memories that are called to mind by a scent—someone walking by wearing a familiar perfume or the aroma of cinnamon rolls in the oven or being enveloped by the scent of vanilla candles. I can't breathe in Estee Lauder's Youth Dew without thinking of my mother.

Fragrance has been a Diva power tool for millennia. The first perfume was incense and can be traced to before 2000 BCE in Egypt. It was used in religious rituals, in national celebrations, and to embalm royalty, and came from the gum resins of trees. Later, other scents from flowers and spices were used and combined with vegetable oils and animal fats to create body oils and lotions.

Egyptian men and women also wore fragrance cones on their heads. They were made of animal fats with scents added. As the heat of the day increased, the cones would melt, covering the body with an emollient cream and releasing perfume at the same time. Fortunately Divas today don't have to go through such a sticky mess to smell good!

Cleopatra, Super Diva and Queen of the Nile, was never a woman of understatement. She loved fragrance so much she had the sails of her ship soaked in perfume so when Mark Antony sailed into port he was already thinking of her. Whoever said less is more was *not* a Diva—excess is sometimes a Diva's best friend!

When Catherine de Médicis went to France in 1533 to marry Henry II she took her perfumer with her. He set up a shop selling perfumes and poisons. Ladies could purchase poisons to dispose of old husbands or lovers and then purchase perfumes to attract new ones! Not surprisingly, he was very successful, and while poison shops have gone the way of the guillotine, perfumeries have flourished and are big business today.

All forms of perfume are made from essential oils (fragrances) and ethyl alcohol. *Perfume*, the purest form of scent, has the highest concentration of oils, more than 22 percent. The scent lasts the longest, three to eight hours, and is the most expensive. Next is *eau de parfum*, 15 to 22 percent concentration; it lasts almost the same as perfume. Then *eau de toilette*, which has 8 to 15 percent concentration and will last four to six hours. Last is *cologne*; it has the lowest concentration, less than 5 percent, lasts two to four hours, and is the least expensive. Essential oils are drawn from flowers, grasses, leaves, seeds, roots, fruits, mosses, and tree secretions (resins), which make up the categories of fragrances—floral, green, chypre (woodsy), fruits, Oriental, spicy, citrus, modern, (synthetic aromas). An average fragrance has anywhere from six to a hundred ingredients, with more complex ones having over three hundred.

As you choose a fragrance for yourself, Diva, there are several considerations to keep in mind. You can have several perfumes—a collection— to be worn for different reasons depending on how you feel or what you want to project. Think about your personality and lifestyle, and what you want in a fragrance—elegance, sophistication, freshness, what have you. Or you may choose to have a "signature" fragrance, that is, only one fragrance that you wear all the time. A signature scent can be wonderful. It announces your presence and brings you to mind whenever smelled by friends or family. Of course, the Diva *loves* to make an impression! Remember, especially on those special Diva evenings, to apply the fragrance to your pulse points—earlobes, throat, between your breasts, at the bend in the elbow, and behind the knees—because heat and perspiration at these spots cause your fragrance to become more pronounced. Scent should always be worn below the waist, too, because fragrance rises. After all, when the lights are out, perfume is still on!

My goal has been simply to find a perfume both my husband and I like. I don't know why this has been so difficult, since he's an easygoing guy, but I've found that what I like he doesn't and vice versa, and what may smell good on someone else doesn't necessarily smell good when I wear it. So I'm always opening up the samples that come in magazines or ads and trying them. Also, I've noticed that perfume doesn't last very long on me, so I've perfected the Diva art of scent layering: With my morning shower I use a gel, scented in my fragrance, then the same-scented lotion, dusting powder, and perfume or eau de toilette (which by the way is not water from the toilet but derived from the practice in France of "performing the toilette" or getting yourself ready for the day).

In my quest for the perfect perfume for both me and my husband, I spray on a different fragrance to try whenever I go shopping. One I discovered that I love is Amarige by Givenchy. When my daughter went to Paris she brought me back Grand Amour by Annick Goutal, which I love also. The other day we received a sample of Obsession by Calvin Klein in the mail, a scent I had never tried. When I opened the packaging, both my husband and I were intrigued. The next day I went to the store and sprayed some on. I went home and we both liked it. Success at last! But in true Diva form, I'm not giving up my other loves.

— Elena

*D*IVA DO'S FOR THE WEEK:

1. Notice during this week what products you use and how they smell. We're lured into buying many different products because of their scent, from coffee (who can resist that great aroma?), to laundry detergents (I love scented fabric softeners), to carpeting. What smells do you react to—good or bad?

2. Plan several trips to the perfume counter, because you shouldn't sample more than three or four scents at a time. Give the salesperson a description of what you're looking for. Then spray the scents onto a mouillette (perfume blotter paper) first. That way if it's a definite "No!" you won't waste a wrist. After you've sprayed the fragrances on, allow fifteen to thirty minutes to obtain the true scent. (What to do in the meantime? Shop! Isn't this a fun assignment?) Then ask for samples of what you like, to try at home before you purchase. If samples aren't available, just spray on yourself and leave for twenty-four hours. Wear each one a full day and note how you feel and other people's reactions to it. Be patient; it takes time to build a perfume wardrobe. But it is important that Divas feel divine. Another great way to go is to visit www.iamdanica.com, and try the "I Am" line of perfumes by Danica Aromatics. This line of fragrances is amazing. It comes in little roll-on bottles with it's own Diva Declaration: *I Am Wild, I Am It, I am Serene*, and so on—perfect for every mood of the Diva!

3. Divas crave scent everywhere, because it relaxes us, putting a smile on our face and desire in our bodies! I have fragrance, either sachet or spray, in my drawers and closets and purse, in my car, and on my sheets, along with scented candles or potpourri in almost every room in the house—plus fresh flowers. You can create an inexpensive sachet by putting potpourri in cheesecloth or pretty fabric and tying with a lovely ribbon. I'm also looking into aromatic plants. What else can you think of? Happy shopping!

*F*RIVOLOUS DIVA DO:

WHEN YOUR SIGNIFICANT OTHER *comes home, turn out all the lights, be naked wearing only your favorite scent, and call out to him, "Come and find me!"*

"*S*NEAKY" DIVA DO:

"ACCIDENTALLY" SPILL YOUR PERFUME *in your lover's bathroom, bed, and car, as a lingering reminder of you.*

*D*IVA TRIVIA:

- An astrologer told Coco Chanel that 5 was her lucky number, so she decided to name her perfume Chanel No. 5 and released it on the fifth day of the fifth month. It was immediately successful.

All That Glitters Is Diva!

I wear glitter every day so on those long hard days if I don't feel sparkly on the inside,
at least I'm sparkly on the outside.
—APRIL NAFTALI, GLITTER GODDESS OF THE FRIENDLY SKIES, CALL SIGN "SPARKLES"

Glamour is my occupation.
—PAUL FRANK, PAUL FRANK INDUSTRIES, INC.

Pixie dust, magic wands, Tinkerbell, and Fairy Godmothers—these are the things little girls dream of. It's time to be a little girl again! Yippee! Divas know we could all use a bit of childlike fantasy in our "grown-up" lives. And to the Diva, wearing glitter is a reminder to lighten up, to laugh, to fantasize, to dream, and to play.

Glitter and fairy dust are magical forces that summon our Youthful Diva. As we humans age it seems we lose our sense of silliness and utter joy at the simple pleasures in life. Our brows begin to furrow and our smiles begin to fade. We are overwhelmed with our responsibilities and want never to get out of bed in the morning. This, my fellow friends, is not the way we Divas were intended to pass our days in Divadom or on earth! True Divas know the definition of *growing up* is not "to become more serious" or "to carry heavy weight on our shoulders and worry about every little thing" but simply to find more fun in more exciting locations as we go along.

Glitter is the tool from the Essential Diva Box of Glamour and Power that we Divas use to banish this superserious-heavy-thinking-very-significant Anti-Diva so that the lightheartedness and playfulness of Diva can shine brightly. Once thought only for special occasions, glitter has become the go-to pick-me-up for the Diva in every moment of life. Not only does it enhance the sparkle in her eye and the glow of her skin, but glitter represents the Diva's inner light. When she wears it her playfulness radiates, her inner beauty glows, and her whimsical fancy-free nature illuminates any room.

Glitter is easy to find these days in a multitude of products, but it isn't easy to use. The Anti-Diva is sneaky in her ways to keep Diva in her predictable little box. She likes to tell Diva when and where it's appropriate to shine, glisten, and be glamorous. At one of my favorite Diva stores by my house, I bought a teeny pack of fairy dust. I treated it like a precious gem and locked it and its magical powers in a drawer and kept it there for . . . well . . . I don't know what, a special occasion I guess. Then my longtime friend and special Diva sister April began giving me gifts of large glittery proportions, one of which was a powder puff by Benefit laced with glitter—everywhere you puff, it poofs glitter. I adore it, but in it went to my makeup drawer, out of sight. I was waiting for the "right" occasion to use it. Fortunately, April came to visit me one day and just her presence was a ray of sunshine. In fact every time I talk to her she brings light to my life. She embodies all that is glitter! She impressed in me the abundance of glitter and its significant importance to the Diva. With her encouragement and infectious playfulness, I finally did use my glitter products. I instantly became giddy with delight and wondered why I'd denied myself this silly yet amazingly powerful treasure for so long. The feeling it gave me of simultaneous giggly youthfulness and Marilyn Monroe glamour brought me back to my Diva reality. A Diva knows the power of these valuable things and of using them. She would never dream of trapping something so precious (just like herself) in a little square box!

I released my pack of fairy dust and vowed from then on to sprinkle it, spread it, and poof it at every opportunity. Glitter has since become my favorite Diva Power Tool; my signature. I have also made a habit of spending time in the Sanrio/Hello Kitty stores. Whether to buy something or not, just being surrounded by these sweet, colorful, sparkly treasures jump-starts my Diva playful side. Now glitter in some form is always in my purse; I take it with me wherever I go and pass it on once I've left. I share my Diva wealth with others. I pass on my glitter pens and glitter body products to friends and women who have touched me in some inspiring way (and some boys, too . . . hee hee). And my reward is my glitter gifts glistening back at me from my friends.

So clear away the stuff in your makeup drawer that has accumulated on top of that fabulous glitter product! Put those youthful pieces of sparkle where you can see them and use them often: a glittery feather pen, shimmery bubble bath, glistening scented lotion, fairy-dust eye shadow, and anything from Hello Kitty and unleash your inner Diva child! A Diva's zest for life, her youthful energy and lightheartedness are contagious, magical, and world altering. Get out the glitter, use it extravagantly, and pass it on!

— Carilyn

Diva Do's for the Week:

1. Take a trip to the makeup counters at your nearest department store. Try on all the glittery, shimmery, sparkly products they have to offer. Treat yourself to the one that reflects your inner Diva dazzle!

2. What products were you crazy for when you were a little girl? Find them, buy them, and use them. Just because you're not a little girl anymore doesn't mean you don't deserve to have and enjoy little girly things!

3. Find some fairy dust at your local crafts store and as you begin each day, make a wish or say a Diva Declaration . . .
   • About yourself and sprinkle it on yourself before you leave the house.
   • About your car and sprinkle it around your car.
   • About your sensuality and sprinkle it in your bed and in your lingerie drawer!

4. Don't save your body glitter for weekend wear! Wear it to work. Hide it under your suit if necessary! Surely your little secret will brighten your day and your night, too!

5. Find a colored glitter pen or feathery glitter pen of your choice. Vow to always sign your Diva signature with this magical pen! Leave the boring, come-in-a-case-of-twenty-four, smudge-your-documents blue ballpoints for someone else.

Frivolous Diva Do:

SPRINKLE YOUR GLITTERY FAIRY DUST *in your wallet and on top of your bills. Spread the wealth when your glitter flies out and showers people with its magic each time you pull out a bill!*

DIVA TIP:

- The brand True Colors by Estey International, Inc., is one of my favorite glitter lines. They give you a tower of different pure shimmery loose powders that you can apply however you want. Mix it with lip gloss, nail polish, hair gel, scented body gel, or lotion, or use as an eye shadow. Its uses are unlimited and so, so glamorous! The products are normally available on the kiosk carts at the malls or online at www.truecolors.com. I recommend visiting their site. It is *amazing!* You can even have True Colors home parties—look out, Glitter Divas!

IV

CONQUERING THE ANTI-DIVA

For the next four weeks we're going to venture into the Diva Underworld, home of the Anti-Diva! Don't be scared. Bring your Goddess with you. You have more power than you think!

"Watch Out, World!"
Vanquish the Green – Eyed Monster!

No one can make you feel inferior without your consent.
— ELEANOR ROOSEVELT

*A*h, jealousy, the green-eyed monster that wreaks havoc on our self-esteem, self-expression, and creativity. Like the Boogie Man and aging, this monster has been a nemesis to us all. Destructive experiences like jealousy are the workings of Diva's archenemy, Anti-Diva. She is an entity that lives in all of us and has many faces. Like a battle between good and evil, she reigns supreme at times of the Diva's self-doubt.

It comes as no surprise that jealousy is all too familiar to women. We are raised in an extremely competitive environment where women are pitted against each other to compete for the men, money, and status. Yet we're told that feeling jealous is a "no-no": Jealous people are bad . . . how dare we "good" girls be so petty . . . and on and on. So when we feel jealous, not only are we feeling bad that we don't measure up to someone else, but we're also feeling bad that we're feeling bad! It's like a downward-sinking spiral that picks up speed as it spins down . . . down . . . down . . .

One night not so long ago I had my own little green-eyed Anti-Diva "episode." My husband and I were talking about business, and he mentioned what an amazing salesperson my friend Bianca was. My reaction (I am embarrassed even to print it) was the absurdly childish: "Well, why don't you marry her, then?" I had reduced myself in a split second to a whiny ten-year-old with hideously low self-esteem (a *truly* Anti-Diva moment). There was no going back, either. Sweet and confident Divarella had been pushed aside by nasty, green-eyed Anti-Diva.

I was in Anti-Diva Hell and needed help out. I called my Diva sisters. They began to ask me questions about why I was even jealous of Bianca in the first place. They wanted to get to the core of my inferior moment. I realized that throughout the two years of my friendship with Bianca, I had repeatedly compared myself to her and decided I was the inferior model. This terrible game of self-comparison I played was a no-win situation. I hated myself, I hated Bianca, and in this case I hated my husband, too. It made me wonder how real my friendship with Bianca was. I had been treating her, or at least thinking of her, as a competitive enemy and not at all as a friend. All this time I had been pretending to be okay in her presence, fighting the green-eyed monster every minute. Certainly not a Diva Do!

As if sticking my finger into an electric socket, my Diva sisters jolted my Diva back from her near-death experience. "How could you possibly think that?" they demanded. "You're a powerful, beautiful, intelligent, and creative Diva. Why choose to feel anything less? How 'bout saying, 'Watch out world, here I come'?"

And in an instant, my body physically shifted into the Diva Power Stance. My shoulders went back, I smiled and stood up straighter. I felt a rush of power. I had forgotten I had a choice in the matter and instead had let my power be sucked away by the Anti-Diva. In that enlightening moment I commanded myself to vanquish this green-eyed monster and embrace the power and strength, beauty and magnificence inside of me. "Yeah! Watch out world, here comes the fabulous *Carilyn Vaile, Diva Extraordinaire*." Just because I say so!

After reviving my Diva status, I decided to be honest with Bianca and shared with her what it was I admired about her. It turned out there were things she also admired in me. It was the beginning of a friendship built on honesty, openness, and true Divaness.

Divadom is a place much like Paradise Island—the exotic and fabulous home of my idol for beauty and strength, Wonder Woman: a place where all women are beautiful, intelligent, loving, and powerful. They see each other as allies, not enemies—helping, encouraging, and supporting each other to help dreams become reality. Women living together in harmony, knowing there's enough of everything for all of them. The Divas in Divadom recognize magnificence, beauty, achievement, and prosperity in others and admire it. They do so because they know all these things are outcomes of women believing in themselves—of women recognizing their own Diva status. Love is one of the Diva's most powerful tools, and she uses it to conquer the Anti-Diva who feeds on hate and resentment. Outwardly admiring another, loving and honoring all humanity are what nourish the Diva's strength.

Next time you start to feel that sinking feeling of the Anti-Diva enveloping you, look at why you're not feeling at the top of your game. Is it because you think someone is prettier than you or someone else got the job/man/status you wanted? Forget it! Instead think to yourself, *Engage, Diva!* and remember, it's in that moment that you have a choice: pity party or Divadom? And after that, let that person know what it is you admire about him or her. It's a funny phenomenon, but when we hold these feelings in, they fester into larger and larger inferiority complexes, but when we speak them to the person, it's as if all negativity is defused and we are actually filled with a sense of power. By doing this we allow ourselves to be vulnerable, opening ourselves up to another, and we get to make someone feel good about him- or herself as well.

Life exists outside ourselves, yet we get so stuck in our own little worlds that we forget what exceptional people with fabulous attributes we Divas are. *Diva* would never sell out on her spectacularness because she wasn't like someone else. She would instead be proud of the uniqueness in herself and others. The Diva is confident and aware of her high value and therefore is never threatened by another. A Diva draws strength from other women, learning from their good fortune, good looks, and good luck, knowing that we're all on the same side, instead of each alone in different corners of existence. Inspired by another, the

Diva learns what she can implement in her own life, acknowledges all people for their contributions, and moves on; no dwelling, no gossiping, no whining (well, maybe a little bit . . . we Divas do allow ourselves a little indulgence here, so long as we adhere to the Diva's One-Minute Whining Rule!).

After all, being committed to living *I Am Diva* is certainly more exciting than I am little-wuss-living-in-fear-of-not-being-good-enough-at-anything Anti-Diva. So there! Dressed in the armor of her magnificence, beauty, confidence, and greatness, no one can defeat the Diva!

— Carilyn

Diva Do's for the Week:

1. Create a Diva Headliner List—like cover stories written on the cover of our favorite magazines, a list of all the reasons why *We Are Great!* Picture your favorite magazines, with you, the Fabulous Diva Babe, on the cover. What would the headlines say about you . . . "Don't Hate Her Because She's Beautiful!" "Hot Legs," or "This Diva Knows How to Have Fun!" Carry with you at all times and refer to them when you feel the Anti-Diva about to strike. If you find yourself stuck, throw a party with your friends. Instead of a pity party where you gossip and talk about all the things you want to fix about yourself, call it the I'm So Great party. Come with magazines, put your own photo on the front, and rework the cover stories so they say great things about each and every one of you!

2. Note the situations in which your "jealousy buttons" are pushed. How are you talking to yourself? Are you acknowledging your greatness or feeling like a loser? Are you throwing yourself a pity party? Are you the "inferior model"? Take time to identify the source of this unhappiness. When you're upset, write it down. Just let it rip. Release your anger or jealousy on the page and use this as a process to release your emotions. Keeping them pent up eats away at the Diva you are inside. When you're done, do a wild Diva dance around the room as you rip the pages to shreds and mix them in the kitty litter box.

3. Make a Diva pact with your friends and find ways to support the Diva in all of you. Have some fun and create your own secret handshake or code words to "Engage Diva!". Choose a mascot that represents your own state of Divaness. (Diva trivia: The official bird of Divadom is the pink flamingo.)

4. Feeling shallow and catty? Make a list of what qualities you have others might be jealous of to pump you up! Make a list in your Diva Diary. Add pictures if you have some, too. I have a picture of my brother, Jason, when he was about three years old dressed in a chic girly ensemble I created for him. It makes me laugh and reminds me I have a fun sense of style, a great ability to dress a moving target, and a close relationship with my brother.

Frivolous Diva Do:

FIND SOME DEVIL HORNS _or a horned headband and wear it during your Anti-Diva moments to bring some humor and maybe even a little laugh to the rescue and then . . ._ scream at the top of your lungs!

"_Bad_-Girl" Diva Do's:

1. Sometimes we just want to be "bad"! When you are feeling this way, revel in it. File your nails to sharp points, paint them green, and poke holes in your fashion magazines. This may sound silly but it fills a need . . . and it's better than clawing a fellow Diva's eyes out!

2. Find or draw pictures of the people of whom you are jealous and deface them . . . yes, very un-Divalike, but sometimes the "Bad Girl" must strike!

Diva Trivia:

- Stereotypical "beauty" and jealousy seem to go hand in hand. This has been taught to us from a very young age—and for a long time. The earliest dated version of the Cinderella story appears in a Chinese book written between 850 and 860 CE. It must be an interesting topic, since seven hundred different Cinderella tales have been collected over the years!

The Diva Emergency Alert System, aka Diva Interventions

The hardest victory is victory over self.
—ARISTOTLE

One night during my college days, some of my girlfriends and I were having a discussion about how it seemed that we all had alter egos—personalities inside each of us who would occasionally pop into our heads and wreak havoc with our outlook on life. My alter ego, or Anti-Diva, is named Holly, and she is a bona fide b-i-t-c-h! She is the worst kind of Anti-Diva because she never lets up once she takes over. Basically she's one big ball of insecurities, constantly defending and justifying why life's not fair and things aren't supposed to be this way. Holly blames other people for why she hasn't made it in the world she's "supposed" to; she constantly thinks she deserves to have a better life. She's a real terror, saying and doing things that she doesn't mean; it's a real life Diva versus Anti-Diva battle personified. The bottom line is that Holly, the Anti-Diva, is rarely happy and never satisfied with her life—how can she be? When she took over, I (my Diva) wasn't even conscious of it until the aftermath. It's really hard to climb out of a hole by yourself, and at that time, I didn't realize that I could get help to get the Diva back again.

Many years have passed since my college days, and I thought that Holly was a thing of the past. Sadly, I learned that this was not the case. Not by a long shot. When I left the corporate world to try my hand at running my own business, Diva was in charge—I was excited, motivated, confident, passionate, and inspired. This is what I had always wanted to do. Initially things went well; I was making lots of contacts, learning a lot, and building my company. But somewhere along the way, my Anti-Diva, Holly, crept in and took over and I lost faith in myself. Holly began to put thoughts into my head that there was something wrong with me and I didn't deserve to have it all. As she cast the spell of doubt over me, I found myself getting angry and beating myself up for not accomplishing the goals I had set. And the more I believed this, the more my power—and life—got sucked out of me. I abandoned my own beliefs and desires and started taking on other people's opinions and ideas of what I couldn't accomplish. I kept waiting for someone to tell me how to make it all work, waiting for my Fairy Godmother to drop the magic key in my lap, but nothing seemed to alter how I felt. As Marianne Williamson wrote in her book *A Woman's Worth*, "There is no diet or doctor that can prevail against a strongly held belief." So true, so true! It's hard to feel love and compassion for yourself when you have such deeply rooted beliefs that you need to be fixed or changed in some way. I felt like I was in a kind of fog that was incapacitating me, rendering me hopelessly apathetic, and it was sucking me into a downward spiral toward eternal *blah*. The worst part is that I was watching Holly weave a path of destruction, and I felt completely powerless to stop her. This was hardly the first step toward the eternal happiness, joy, and Divadom that I had imagined when I started out. The Anti-Diva had not only arrived but was in full control of all my fears. With each passing moment of denial and fear, I gave more and more of my power away until I was left feeling completely bankrupt—financially, spiritually, emotionally, and physically.

Then one morning I woke up and thought to myself, *This is sooo boring; this suffering is completely overrated!* It was time for Holly to go! By this time months had passed, I'd gained fifteen pounds, I'd spent almost all of my money, and I was out of contact with many of my friends. I had reached the emergency stage. That's when my Diva sisters stepped in with the DEAS—the Diva Emergency Alert System. It's like the Bat Signal that Batman and Robin used to let each other know if there was trouble. Sometimes when we're in the pit of despair it's hard to recognize that we need help, but the DEAS ensures a Diva Intervention, a way to let your trusted friends and/or family come to your rescue when you need them most, even if you're not aware of it.

Now is the time to make your own Diva distress signal, a code to signal your sister Divas that trouble is afoot. For example, set up a plan with several of your friends for different types of situations. Have one or two people who are on your Diva hot-line emergency list—you can call them at any time, no matter where you are, if something bad happens. My friend Gina lives two thousand miles away, but she knows that she's on my Diva Emergency Speed-Dial List; she's someone I can call if I've hit rock bottom, and she'll be objective and just listen to me. It's also important that you are on your Diva sisters' Emergency Speed-Dial List. When my friend Erica was in trouble with a relationship, I was "on call" for about a week and made myself available at any time for her to call me so I could talk her through the rough times. With other friends who are in the same town, set up a plan where they know to call you and check in if they haven't heard from you in more than two or three days. Or schedule a weekly play date for coffee, drinks, or a meal with one or more friends, and include time to discuss what you've accomplished in the last week, what you didn't accomplish that you said you would, and what your goals are for the next week. With several backup plans in place, you'll have a safety net in case one falls through.

Here's what I learned from my own Diva Intervention: Look to others for support, but not for answers. It may take time to gain clarity on a situation, so don't rush through it. The less you resist the process, the easier the answers will come to you. This approach to life will have us all gain back our power by enabling us to accept life for what it is—and isn't. That, and a good Diva Intervention from time to time to exorcise your Anti-Diva.

— *Molly*

Diva Do's for the Week:

1. Make a Diva Intervention emergency phone list. Have it handy next to your phone—or better yet, programmed into your phone. I usually memorize most of my friends' phone numbers, but I have my Diva Emergency contact information programmed into my cell phone, just in case.

2. Identify who your Anti-Diva is and what her character traits are. Give her a fitting name if she doesn't already have one. Be on the lookout for when she rears her ugly head unexpectedly. Now that you've identified these problems, start to embrace the things you are afraid of that hold you back. If you really want to break through a specific fear, act it out. Pick a fear—for example, the fear of being successful. Act out this fear in the mirror or with a friend (choose a friend with whom you feel comfortable being a drama queen on purpose!). Really exaggerate it—act as if you're auditioning for a movie and give an Academy Award–winning performance. Now do it and be ten times more dramatic! Oh, woe is me—I am not successful, I will never be successful, et cetera. Have some fun and let it rip! The next time this fear comes up for you, you'll remember your showstopping performance, and it will make facing the fear easier. Or at least it will make you laugh. *Note:* If you feel you can't snap out of the doldrums or if you feel that merely talking to friends or family isn't the right answer for you, then you may want to consider getting professional advice from someone who is specifically trained to give you proper feedback.

Super-Diva Bonus Round:

Spend time with people who love you unconditionally. Said another way, stop hanging out with people who consistently bring you down, tell you that you can't/won't accomplish what you want, or disempower you in your everyday life. Of course, you can still love, honor, and respect these people, but start to notice the effect they have on you in the long term.

*F*RIVOLOUS DIVA DO:

CREATE YOUR OWN DIVA EMERGENCY KIT *complete with different items that make you laugh (funny pictures, cartoons), favorite foods and music, and mindless movies.*

Defusing the Time Bombs

. . . chance, the very worst guardian a man can choose for his personal comfort.
—MARGUERITE BLESSINGTON

There are many types of frustration and, like cholesterol, some are good and some are bad. Learning to discern which types work for the Diva and which work against you brings great power. While it is sometimes hard to tell them apart, a little work on your part will go a long way.

There are simple frustrations, like a run in your stockings, leaving late for an appointment and being stuck in traffic, or burning the rice. Annoying, but not earth shattering. That is, unless your frustration meter has been building over time. If that happens, watch out. "There she blows" will be all that's left after one of these minor frustrations pushes you over the top.

These, however, are the easy ones to defuse, because we cause them to happen. Usually we've jammed too much stuff into our schedules and not allowed enough time to take care of things. A little foresight and all of us can begin to dismantle this frustration process.

"Diva-shaping" frustrations are a whole different kind of animal. These frustrations are our internal guidance system; we may be expanding our personal power, learning new skills, or—more important—we may have given our power away. Over the years I've come to realize that my Anti-Diva, the one who likes to keep me small and insignificant, is the most powerful force I will ever have to reckon with in my life. This woman is a terror! I call her Maralysis Paralysis, because she's made up of all my fears, failures, and mistakes. Maralysis is the one who whispers in my ear, "It's okay, you don't have to worry about anything. Sign up for that new credit card and get the 10 percent discount on all that stuff you really don't need anyway." Where Maralysis has her way with me, my frustration level begins to grow.

Whenever Diva is sacrificed, we cultivate an environment of despair, depression, and weakness. Our frustration is actually a gift from the universe: It's a spotlight shining to show us that Anti-Diva is having her way with us. Seen in its proper light, as a warning beacon, frustration becomes the point of demarcation between our Diva and our Anti-Diva. The laws of the universe provide us with this contrast between frustration and freedom to teach us to discover what it is we really want in our lives. When we get trapped in the frustration zone, we become powerless, angry, and bitter. The lesson is for us to discover the habits that no longer work for us, so that we can replace them with habits that bring us joy.

This week let's explore the ways that we set "time bombs" for ourselves. A time bomb is any action or nonaction that will cause a problem for us in the future. A decision to be late on a payment for our health insurance, for example, causes us to lose the insurance. At some point we might need the insurance, and so on. A less dramatic example is putting off doing the laundry. Then your child needs his or her favorite shirt for a special school day. The morning of the event, you feel like the worst mother in the universe. *Bang!* Your time bomb has just gone off. This week, we declare a "bomb-free" zone in your life—and you have a buddy to help you with this process, your intuition.

Your intuition knows everything you should do and when. This internal voice whispers to us all the time. What is the whisper? It is all those little thoughts and messages that pop in your head from nowhere. Sometimes the whisper comes in your dreams and you wake up astonished at the clarity of your dream. This week we want to strengthen our relationship with our Diva intuition. Listen this week and act on every whisper no matter how ridiculous it is for you. We will also begin to develop a new habit in the area of our intuition: From now on we will listen. Here are a few "time bomb" examples.

1. **Old Habit:** *Intuition:* "Check the tires." *Anti-Diva:* "You don't have time."
   Result: Flat tire when the kids are in the car and you are stranded.
   Diva Practice: *Intuition:* "Check tires." Stop the car and check the tires. You

see that the left rear tire is soft. You drive to the nearest gas station and put air in the tire until you can get home and take care of the problem. *Result:* Disaster avoided, time bomb defused.

2. **Old Habit:** *Intuition:* "Take a right at the next corner." *Anti-Diva:* "This is the long way and you're already late." *Result:* There's an accident ahead and you sit in traffic for an hour, making you miss your appointment.

   Diva Practice: *Intuition:* "Take a right at the next corner." You take a right and there's no traffic at all. *Result:* You arrive at your appointment early with time to refresh your lipstick and breathe.

3. **Old Habit:** *Intuition:* "That woman looks interesting. I should strike up a conversation." *Anti-Diva:* "She's attractive and looks intelligent—a woman who looks so together doesn't need your friendship." *Result:* You don't talk to her and miss out on a promising friendship.

   Diva Practice: *Intuition:* "That woman looks interesting. I should strike up a conversation." You strike up a conversation and discover a shared love for literary fiction. *Result:* You join a book group with a new friend and discover a group of women who share your interests and intrigue you.

It's fun to listen and develop a strong relationship with our intuition. Give her a name; she's your own personal guardian angel or Fairy Godmother. Imagine that the whispers are secret-coded messages just for you. Like a spy on a mission, write down her secret messages to you every day. To create a solid, new habit, do it at the same time every day. After twenty-one days of doing this, or any other new Diva practice, you will have created a new positive habit in your life.

A Diva uses frustration in a positive way. It will show you where you need to go, to change, and to grow into the fullness of who you are. Life is a journey, and frustration is only a bump along the way; make it a bump that launches you from the valley to the top of the mountain.

— *Maureen*

$\mathcal{D}$IVA DO'S FOR THE WEEK:

1. Keep an accounting of all the things, big and little, that frustrate you this week. This will become your guide to where your power is being given away.

2. If you find yourself frustrated, take a Diva break. Walk around the block, sit in the sun, or rearrange some pictures on a shelf. Do anything to re-create yourself with an action. Your energy will shift immediately.

3. For every frustration, look to discover the source. As you begin to unravel the actions from the drama of your emotions, you'll gain power and mastery over your circumstances.

4. Celebrate every "time bomb" that you dismantle. To create mastery over the time bombs, you have a new assignment—welcome to the Anti-Diva Bomb Squad! Get a bowl; any bowl will do, but Diva prefers a large crystal bowl that she picked up at the local discount store. Then arm yourself with brightly colored paper cut into one-inch strips. *Tasks* will get one set of colors: yellow (caution) for things that should be done in the next week; red (urgency) for overdue; green (growth) for those items you keep putting off. *Treats* will get the Diva color: pink.

Make a list of all the tasks you're avoiding and haven't found time to do and all the treats you've been wishing to do. Then take one strip from the task set and one from the Diva set. For example: Let's say the task you are avoiding is balancing the checkbook. Not earth shattering, so it gets the yellow strip for caution. On the Diva strip write down a treat for yourself, like "a fifteen-minute foot massage." Fold the strips and place them in the bowl. Use the power of color as your Diva alarm system. Too many reds—time to take action, you're headed for trouble. Too many pinks, time to play. Remember, for each "thing to do," you earn a Diva pleasure; this is where the honor system comes into play.

$\mathcal{F}$RIVOLOUS DIVA DO:

MAKE A FAIRY WAND AND A CAPE. *Call it the "Diva Defuser Cape & Wand Set." Fly around your home defusing the time bombs you've created. Make sure to give yourself some fabulous Diva superpowers.*

From Regret to Opportunity

You miss 100 percent of the shots you never take.
—WAYNE GRETZKY

One of my strongest talents is following my life when it takes a turn. I think you have to be open
to happy accident. That's really where your life lives.
—SUSAN SARANDON

Do you spend too much time on regrets— wondering why you did what you did or didn't do, or wishing you hadn't done this or that you "should of, would of, could of"? Who hasn't spent hours in her head going over past conversations with people? *Why did I say that, why didn't I say this, if only I'd thought of . . .* These thoughts are the tools of the Anti-Diva. They rob us of our ability to enjoy what's great about our present moments. Now is the opportunity to erase this congestion from our minds. Instead of driving herself crazy rehashing every little thing, the Diva learns from them!

Some of us may regret not finishing school, marrying or not marrying someone, taking or not taking a job. My biggest regret was that my divorce caused my children to grow up in a single-parent household. The divorce was the right thing for us to do, but my kids didn't have the mommy and daddy in the house with the white picket fence and the dog in the backyard, the vision of my main goal in life. Being there, mentally and physically, for my children was more important than anything, so I made a powerful decision and changed my life. This wasn't easy, but I was committed to giving my children the best life I could for them, and for me. And I wasn't going to pile regrets on top of regrets. So for more flexibility of my hours, I also changed careers from nursing to sales. A Diva always has choices in how she lives her life. The Anti-Diva will whisper in her ear, "It's more secure to stay and put up with it." Other people will say, "Why do you want to do that? It's going to be so difficult for you!" But instead of "Woe is me. How will I survive?" the Diva turns her energies into "What are my new opportunities?" With perseverance and my loving support system I learned I could take care of myself. I would survive on my own! What a sense of freedom! My Diva was surfacing.

Regrets are heavy weights on our shoulders, making us unable to walk, even crawl, forward. You have to take these off—one by one—until you're free to run ahead into your dreams. A true Diva seizes new chances where she may, so be on the lookout for ways to undo these needless thoughts. My mother, even into her late seventies, was still regretting the college education she didn't have. Imagine that, after all those years, it still affected her. It's never *too late* to go back to school. There's night or weekend school, school by mail and on the computer. Or if you've always wanted to sing or dance or act à la *The Sound of Music*, you can turn your local theater into your own Broadway stage. You may have pictured yourself a drummer in a rock band; now's the time to get some skins and scare the neighbors. Whatever you feel you missed, find an opportunity to do it now. If your regret is that you hurt someone in the past, instead of continuing to feel bad over it, make amends; write a note or call the person.

Give it up, Diva sisters! It's necessary to live in the present moment to be aware of the opportunities to create your future. Take a look at where you are and where you want to go and what you need to do to get there. When a fear or negative thought or self-doubt arises, sit quietly and let it pass through your mind. Do *not* grab on to it and bring it into your life. It's just the Anti-Diva trying to stop you from your dreams. There are *always* opportunities for Divas. To avoid regrets we will now be open and capture those that intrigue us. While being a writer always sounded exciting to me, it certainly wasn't one of my life's goals. So when my daughter asked me if I wanted to join her and Maureen in writing a book, I could have said, *I can't do that. I have no experience. I've never written anything. I have no time. I have a business already*, and so on. I said, "Okay!" I didn't want to look back and say, *Why didn't I do it?* And here we are! A Diva makes adjustments in her life to experience new things. She loves to take on fun challenges and is careful not to drop her other commitments to make it happen. She is a multitasker, capable of excelling at many things.

Right now that's where I am. I have my own business, plus I have a deadline for writing this book. Plus I have a husband at home. Because my schedule is so full, I can't spend as much time with him as I'd like, but I don't want him to feel left out. What would a Diva do? Give extra-special attention in unexpected places. When I went to New York on business I cut roses from my garden for him with a note expressing my love. I pick up and bring home his favorite foods for dinner. Some evenings I make him popcorn, his favorite snack. Sending cute cards to him at work brightens his day. And I call him almost every day to keep the closeness between us. Because of this, he's very understanding and supportive of my busy schedule. He goes to the market, sometimes cooks, and does laundry to help out. And best of all—he planned a cruise vacation for us to celebrate after the book is completed!

So, my Diva darlings—here is Grandma Diva's second rule:

Stay open to opportunities that come your way. Bite your tongue before saying "No" and say, "Let me think about it." Your life will be grand!

— *Elena*

*D*iva Do's for the Week:

1. Write down your regrets, "what ifs," "wish I dids"—all of them. Choose one to take action on this week. For example: If you've always wanted to go back to school, call your local school and get a catalog. If you wish you had followed your dreams of becoming an artist, go out and buy some paint and brushes. Put them physically in your life in an obvious place so you see them often—see if they call you to action. Or maybe you'll realize that dream isn't still important to you. Remember Carilyn's desire to be a rock star? She found out it wasn't really a rock star she wanted to be; instead, there were a few qualities of a rock star that she found she could implement in her life as a Diva! Either way, you will banish the terrible "what if" that's been draining your Diva.

2. If your regrets have to do with decisions you made, work on accepting that your decision was the right one at that time. If there is something to be learned from this decision, learn it and practice it. For example: If there was a time that you wish you had said something but were too afraid to, from now on speak up, don't suppress yourself.

3. Burn your list of regrets, write your new opportunities in your Diva Diary, and make a toast to yourself, the Opportunist Diva!

*F*rivolous Diva Do:

IF YOU'VE ALWAYS WANTED TO BE A DANCER *(most Divas do), buy some ballet slippers and a fluffy pink tutu and dance around the house!*

V

*L*ESSONS IN STRENGTH

The goal of being a Diva is to build our strengths—inside and out—over time. We learn from our sisters the tips, tricks, and qualities that speak to our Inner Diva, and we share them freely with each other. As we repel the forces that bring us down and attract the virtues that make us stronger, we become more fearless, knowledgeable, genuine, and brilliant. We're all in this together on Planet Diva.

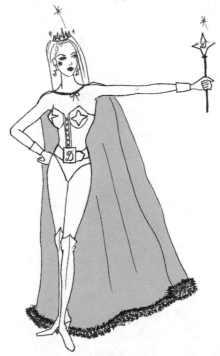

I Am Diva, Hear Me Roar!

My mother gave me really smart advice—you can do and be anything if you're willing
to deal with how other people respond to you. I was willing to take
whatever anybody would dish out for the right to be myself.
—Whoopi Goldberg

What good is fear? While fear has some positive qualities and can sometimes be a good motivator, it's more often than not the thing that holds us back and prevents us from moving forward in our lives. Do you ever notice if you use strategies or have developed habits or patterns to avoid the feelings you don't want to feel? Are you wasting time fortifying the strategies that keep you playing small or being afraid? To dwell in apprehension can be daunting and energy sucking, but only if you look at it as a roadblock instead of part of the highway. Get to know your fear; love it and embrace it like your best friend. Instead of having the negative aspects like trepidation, uncertainty, and negativity slow you down, use these things to propel you forward.

When I look for Diva role models, it's those who are fearless that I admire most. Two of my favorite examples are Eleanor Roosevelt and The Divine Miss M, Bette Midler. These Divas embody fearlessness, determination, and compassion. Their strong beliefs in themselves became their driving forces. The combination of tenacity, courage, and compassion made them strong leaders in the male-dominated worlds of politics and show biz; they were respected and admired for the strength of their character, possibly more than for specific accomplishments. Their successes stemmed not from being ruthless and running over others, but more from believing so fiercely in what they were committed to creating in their lives that they were willing to fight for it no matter what. They also reinvented themselves, building on strengths as well as failures. But above all, they remained true to themselves even when others doubted them. Eleanor Roosevelt was not out to decorate the White House; instead, she radically redefined the role of first lady, fighting tirelessly on behalf of the poor and disenfranchised and becoming arguably the most influential American woman of her time. Bette Midler didn't fit the Hollywood style and look—and to push the boundaries even more, she was so bold that just as she reached the peak of her career, she took an extended vacation and disappeared from the spotlight for almost a year—completely unheard of in the industry. Fans and critics alike doubted her ability to make a comeback at all, let alone a successful one. When she returned, much to everyone's surprise, she was just as captivating and saucy—and popular—as ever. I think Ms. Roosevelt summed it up best when she expressed the importance of believing in yourself: "You gain strength, courage, and confidence by every experience in which you really stop to look fear in the face . . . you must do the thing you think you cannot do." Right on, Diva!

On my path to fearlessness, I have given myself permission to reinvent who I am. This stems from being willing to trust myself, follow my passion, and listen to my gut instincts like a true Diva does. When I do, more often than not I'm on target. I've always had the little voice in my head (you know, the Inner Diva voice telling you, *I know I can do this*), but somehow I ignored it in favor of the opinions of others who were more "experienced" in life and whom I thought knew what I should do with my life better than I did. There's a tendency, Divas, for others to tell you why something can't/won't/shouldn't work out and to let those voices drown out your own—don't allow this to happen to you! Years ago, when I was getting ready for a blind date, I called a friend of mine to ask for some advice to calm my predate jitters. My friend replied, "Just be yourself—your sweet, demure self." At first I got angry. Then I got upset. Then I got worried: Would people like me better if I were more soft-spoken and feminine? This wonderful woman didn't actually see me as sweet and demure, she just thought that things might work out better for me if

I showed up that way. I made several attempts at being a kinder, gentler woman, but it was all so fake. It was then that I came to the realization that I am not a sweet and demure person; I am loud, affable, and funny. This may be a turn-off for some, but if that's the case, then those are not "my people." Now I'm learning about what *I* like to do and what I don't like to do. And it doesn't matter to me what others think about it. At the end of the day, what I think of myself is far more important than what others think of me.

When it comes to being true to myself, I have found that not taking a risk is more dangerous and scary than actually taking it. For example, most of my Diva lifelines felt very strongly that moving to Southern California was a bad idea. A very bad idea. And they weren't afraid to remind me of it regularly (my family frequently refers to this area as La-La Land). I had always wanted to live out west, and the little voice inside me told me to take the leap of faith and do it. Although most of my friends and family are in the Midwest, I knew in my heart that I would regret not at least giving Los Angeles a try. I'm glad I trusted myself—eight months after I moved here, I met my husband. No longer will I let the Anti-Diva snatch defeat from the jaws of victory by whispering to me that I can't or shouldn't say or do something; if she tries, I will thank her for sharing and tell her politely but firmly, "It's my life, and I am the only one who can live it!" It may have taken me a few years longer to develop my own fearlessness, but now that I am on the path, I am no less determined.

The consummate Diva is a risk taker, a trailblazer. She knows that she can accomplish what she sets out to do, whether it's planting flowers, running a business, or starting a new family. A Diva is the CEO of her life, and she doesn't intend to let it become a nonprofit organization. Where in your life are you a trailblazer? Where are you more concerned about other people's opinions than about following your own dreams? Have you ever given yourself permission to take an extended vacation from your career? From your life? Have you lost your moxie or your courage? Whether it's fifteen minutes or five months, take some time to reassess where you're being true to your own standards and ideals and where you're settling for someone else's. Allow yourself to reinvent who you are and who you want to be in the world. Don't allow yourself to get caught up in the status quo. A Diva knows that there will always be people who will freely give their advice and opinions about how you can't/shouldn't do, be, or have something in your life. As long as you follow your heart, no matter what that looks like, then being true to yourself is what will allow you to reap your rewards.

— Molly

$\mathcal{D}$IVA DO'S FOR THE WEEK:

1. Find one unique trait about yourself—a talent or ability that separates you from the rest of the pack. If you're not sure, ask friends, family, and people who know you well. Most important, make sure it is something you believe in and is genuinely part of you. For example, Oprah loved to talk; Madonna loved to perform. Get out your Diva Diary and create a new venture for yourself. What's something you could do that would focus on this talent?

2. For you Divas who are not completely enthralled with what you do, get out your Diva Diary and create a Diva Declaration. One that I have used recently is: *My vocation is my vacation.* In other words, pretend that every day this week at work is like being on vacation. Let this be your mantra for the next week; say it to yourself morning, noon, and night, and look into the mirror as you do so whenever possible. Then, as you incorporate this Diva Declaration into your daily routine, start to notice what happens and write it down.

3. Make a list of your fears—be honest about them. Identify where you deny yourself permission to have it all. Then start to notice what you say to yourself, what strategy you opt for when you get that sinking, uneasy feeling. In the words of my esteemed Diva friend Carilyn, "If you feed the dragon it won't go away."

$\mathcal{F}$RIVOLOUS DIVA DO:

DECLARE TODAY "IT'S ALL ABOUT ME DAY" *and let people know it. Have fun with it; tell people with whom you are having conversations, "Well, enough about me; tell me about you—what do you think about me?" On this sacred day, don't do anything you don't want to do.*

The Diva's Pot of Gold

I have all the money I'll ever need—as long as I die by four o'clock this afternoon.
—HENNY YOUNGMAN

The prince leaned over and kissed the princess. She woke up and they lived happily ever after. Or the knight slew the dragon and he scooped the damsel in distress up onto his horse and they rode off into the sunset. We all grew up with these fairy tales, so we were all waiting for our knight in shining armor to come riding up on his white stallion and carry us off to his castle, where we would be taken care of forever. Ah, fairy tales.

There are many myths about money, but the truth is, none of us gets rescued by a prince unless we're Princess Grace or Princess Diana—and it turns out they weren't so happy, either. The rest of us woke up at a certain age and realized we were on our own and needed to learn how to take care of ourselves. We must become astute in money matters and take charge of our future and providing for it, whether married or single. The odds are we're going to be alone at some time in our lives, and a true Diva knows that she must bury her own pot of gold to be prepared for life's curves. Having control of our money and taking care of our financial future are among the first and most important steps in our evolution as Divas.

As with everything else, our belief system about money was learned in childhood. What are your earliest memories regarding money? What are your fears? These will affect how you handle money today. My parents grew up during the depression. My mother's family was especially affected; they ate a lot of spaghetti to get by. (Now "pasta" is trendy bistro food.) She believed there was never enough money even when my dad was doing well. Their freezer and pantry were full of food that could have been there for months, maybe years. Carilyn was afraid to eat anything from it, because of the freezer burn.

Whatever your history with money is, we're going to start fresh right now! That's the first thing you need to know—you can make a fresh start at any time! We're going to have a healthy and friendly relationship with money. Your Diva Declaration is *I love money and money loves me*. Repeating this is the first step, but it's not enough. We want to get very comfortable and cozy with money, so we're going to play the "Diva Does Money" game. Never played it before? No problem. Just go to the bank and get a hundred dollars in one-dollar bills. Bring it home and spread it out on your bed. Touch it, hold it, talk to it like it's your best friend. Remember how best friends help each other.

Now begin a discussion about how it's spent.

"The first group of you will be going toward my monthly bills—rent or
mortgage, food, insurance, utilities, phone.

"Another group will be going into a money market account for emergencies.

"These dollars will be going to pay off a debt, whether credit card or
a student loan.

"This is my Diva maintenance pile for my clothes, nails, and hair.

"Others of you will be going on vacation with me.

"This pile is for my future, to buy a house or car, or start a business.

"Some of you are going to help me retire and still enjoy my life.

"Last, but certainly not least, is my frivolous spending section to keep me in fun."

Draw a game board with eight dollar-bill-size rectangles, one for each of the categories listed below. With markers color each rectangle:

1. Red for monthly bills
2. Orange for money market
3. Yellow for debt
4. Pink for Diva maintenance
5. Blue for vacation
6. Purple for future
7. Green for retirement
8. Silver for frivolous

Look at how you spend your money now and put this money into representative piles. Are you happy with how it's distributed? Are there some categories that are empty?

Now redistribute the money into the way you would *like* each pile to look. These are now to become symbolic reminders of your goals. In true Diva style, cut out the rectangles and wrap each little pile in pretty ribbons and thank them for what they are doing to help you. On top of each pile put a cover paper and draw a pot of gold in gold ink. Then write what your dollar goal is for each pile. Put them in a drawer so you can pull them out at any time to get reacquainted with your friends and your goals. If you need them out, place them in a clear plastic box as a constant reminder.

The next step in our game is to take colored index cards and write on them BUDGET, USE A DEBIT CARD INSTEAD OF A CREDIT CARD, PAY OFF YOUR CREDIT CARDS, and PAY YOURSELF FIRST. Set up a budget first. On second thought, *budget* is such a dreadful word, so let's banish it and call this concept "Wise Spending" instead. In order to win the "Wise Spending" Sweepstakes, you need to know what your expenses are. Write down everything you purchase impulsively during this week, even that three-dollar cup of coffee or Krispy Kreme doughnut. Make another list of your fixed expenses—house and car payments, medical and car insurance, utilities, taxes, food, and so forth. Finally, list all sources of income—salary, bonuses, interest, what have you. Add up the columns. Yikes! The money isn't going as far as you thought!

The second card offers a way to overcome this. It says, USE A DEBIT CARD INSTEAD OF A CREDIT CARD. This way you're spending only what you have, instead of increasing your debt, plus you see where your money goes. The next card says, PAY OFF YOUR CREDIT CARDS. Only keep one for emergencies. I learned this the hard way. When I was single and money was tight, I took a trip with my two kids up the California coast. On our way home in the late afternoon, the water pump went out in my car. We walked to the closest town—a little place appropriately named Lost Hills. The mechanic informed me that he would have to get the part from another town the next morning. He wanted to be paid first, but my credit card didn't have enough room on it and they wouldn't take a check. What to do? I called my dad and cried. A Good Samaritan overheard me on the phone, offered to give me the cash, and said he'd take a check from me. Hallelujah! I vowed never again to let myself get into that position. When I got home I paid off the credit card and kept it for emergencies only. If you don't have family, this is where the Diva Emergency Phone List that Molly mentioned in Week 14 comes in. Always have their names and numbers with you.

The fourth card says, PAY YOURSELF FIRST. When you get your paycheck, right off the top put 10 percent of it into a savings account. If you have a 401(k) plan at work, take full advantage of it. What you don't see, you won't spend.

After you pay yourself, pay your fixed expenses. Allow yourself a certain amount, say fifty or sixty dollars a week for spending money. With what's left over, pay down a debt, and when that's paid off, divide the extra money among your other goals. Open different savings accounts at your bank, one for each of your original stacks in your drawer. Put a sticky note on top of each pile (account) at home and write the totals of each account so you can see it growing. Then to encourage yourself to reach the pot of gold at the end of your rainbow, use the same-colored index cards (your Rainbow Reminders), cut them in half, and tape them in different places—the phone, car, refrigerator, wallet—as a reminder to Save! Save! Save!

Also, the Diva finds creative ways to increase her income. Maybe it's a new job, or asking for a raise where you are. Pack your lunch at least once a week and save the money. Skip the purchase of coffee on the way to work and make it at home, putting the money you save in an account. Purchase your clothes during store sales, at discount stores, or at designer outlets—finding a great bargain is a true Diva thrill. Or turn a hobby into extra money; if you make jewelry or some other craft, start selling it to others. Once you start this game with yourself, and see the money add up, the discipline will become more fun and you will challenge yourself more. When it comes to your emergency fund, decide what's a comfortable amount for you, and never let it drop below that (recommended is three to six months' income).

While the Diva Money Game can be played alone, it helps to play with others for support and encouragement. Money has always been a taboo subject, nothing we women are supposed to talk about, because it's not "feminine." To counter this, select honest, trustworthy, and nonjudgmental friends for your "Diva Does Money Discussion Group." Here you can share your fears, past experiences, mistakes, what you each have learned, and what your money goals are. We, The Four Divas, are now doing this and we have had long, enlightening discussions regarding money. Come up with creative earning and saving strategies to find the way to your own pot of gold!

— *Elena*

𝒟IVA DO'S FOR THE WEEK:

1. To help you get started with your "Frivolous Account," find a beautiful hatbox and put a slit in the top, or use a large pretty glass vase, empty all your change into it at the end of each day, and watch your money grow. Do it for the next thirty-five weeks as you're reading this book. At the end of that time reward yourself with a fabulous frivolous Diva treat.

2. Take the Diva Money Challenge. Empty your wallet of all dollars and change. Put in twenty dollars and see how long you can make it last. Write down what you spend it on.

3. If you have a significant other who handles your finances, tell that person you want to be involved in the process from now on.

4. Keep your checkbook balanced, so you always know where you stand.

ℱRIVOLOUS DIVA DO:

TEST-DRIVE YOUR FAVORITE *luxury car. Don't be afraid to smile and say,* *"Just looking."*

The Bionic Diva

People always say I didn't give up my seat because I was tired, but that isn't true.
No, the only tired I was, was tired of giving in.
—ROSA PARKS

I don't let anybody push me around. I would stand toe-to-toe with any guy,
but I want to make sure I've got my fishnets on when I'm doing it.
—CHER

As with the lives of all Divas, we are sometimes tempted into the trap of "selling out"—sacrificing our individuality to gain mainstream popularity, sometimes at a cost of our own authentic expression. It's as if acceptance from those around us proves our own worth. We seem to always be fighting for the respect of others, forgetting that the most important person to be respected by is the Diva we see in the mirror! This self-respect comes from standing up for what's important to us. By doing this we tell ourselves *We are worth it!*

Boundaries are necessary for the Diva to feel the strength and power that come from respecting herself. As Divas we must learn to honor that little voice inside that says, *This is not okay with me, say no, leave,* or *I can do it.* When we don't, we feel victimized or convinced by someone else to question our own intuition. What is happening in these moments is the destruction of our Diva Force Field, which, like Wonder Woman's invisible plane, deflects any harm that may come to us. Thinking someone knows better about you than you do; doing somebody else's work because you don't want to ruffle feathers; overworking yourself to prove you're smart, capable, worthy; canceling time with your friends to be at your husband's beck and call to show you "love" him . . . all these things I like to call the wimpy workings of one of the Anti-Diva's many faces, "Pussywillow." Pussywillow is the measly, whiny, roll-over-and-flatten-me wimp who succumbs to everything and stands up for nothing. When she's present, who we truly are is sacrificed and we're left with a terrible, uneasy feeling. This feeling is an indication of a boundary being crossed. Sometimes the signs are more obvious: We feel angry, bitter, unsettled—we're eating too much or too little—we hate our boss, coworkers, or husband. It's really quite an ugly scene when Diva does not honor herself!

Fortunately there's great power to be found amid the ugliness. If it weren't for these uneasy moments it would be difficult to define where our boundaries are. I have my father-in-law to thank for giving me the opportunity to define a major boundary. It used to be that whenever I was in his presence, Pussywillow seemed her strongest. After almost every conversation with him I felt like such a wimp. He's a very opinionated person who comes across like his way is always the best way, and he always managed to threaten my Diva Force Field. More times than not, I squashed the little voice in my head whispering, *You don't agree . . . you don't believe the same thing . . .* or *. . . ouch, that hurts.* I was left feeling violated, weak, and wimpy. And in those moments, my Diva love for humanity was lost and replaced with hate and anger.

I knew I needed a force stronger than myself to end this ongoing destruction so I created a vision of the Bionic Diva. My superhero alter ego—a morph of Wonder Woman and Jamie, the Bionic Woman—Bionic Diva is courageous and stands her ground even at the risk of looking tough, ruffling feathers, and not being liked. She stays confident when others try to reduce her Diva Force Field to rubble. Bionic Diva admits her fears and proceeds anyway. She may have weaknesses but her power shines through because she recognizes her own worth. She has the ability to see through people's rough outer core into their hearts and find compassion for even her worst nemesis but *not* at the sacrifice of her own values. Above all else Bionic Diva respects herself, believes in herself, and honors her boundaries at all times.

To distinguish the boundary crossed with my father-in-law I had to step outside myself to release the emotion I had wrapped up around past conversations with him. I pictured myself as the Bionic Diva watching a movie of the scene to visualize the situation objectively. I saw that at the cost of my own self-respect and esteem I was trying to be liked by my father-in-law, which left me instead feeling like a puny peon . . . the true vision of Pussywillow's ugliness. I recognized that he and I simply saw things differently; neither one was right or wrong. And a Diva certainly knows there isn't one way to look at anything; all beliefs are valuable to the holder. The truth is, everyone has different opinions, and the Bionic Diva realizes that is what makes the world an interesting place. If everyone felt the same way and did the same things what a boring world this would be!

The time had come for me to flush the poisonous need to care about the opinions of others at the cost of my own self-respect. In visualizing the "movie" of our interactions, I realized I'd never thought to trust my own values. In these conversations it became clear that if I didn't honor myself it would lead to my unhappiness and a feeling of inferiority. I also learned that it wasn't the other person *making* me feel terrible. It was the fact that I wasn't respecting myself and honoring the beliefs unique to me!

It's the Diva's burden and privilege to take a stand for herself. Define your boundaries, be clear to yourself and others, and stick to your guns. With this knowledge and practice we will see ourselves in the empowering light of the Bionic Diva, and assume her role as our Diva birthright. Although sometimes it may be easier to let Pussywillow have her way with us, wallow in our own misery, and blame others, constant yielding to Pussywillow erodes our Diva Force Field, taking with it our self-esteem and positive image. Taking responsibility and action are the antidotes. They are the Diva's prized weapons in her ever-expanding arsenal—she's got a huge set of guns that she keeps at her hips and sticks very close to them. Say "Bye-bye" to our well-known friend Pussywillow, and "Hello" to Bionic Diva! Her bionic ears listen to herself first before reacting. Her bionic heart is filled with self-love and self-respect. All that fills her veins are cells of honor, valor, confidence, and strength.

THE DIVA'S BILL OF RIGHTS

We all have the right to have our own space, our own life values, self-expression, and opinions. We all have the right not to do someone else's work, to stand up for ourselves, to laugh loud, to keep our house messy, to hire a nanny, and to leave the office at five o'clock. We have the right not to kiss ass anymore. We have the right to believe in ourselves. We have the right to be everything all at once: good, bad, ugly, beautiful, sensitive, tough, smart, challenged, sweet, and strong. We have the right to be Divas!

—Carilyn

$\mathscr{D}$ARING DIVA ACTIONS:

1. When you find yourself feeling angry, upset, hurt, used, or violated, write it down. Since we don't know what our boundaries are until they're crossed, we depend on these signs to alert us. Play back the scenario in your head as if you were watching a movie. This will help you detach yourself from your emotional buttons, gaining strength and clear vision. How would your Inner Diva have behaved in those same situations? What are your boundaries? What is okay with you and what is not? What will you accept and what will you not? What are you committed to having and being in your life: fun, freedom, expression, and love; or suppression, dominance, and manipulation? Take a stand for yourself. You are worth it and you have the right to be the driver of your own bus in life!

2. Create your Bionic Diva or superhero for the times your Diva needs some strength. What does she represent? What are her special weapons and her powerful strengths? If you'd like, draw her in your Diva Diary (maybe give her glitter hair!) and visit her when she's needed. Or if you want something more visual, get a small doll or Barbie. Dress her in superhero gear: guns at her hips, a big D on her chest, and so forth. Keep her with you and talk to her when you need strength!

3. Create a game court with boundary lines and draw in your boundaries from above. Make it as personal and visual as you like. Maybe the court is hot pink and the boundary lines are royal purple . . . When you're in the midst of a Pussywillow moment, get out the court and draw yourself onto it to represent your current stance. Now move yourself to where you'd like to be. Remember, nobody can cross the Queen of the Court!

4. Create a Diva Declaration for yourself to replace these Anti-Diva Downers and add them to your game or the powers of your superhero.

$\mathscr{F}$RIVOLOUS DIVA DO:

BUY YOURSELF *(from a costume store or get a child's model) a holster and guns to put on when you need to "stick to your guns!".*

Integrity, the Foundation of Power

Always do your best. What you plant now, you will harvest later.
—OG MANDINO

I was working on a graphic image for a Web site recently and I was struck by a ragged edge that was intended to be a smooth circle. As I was looking for a solution, I discovered a technique called "feathering." What happens is one block of color, called a pixel, is softened and merges with a block of white to form a smooth-looking surface. That's how I think of the concept of integrity. Strengthening our resolve and keeping our word, one act at a time, builds a foundation for our lives so strong that nothing can shake it and our rough edges become smooth.

Most of us have been raised to think of integrity as an assessment of moral character. In fact, the definition of *integrity* is the "adherence to a code of values," with the second definition being "soundness and completeness." When I think of integrity as a moral judgment, as a code of values, I get stopped in my tracks. I'm always doing something wrong. If I don't bake the cookies for the bake sale at school, I'm a bad parent. If I forget to mail the check, I beat myself up. In this world there may be some winner of the moral judgment sweepstakes, somewhere, but it certainly isn't me.

I grew tired of the no-win situation and longed for a life that had *soundness* that was not a function of my schedule or bank balance. The Diva in me was in search of a lifestyle that went beyond right or wrong, and I found a new opening in the work of Diva Marta Monahan in her book *Strength of Character and Grace* that helped me anchor my life in the second definition for integrity—soundness and completeness. Marta points out to us that we live our lives in a state of (say it ain't so, Joe) *mediocrity*, less than sound for sure. What a horrible word, *mediocre*. Wouldn't you want to be anything except that! I started to imagine how we might have ended up this way. No little children look up beaming to their mom and dad and say, "When I grow up, I'm going to be mediocre." No high school valedictorians say, "I can't wait until I finish college and have an ordinary life." We may never consciously choose this path, but many of us end up there anyway. How did this happen to our Divaness? More important, how can we restore the grandeur in our lives? The answer, dear Divas, lies in our ability to face the shortcuts we take and, as Marta says, "Develop the courage to be brilliant." She defines *brilliance* as taking any task, even the smallest one, to the level of mastery. In reading her work, I decided that a true Diva lives a brilliant life—and I wanted to be living such a life.

I began my quest for brilliance in earnest, by choosing the smallest of tasks to master. Cleaning the kitchen after dinner can be arduous. Some nights I'm so tired, I just can't bring myself to do the dishes. Whenever that happens, however, what awaits me the next morning isn't joy and a sparkling kitchen, it's a cold, greasy sink full of dirty dishes. Yuck! When I do summon up the discipline to complete the cycle of the meal, I'm greeted by a fresh new start every day and I feel good waking up. What about you? What are the areas of your life where you are letting the misery drag on and on by keeping things incomplete?

This week you will explore your relationship to integrity, in search of your Diva brilliance. Now we must remember the Diva's mantra, *If we want it done, it must be fun.* Take on your integrity in Diva style. Time to clean the toilet? Put on your sexiest high-heel shoes, lipstick, and French Maid apron. Clean it better than you've ever cleaned it in your life. Time for dinner? Become Diva Chef Julia Child or Nigella Bites, the fabulous Domestic Goddess Chef from England. Create the most magnificent Tuesday-night dinner you have ever served. Don't change the menu, change your attitude. Celebrate the opportunity of the gift of life. Meat loaf, mashed potatoes and gravy, carrots, and salad served on your best china, with your best glasses, and the candles you save for a special occasion. You are the special occasion, Diva, living life with attention to the details.

When you elevate the importance of the most mundane activity, you elevate your entire life and the lives of those around you, effortlessly. As architect Ludwig Mies van der Rohe once declared, "God is in the details," and the Diva is in the shine that surrounds a job well done. You will quickly see that every time you keep your word, make and keep a commitment, be true to yourself, and do your best, your Diva becomes stronger. Live a life that is bursting with brilliance; your shining star awaits. As for me, it's time to do the dishes.

— Maureen

ᗪIVA DO'S FOR THE WEEK:

1. Find an area of your life that could use a little sparkle. This will be the area in which you develop mastery. Start small. For example:

   - Clean the kitchen after every meal. Did you ever notice how one cup in the sink draws more dirty dishes to it? Keep the sink empty this week. After twenty-one consecutive days it will become a habit.
   - Keep your car spotless this week. Wash and have it detailed. Clean it out every time you get to your destination. If possible, try not to eat in it. I know, that's a tall order some days, so just do it for one week—you'll probably like the way it looks enough to keep it clean for good.
   - Declare war on junk mail. Look at your mail between your front door and the garbage can. Do not save anything for "maybe later." Throw out everything you can't use in the next seventy-two hours. Better yet, sign up to opt out of all those "pre-approved" credit card offers.

2. Keep track of your experience in your Diva Diary. Note how you feel when you catch yourself not doing what you said you would do. Get it finished or take back your promise. Make a note of how you feel when it's complete. To access your power, finish something you've promised to do.

ᖴRIVOLOUS DIVA DO:

IT'S TIME TO PLAY DRESS-UP. *Create some outfits for your boring tasks: the French Maid for household chores, Wonder Washer Woman for cleaning the windows, Chef Creme Ooh La La with a Chef Hat, brilliant white apron, and your "special" set of spoons and spatulas—and don't forget Della Street, secretary to the famous Perry Mason, for keeping your household or office papers nice and neat.*

VI

A Diva's Surroundings

In the Diva's castle, she reigns supreme. Like the Midas touch, where everything he touched turned to gold, we declare you now have the Diva's touch: Everything you touch turns to beauty, love, and fun.

From Clutter to Clarity

Action is the antidote to despair.
—JOAN BAEZ

*M*y name is Molly and I am a recovering pack rat.
I've spent the better part of two weeks cleaning out my Diva den, otherwise known as my office. Really. And it's no bigger than an average-size bedroom. Actually, if you count the "charity attempts"—those times when I set aside time to clean and, within the first ten minutes, found something completely fascinating to do, like reading old magazines, staring into space, or checking my e-mail for the fourth time that morning—I've been at it for months. But since I started, I have managed to throw away at least a dozen boxes of stuff, even more bags of garbage—including some things that for sure I once treasured—and about five pounds of dust.

I've always been one to attract clutter. Having lots of stuff around is almost like a security blanket (I still have the yellow blankey I carried with me at all times during my childhood). I can look around at all of my treasured belongings and never be lonely; they are comforting and make me feel good. My mom, on the other hand, has always been what I consider a fastidious Diva; in other words, my parents' house is always clean and she is always superorganized. She believes there's a home for everything in the house, and if there isn't, then it should disappear. I've always envied and admired that about her. During my cleaning spree, I repeatedly recalled her favorite refrain, which she has tried to instill in me since my youth: "Purge, honey, purge; you'll feel so much better!" To avoid confusion, let me be clear that she was *not* saying this after a large meal; rather, she was urging me to get rid of the massive amount of stuff I regularly brought home. My parents are constantly shocked and amazed at the fact that I can bring home multiple suitcases for a long weekend. Every time, I'd show up to visit with all my worldly possessions and enough things to keep me busy for weeks in my three carry-on bags and two suitcases. And every time my dad would say, "Geez, honey, did you bring all your silverware *and* the kitchen sink?" It still makes me laugh today thinking about it.

My mom's plea to "get rid of crap" used to drive me crazy because I was convinced that I somehow needed to have a wicker basket containing 379 matchbooks (regardless of the fact that I'm an *adamant* nonsmoker), seventeen books from business school that I hadn't so much as opened during the last ten years, thousands of dollars' worth of clothes that I hadn't worn in years (or even at all), two Walkmans that didn't work, tax information including unused envelopes to the IRS from 1992, about two thousand business cards from various jobs I had left more than three years ago, and other "really important" or "really nostalgic" stuff.

This ruthless cleaning was a cathartic experience. With my office clean and organized, I was able to focus on producing results in my business, and I started to keep track of all the business I conduct on a daily basis—and I love seeing what I have produced! It's empowering and it makes me want to produce even more! Now it's a pleasure being in my office and working here—is it any wonder that my businesses are starting to take off? In fact, my whole life seems less heavy and serious; joy, fun, and laughter have returned. The Diva was restored to that area of my life. Even my husband noticed a big change. Oh, and I finally gave away that yellow security blanket . . . my cats now use it as *their* blankey.

Okay, Divas, now is the time to look into your own life and see where things are cluttered—whether it's your physical space or your emotional/mental space. Whether it's cleaning out a room or going for a walk to clear your head, removing excess clutter from your life feels good psychologically. The sense of accomplishment acts as a sort of validation in your life and frees you up to concentrate on more important and fulfilling things. Notice where you're avoiding projects you said you wanted to complete. When you think of organizing your finances or cleaning the bathroom, does the mere thought make you feel sleepy or tense or even sick to your stomach? If so, then go back to Week 20 and think "brilliance"; it's time to declutter so you can focus on the things that are important to you and get your life back in balance.

One way to get started is to begin your own DAC (Divas Against Clutter) group. Plan regular meetings each time at a different member's house to help each other toss away all the energy-sucking stuff! Whoever hosts the meeting gets to pick the project to tackle that day. Plan ahead and make specific goals for what you intend to accomplish at your DAC party so you can have any necessary supplies ready to go when the group arrives. The project can be anything from reorganizing the furniture in a particular room to improve the energy (otherwise known as Feng Shui) to cleaning the garage to painting the kitchen to planting a garden. Whatever the project, trust your Diva sisters to steer you in the right direction. Make a celebration out of the day; for example, have T-shirts made that say FASTIDIOUS DIVAS UNITE! Select different Diva topics to discuss, such as favorite Diva moments, best tip for defeating the Anti-Diva, or your favorite Diva Declaration. At the end of the day have a wrap-up meeting to see if you accomplished all of your goals for the project. Celebrate your accomplishments!

Purge, Diva, purge; you'll feel so much better!

– Molly

$\mathscr{D}$IVA DO'S FOR THE WEEK:

1. Enlist the support of friends, family, coworkers, and so on to help you do your "dirty work." Have them help you with updating your computer, doing your bookkeeping, even organizing a filing system. The key here is to delegate, delegate, delegate. Even if you know how to do some or all of these tasks, take as much as you can off your plate so that you can put the time and effort into what you really *want* to be doing.

2. When you do decide to tackle a large project by yourself, divide it into manageable pieces. Schedule in one- or two-hour increments per day. If it's cleaning out a large or particularly disorganized room, start with a small area first and completely clean or organize that before moving on. This will make a big difference psychologically and make it easier to tackle the rest.

3. Time to do something with all those photos you've been holding on to for no good reason. Offer any pictures you don't want to family or friends before tossing them. Put the rest in photo boxes or shellac them to a tabletop, stool, or other useful piece of furniture. Pick out a few favorite photos of your girlfriends, sisters, Mom, or Grandma; make them into magnets or find "homes" for them, either in frames or on a bulletin board, and place them prominently where you can be surrounded by Divas every day.

$\mathscr{F}$RIVOLOUS DIVA DO:

HAVE A BONFIRE IN YOUR BACKYARD *using your old papers that you've just purged as fuel to fan the flames. Invite your Diva sisters to join you and make s'mores to celebrate!*

Closet Clutter: Out with the Old!

Good clothes open all doors.
—THOMAS FULLER, AN ENGLISH PHYSICIAN WRITING TO HIS SON ON LIFE'S LESSONS, 1732

What to do! What to do! A closet full of clothes and nothing to wear. Sound familiar? This week we're going to attack that cluttered closet so that we can see the beginnings of your Diva wardrobe. Do you feel the anxiety growing? Calm down, we'll go slowly. You might even enjoy yourself!

The Diva surrounds herself with clothes she loves—clothes that lift her spirits and inspire her! Most of us can't find these items—if we own them—in our closets because of the abundance of extraneous outfits that we have collected there. There are many reasons we've allowed ourselves to accumulate so much stuff. Psychologists have stated that clutter means we're afraid of losing things and that we won't be able to provide them for ourselves in the future. Having a closet full of clothes may give us a sense of fullness or comfort because of some childhood deprivation, such as of food or love. Also, we may place sentimental meaning on our clothes so when we let them go, a part of ourselves is being lost. I still cling to the navy blue polka-dot dress my husband gave me while we were dating eleven years ago—although it hasn't fit me in five years! Whatever the reason, clutter blocks the energy flow. It keeps us stuck, a situation we may subconsciously create because we're afraid to move into the unknown. But even a small amount of cleaning out will make you feel so good that you'll be encouraged to go on. Because when you're cleaning on the outside, you're cleaning on the inside, too. Eliminating unnecessary items will also create more energy to enable you to do other great, fun things in your life for yourself and for others.

I realize this is a very emotional experience, so let Grandmother Diva guide you through this treacherous maze. And if the Anti-Diva should whisper in your ear, "Keep it! You'll wear it again," slam the closet door on her. If you feel you'll have difficulty making decisions on what to let go, invite one of your honest Diva sisters to help. Now is the perfect time to do this, so let's get started!

There are several things to consider as you go through your closet:

1. Good lighting is very important, so it's easy to distinguish colors.
2. Pull out all items that no longer fit. You'll probably never be that exact shape again, and if you are, you deserve new.
3. Toss any items you haven't worn in the last two years. News flash! There's a reason you haven't worn them.
4. Examine each item for fading or spots, and to identify those that need repair. Toss or fix. If you haven't missed wearing them, you don't want them.
5. Evaluate any lifestyle changes. If you no longer need business suits, girdles, or bodyslimmers, out they go!
6. Take a break. Have a cup of chamomile tea to calm you, and chocolate chip cookies for energy.
7. Finally, look at styles and colors. Keep only what you love and makes you feel Divaesque! When in doubt, throw it out! Those items bought on impulse with the tags still on them, *out!* That purple plaid jumpsuit that may come back in style—*out!* Who knows when, and it won't be exactly the same. Those baggy, spotted, holey, comfy sweats I still see hanging in your closet *gotta go!* A Diva relaxes in *flattering* comfy sweats.
8. Sort what's left by tops (sleeveless, short sleeves, long sleeves), pants, dresses, and jackets. Then in each group, sort by color.

Don't you feel much better now? The more items in the closet, the more difficult it is to make a decision about what to wear. It becomes easier to go out and buy a new item than it is to find it in the closet. If you aren't happy with how you look and are buying baggy, matronly items until you lose weight—give it up! Love yourself! Accept yourself as you are. Find something fabulous that you love, and you'll feel good *now!* I have a dear friend who is older, the mother of five, grandmother of nine, who dresses in fitted tops, short leather skirts, and high heels. She always looks so feminine and attractive—a real Diva! Her age and weight don't stop her from expressing her beauty and magnificence and from letting her true Diva inside shine through. Wearing loose clothes can actually make you look larger. When I decided to give up baggy clothing and wear more fitted clothes, people were certain I had lost weight. So getting rid of ill-fitting, unflattering items will actually save you money, in addition to saving time on those frantic what-to-wear mornings.

Keeping only what inspires you increases your positive energy, which in turn affects you and everyone around you. And it also affects the type of people you'll attract into your life. Divas don't want people who pull us down and drain all our energy, but if that's how you feel, that's what you'll attract.

When you take care of your clothes, you're caring for yourself! Cleaning out is also an opportunity for the generous Diva to shine. Donate your items to charity (and get a tax deduction), give them to a family in need (share your good fortune), or give back to yourself and take your discarded clothes to a consignment shop and get some of your money back. It may take several times going through your closet before you get it where it needs to be. That's okay.

A Diva knows that the spiderwebs in her closet are *not* connected to the Goddess and must be cleaned out along with the old clothes! Think of your closet as another room in your house and decorate it as such. How would it look?

Cleaning out my own closet was such an empowering experience. It took several tries, but the more I worked at it the better I got—I started tossing everything. I can now go to the closet, pick a top, and immediately see what I have to go with it. While I used to have to summon up all my energy to pick out an outfit, now I actually feel energized when I open those once forbidding doors! People I love at work have commented on how great I've been looking and dressing lately.

Most important, reward yourself at the end of the week—a massage, a special lunch, a leopard hat, and zebra purse. You're on your way to your total Diva wardrobe!

— *Elena*

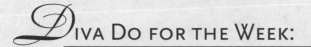 Diva Do for the Week:

You've already done it! Yea for you!

Frivolous Diva Do:

MAKE YOUR CLOSET A SPECIAL ROOM. *Place a beautiful hat or drape a colorful scarf over a shelf.*

Diva Tips:

- Use adjustable shelves in your closet to hold your sweaters, tees, and knitwear so you can change them as your wardrobe changes.
- If you've been holding on to something you like, but need something to go with it, start a list and keep it with you. Usually you find it when you're out looking for a gift for someone else.

Home Sweet Home

The library of my soul overflows with so many happy memories, I refuse to deny them any longer, or the truth of what came before or after their creation.
— SARAH BAN BREATHNACH

I **am a woman lost.** I know how to create a home for a husband or children, but when I sit down to create a home that reflects who I am as a Diva, I come up short. It isn't that I don't know how to "Martha Stewartize" my surroundings; I owned a crafts store and can create beautiful decorations. And it isn't that I don't have the time or the talent. When I was married I canned fruit and vegetables, made jams and gourmet meals, knitted, made slipcovers, and once, I made my husband a designer suit for work. But when my marriage ended, I somehow felt I no longer could have a life anchored in domestic bliss. Somewhere I lost my heart, and here I am, at fifty-two, with a work in progress that I call Home Sweet Home.

When I moved to California I left all my physical belongings behind. Gone were the days of making do. I vowed that I would only live with items that I truly loved. A noble thought indeed. As I sat on my mattress on the floor, with my clothes in a plastic filing cabinet from my new best friend, Target, I asked myself, *What are you doing?* I went into my son's room, examining the fifteen-hundred-dollar bedroom set, complete with desk and dresser, because after all, I had just changed his life; he needed to feel secure. What about me? Didn't I deserve a bed? But as I sat and thought about the furniture I lacked, I made a huge discovery. What was missing was a strong relationship with my true self. What about you? Can you find evidence in your home of putting others first? I sure did.

The truth was I had lived my life for the approval of others. I knew how to decorate as a young woman wanting a husband, as a wife, and as a mother. As a fifty-year-old woman starting a brand-new life, I had no idea where to start. In the world of design, I was a ship without a rudder. It was time to start living now, just for me.

On my Diva journey I began to explore the concept of the outside being a reflection of the inside. When I looked around at my carefully designed home—at least the part that others could see—I was quite dismayed. I seemed to have a knack for creating a beautiful space and then cluttering it up. As a single parent, my life is on the run juggling soccer practice, my son's homework and my own work, and that never-ending chore of cleaning my house. I remember always feeling I was losing the race. I was so discouraged I lost hope of any change—that is, until I met Donna Bell, founder of Crown Rose International (www.crownroseint.com) and creator of the Organizing Principles of Beauty. Donna is called the Closet Prophetess, because she can look at your closet and tell everything about you. (Scary thought, isn't it?) As Donna explained, we live with intergenerational patterns, so my collection of broken-objects-waiting-to-be-fixed-one-day was a reflection of my parents' depression-era mentality—there isn't enough, and there will never be enough. The notion that we must hang on to what we have was a deeply ingrained belief. Once I realized that my life was filled with hanging on, both metaphorically and physically, I threw out or fixed everything that was broken, ripped, or worn out. I was then able to see I had more than enough—I had an opulent life, the life of a Diva. I was ready to embrace my original thought, to live surrounded by the treasures I loved, and my journey into beauty began.

Donna says that if you can clear the space—a wall you want to redecorate, for example—the room will tell you what you need. I thought she was crazy, but I was wrong. The room *will* tell you what it needs to be complete, if you will only listen. It might show up as an impulse to stop at an art show or furniture store. For instance, I had an empty wall by the front door. It was used as a receptacle for junk as we entered the house. I started to imagine that wall as an expression of my Divaness; I fixated on it, noticing it more each time I passed it. One day I went to my favorite store, the Bombay Company, and there I found the perfect table, on sale, to go against the wall in the front entrance of my home. After I brought the table home, I discovered a beautiful orchid to go on the table and later a ficus tree to complete the picture. What I discovered is that as you keep listening, the adventure becomes spectacular, full of surprises and delights. Donna calls the experience "synchronicity," the coming together of things meant to be.

I use many tools to discover who I am today, and how that is reflected outwardly in my home. Start with what's important to you. For me, mothering is a priority right now. I have a ten-year-old son, and I want our home to be a place of comfort, beauty, and joy. I don't want to be worried that Alex will break a precious heirloom or won't feel at ease in his own home. Still, most important, it is the home of the Diva. My decorating is my self-expression, to demonstrate the beauty I feel and the colors I love. Regardless of this stage in my life; this time, I am creating the home for me. Your home will reflect the many stages of your life. When you can freely express yourself, you will be expressing the Diva within you. Seek guidance to discover your true voice.

One of my guides is *Mrs. Sharp's Traditions*, by Sarah Ban Breathnach, author of *Simple Abundance*. In this wonderful book Sarah brings us family traditions from the Victorian era. The book is full of unusual, easy activities that are home and family centered. I use these traditions to ground me and to provide Alex with an experience of family, for a family of two most of the time, three when his older bother Patrick comes to visit.

This week we explore the home of the Diva. Where does your self-expression live in your home? Even in the midst of activity and chaos, the Diva needs a space to call her own.

— Maureen

*D*IVA DO'S FOR THE WEEK:

1. Choose a room (or space in a room that you share with others) that is just yours to create. Remove everything from the space. Do it one wall at a time if you need to for space reasons. Listen to the space. Does the wall cry out for a new coat of paint, a new color, a wallpaper trim? Look at some decorating magazines; don't forget *Architectural Digest* and *House Beautiful*. What style speaks to your Diva?

Now create your room on paper. Cut out pictures of furniture, paintings, flowers, and other adornments for your Diva Diary.

2. Make a promise to keep fresh flowers in your space. You can find beautiful and inexpensive flowers at the grocery store or farmer's market. The Chinese discipline of Feng Shui tells us that dying flowers call on the chi, or energy, of the dead and bring in negative, inauspicious energy, so change your flowers as soon as they begin to fade.

3. Begin to create the space for yourself. Purchase or make one item this week that calls to you. Be open to the gifts the universe has for you. Over time, at your pace, complete your space.

*F*RIVOLOUS DIVA DO:

SAVOR YOUR DIVA SURROUNDINGS. *Make a date with yourself, clear the house, send the kids or husband out for the evening. Buy bags of tea lights—those little tiny round candles that go in diffusers—and place them all around your space; the more the merrier. Make yourself a cup of tea or pour a glass of wine, light the candles, and relax in the glow of who you are.*

Illumination: Ignite Your Creativity

You can't depend on your eyes when your imagination is out of focus.
—MARK TWAIN

To start a fire we need three things: combustible material, oxygen, and a spark. These same three things are what's necessary to ignite a Diva's creativity. All of us have the possibility of being creative whether we believe it or not—yes, even the left-brainers. It's a simple law of Diva Physics. If it doesn't seem to come naturally, it doesn't mean you can't do it. All you need is to combine the three magical components.

Our combustible material, the first ingredient for a Diva's fire, is the Diva herself. By now she is ready and looking to be lit up! Oxygen, the second ingredient, is the space for the imagination to breathe. We block the floodgates of inspiration with our cluttered minds and busy schedules. Uncluttering our minds is the secret to this component of fire, and it works hand in hand with the third and most mysterious of the three elements, the spark.

There are many ways we Divas can free our minds and summon the spark. Taking a drive is a great place to start. Groundbreaking, amazingly original ideas or ingenious problem-solving skills have already come to all of us at some point in our cars, in the shower, on the toilet, or just before going to sleep. During these times there is nothing else for us to do but be with ourselves. The mind naturally wanders, searching for ways to entertain itself. The magical gates of imagination open and allow us to tap into their entire universal resource. The Diva's ultimate secret is that these ideas and inspiration are inside us all the time. We just need to get out of the way. I was tired of having all my fabulous flowing ideas from my commute home be forgotten, so I purchased a mini recorder to carry with me at all times! Taking a walk or a long shower or bath, spending time in nature, visiting a zoo—these are other ways to oxygenate our minds to the spark of inspiration.

Another way to summon the spark is to talk to people. A true Diva really listens to other people and is present in every moment of life. She knows sparks can fly from every encounter, so she pays attention.

I got into the fashion business after designing a top no one had ever seen before. I cut the crotch out of a pair of Calvin Klein men's underwear, turned it upside down, finished it off, and it became a little tank top for women. The idea was inspired by a photographer I was working with who asked me to bring a pack of men's underwear to the shoot for the female model. I thought that was so boring and challenged myself to create something more fun out of them. The top was such a success that I set an unbelievably high precedent for sales with my sales reps and buyers. This early success overwhelmed me as I tried to force myself to create something else equally unique. I was so worried all the time and under so much pressure from myself that I came up with nothing but frustration. I went to a scheduled meeting with one sales rep feeling quite glum but still open (because *I Am Diva* after all). She showed me a photo she had cut out from a magazine of a woman wearing a top; the cuff was striped in a way that looked like a sock. She said, "Who knows, maybe your next thing will be from socks." In that moment I was struck by the biggest spark I had ever felt. My imagination fire was roaring and the creative juices were rushing in. From that one powerful sentence came a hugely successful top collection I designed from men's striped athletic socks that I initially bought as a six-pack from Kmart!

Feeling overwhelmed is the warning sign that your creativity tank is on empty. When your body gives you this signal, you must stop and take a break no matter how busy you are. You simply cannot think creatively until you free your mind. I learned that from the meeting with my sales rep. I needed to get out and talk to people instead of driving myself crazy locked in a room trying to create. I have since made a promise to myself that whenever I begin to feel bitchy, angry, or overwhelmed, it's time to stop what I'm doing and refresh myself. I won't take any calls and I'll do something fun like spending fifteen minutes looking at fashion magazines, drawing, skipping, singing (now ruled out by my coworkers—apparently my off-key voice is disruptive), or walking. I encourage everyone in my office to do the same. If eyes are rolling to the back of heads and they seem to be dragging through the day, it's time for a fifteen minute fun creativity break!

Creativity is not a luxury. It's a necessity. It's our natural energy. It's the way we refuel and continue. It's the alkaline we need to balance the acidity in our lives. Unclutter your mind, surround yourself with new things, and watch the fire of imagination ignite you!

— Carilyn

$\mathcal{D}$IVA DO'S FOR THE WEEK:

1. Spend thirty minutes somewhere quiet, like the space you created for yourself in Week 23, with just your Diva Diary. Think about the things that you love. Jot down any ideas, questions, or thoughts that come to you without judgment or assessment. Just brainstorm. An amazingly powerful book I read is *The Artist's Way* by Julia Cameron. By simply writing freely I released the clutter in my mind. I even got to the point where I wrote down a question concerning a problem I had—and the next sentence I wrote was the answer! Bizarre but very powerful. I recommend the book to all Divas!

2. Visit creative places: the library, the park, a museum, the theater, a bookstore, a fabric store, a crafts store, a music store, a concert, a candle store, a bath and body store, any boutique. Look around and enjoy what others have created for your enjoyment. Watch Home and Garden TV or the Style channel. What ideas come to mind? Do you feel like playing yet? Remember, we're not out to reinvent the wheel or turn you into Einstein (although anything *is* possible); we're just out to have some fun and wake up our creativity.

3. Look in your life and see where you're already being creative and perhaps haven't yet acknowledged it. My husband will tell you he isn't creative. "Carilyn is the creative one," he'll say. Yet he's a master at merchandising his retail stores and a whiz with numbers and with financing his businesses—and all these things are expressions of creativity.

4. Express yourself creatively without judgment or evaluation for at least thirty minutes this week. Just have fun! Experiment. At a loss for ideas? Here are a few:

- Write a poem (with a pink glitter pen, of course).
- Bake cookies out of the box, if you're not the "from-scratch Diva" like me, forming the dough into silly shapes before you bake . . . cookies don't *have* to be round!
- Freeze raspberries and mint leaves in ice cubes.

- Make Popsicles using Dixie cups and toothpicks.
- Paint clouds on the ceiling or get those glow-in-the-dark stars . . . be with nature every night!
- Put your photos in an album with fun stickers or a silly narrative.
- Arrange a vase of flowers: real, silk, or glass.
- Sign up for a dance class, a language class, a sculpting or painting class.
- Hold a fabulous themed dinner party in your home—say, Dazzling Divas of the Century.

5. Start a list in your Diva Diary of all the things you can think of doing that sound fun, silly, and creative. Really use your imagination—no judging and (believe me) nothing is too wild! This will be known as your Diva Delight List.

6. Make a commitment to yourself that when you feel frustrated, overwhelmed, stuck, or dull, you'll stop and do something fun and creative. Whatever you're working on can wait. It will certainly be there when you return, and you may have a fresh new look afterward. Take a walk outside, daydream, or pick something from your Diva Delight List.

*F*RIVOLOUS DIVA DO:

CREATE A SPONTANEOUS MASTERPIECE *with your feet (an idea from my left-brained husband). Paint your toes and feet and walk along some paper or canvas in multiple colors! Feel the cool paint squish between your toes!*

VII

Self-Expression

The life of a Diva is much more art than science, although the experiments can be quite fun! In this step we explore your voice, your creation, and your self-expression in the world. Remember, you can't go wrong, because the Diva is larger than life and doesn't fit in anyone's box!

Breaking the Rules— or Better Yet, Redefining Them

The most damaging phrase in the language is, "We've always done it this way."
—GRACE HOPPER

From the time that we're tiny tots, full of joy and exuberance for life, the world and its rules begin to shrink us from beings of huge possibility to tiny shrews of doubt. It starts out with the little things, the essential cautionary advice—"Don't run into the road and don't talk to strangers." Slowly but surely the rules creep into areas where rules were never meant to go. Remember the kindergarten teacher—or even worse, your mother—who spoke those infamous words, "Honey, don't color outside the lines"? Those words tortured me. I was trying so hard to stay inside the lines that I believe in that moment I created lines everywhere and my lines became impenetrable walls, not healthy boundaries. Now, I'm sure that whoever created coloring books didn't intend to thwart the creativity of every child. And not all of us created walls—some took flight. I look at artist Peter Max's cows— no black and white here, but bright blues and vivid colors—and know this was a child who probably threw away the coloring book.

What road did you take, the good girl or the bad? You know there really wasn't any gray area; we had to be one or the other. I've been both. During the first twenty years of my life I colored inside the lines; I tried to be perfect. It was hard work and a job that I constantly failed at. Then, for about five years in my twenties I lived a harrowing existence as a bad girl without any rules at all. Dante writes that over the gates of Hell are the words ABANDON HOPE ALL YE THAT ENTER HERE. That about sums up my experience of the life of a wild one. Around the time I turned thirty I bought every rule book that was published—*Our Bodies, Ourselves; The Feminine Mystique; The Dance of Anger; Making Peace with Yourself; I'm Okay, You're Okay.* To tell you the truth, I wasn't even close to being okay. I needed help. You name the program, I was in it: Al-Anon, Weight Watchers, Overeaters Anonymous, traditional therapy, primal scream therapy, transactional analysis. Yikes! I was a self-help junkie trying to perfect the amazing imperfection that was me. Dante's words could still have been hanging over my life because I was never going to get me right, so I did what every good imperfect American woman of the 1980s did: I got a really good career, and an MBA. Now I had to *prove* myself, so I didn't really have time to improve myself.

When I was forty-nine (and I hope it doesn't take you that long) I discovered that I no longer cared about living the life that everyone else thought was great; I was interested in living the life that I thought was great. Like when I moved to California. It was the act of a desperate woman, one that today I'm thrilled I took. Why do we have to have our backs against the wall before we take decisive actions? I don't want to be desperate; I want to be a Diva. The Diva stands in the middle of the road, going wherever she wants to go because that's where she chooses to go. The Diva follows the rules of her heart.

Let's explore how the Diva spices up her life. Imagine that you're a food server balancing a tray on one hand. Look at each area of your life—family, self-care, career, intimate relationships (spouses/lovers), fun and recreation, friends, spiritual growth, and personal growth. Now, if each area was a family-size bowl (remember those great restaurants where they served everybody at the table family-style?), how balanced is your tray? Are you doing the balance dance just to keep everything going at the same time? Is your tray so out of balance that it's on the floor? Have you pulled the muscle in your shoulder because one side of the tray takes up all your time? Now put the tray down on one of those handy tray stands they have in restaurants and look at it. Make each area of your life a selection from our basic food groups. How would they match up? Well, Diva, we're going to find out right now.

Step 1: Number the life areas in priority order with number one being *the most important to you*. Now list all of the foods in priority order, starting with your favorites. Remember, Divas, there are no calories here; indulge!

Step 2: Draw a line from the life areas to the appropriate food group for yourself:

LIFE AREAS	FOOD GROUPS
Family	Soda, chips, and dips
Self-nurturing	Champagne, spirits
Career	Caesar salad
Intimate relationships	Green beans, carrots, brussels sprouts
Fun and recreation	Filet mignon, sushi, lobster
Personal growth	Chicken, fish, beef
Spiritual growth	Dessert, baked alaska, chocolate
Friends	Butter, sour cream, milk, ice cream
Exercise	Bread, pasta, mashed potatoes
Life maintenance (bills, shopping)	Apples, peaches, melons

If you only have time each day for the top five, how balanced is the diet you're feeding yourself? Are you starving in some areas and overexpanded in others? Balance your life with the Diva plan of action—eat dessert first. Imagine what your life would feel and look like if you took care of yourself first thing in the morning. Pretty radical thought. The rules police would surely find you and track you down. You would be sentenced to days of solitary confinement with your dirty laundry. The number one rule for women to break: Take care of everyone else first. The airlines have it right: Put your own oxygen mask on first. The Diva Rule is to take care of yourself first and then take care of your child, or spouse or boss or lover. If you don't have the oxygen to live, you have nothing left over to give to anyone.

If you took care of yourself first, here's what would really happen. You would be happy and so would everyone else in your life. If you don't believe me, that's okay. Just suspend all judgment and try it on for a day. You can always go back to putting everyone else first and yourself last tomorrow. Put down the overloaded tray of your life for just one day and pick up just the dessert. Break these ridiculous rules today: *Fat women and older women can't be sexy. We can only have cake on our birthday. We can only make stuffing for Thanksgiving. Big women have to wear baggy clothes. Be ladylike. Keep your voice down. Don't draw on the walls.* (Okay, moms, cover a wall in the bathroom with white wallpaper.) *What will other people think? Don't tell anyone. Don't chase men. Do chase men.* Break all the rules that tie you down. As an aid, repeat the following mantras when you feel compelled to sacrifice yourself for another:

I color outside the lines.

I eat dessert first.

I swim right after lunch.

I have no bedtime!

You are not the boss of me; I am the boss of me.

Today give yourself permission to live the life that you love. If anyone asks what's going on, just tell them you're in Diva training.

— *Maureen*

Diva Do's for the Week:

1. Buy yourself a Diva doll. Mine is Cher; she's fabulous. Now find the ugliest string you can find and cut it into pieces about twelve inches long. Tie a piece of string on your doll for every rule you can think of. This represents all the rules of everybody else that you live with each day. Every time you break a stupid rule, untie yourself, one rule at a time.

2. Buy yourself a box of sixty-four Crayola crayons. Smell them and go back to your childhood, then color outside the lines.

3. Encourage at least one other Diva to go outside her lines. It's so much fun to be bold together.

Frivolous Diva Do:

BREAK THE RULES. *Wear your shirt inside out. See how many people tell you it's wrong. Just tell them you're superstitious and it's bad luck to change the shirt once you put it on inside out*

Humor—Lighten Up, Divas!

The person who knows how to laugh at himself will never cease to be amused.
—SHIRLEY MACLAINE

Do you ever think about a funny line from a show or movie you've seen, or something funny a friend said to you, and then just start laughing out loud? I do. All the time. And that makes me laugh even more. I love to go into card shops and read the greeting cards that make me giggle out loud. Other people may stare, but you know they're secretly jealous that I get it and they don't. In fact, rarely do I ever send a humorless card to friends or family; it's just not my style to be overly serious.

There are few comedians who crack me up like the boys from Monty Python. I used to stay up really late (well, twelve-thirty in the morning may not be that late for some, but it is when you're thirteen!) to watch them with my brother, John. On occasion we'd get "shushed" by our parents for laughing too loudly in our very loud and identical straight-from-the-belly guffaws at their completely absurd, over-the-top humor. Carol Burnett is another one of my all-time favorite comediennes; some of the funniest parts of her show weren't the skits themselves, but the mistakes and blunders they made and kept as part of the show. Ad-libbing was a regular part of the program, and they would make things up on the spot just to see if they could catch each other off guard and make the others laugh. And they did so quite successfully and often. I loved it that making each other laugh was almost as important as getting the audience to laugh.

But before my rise to Divadom, I didn't laugh at myself very easily. On the contrary,

I took myself just a little too seriously for my own good. I let my humor out in measured doses and only if it didn't make me look foolish in front of others. Fortunately, I got over that. I've been involved in too many borderline-excruciating situations not to find at least some humor in them. One particular occasion comes to mind when I was recently a bridesmaid in a Diva sister's wedding. I was the last to come up the aisle before the bride. Just as I was walking up the aisle, I tripped on the wooden floor and stumbled, grunting loudly and flailing my arms wildly. I managed to regain my balance just as I was about to fall flat on my face. Before becoming a Diva, I would have found this experience humiliating and upsetting. But mindful of my Diva status, I regained my composure and curtseyed in my floor-length gown and flowers to the applause and laughter of the audience. And it was all captured on film! It lightened the mood of an otherwise nerve-racking moment.

One of the Diva's most important tricks of the trade is her sense of humor. Incorporating humor into everyday life makes us feel better about ourselves, our lives, and everything around us. Humor also brings levity to a tense, uncomfortable, or difficult situation by disarming the severity of what's happening. For the most part, the pain and suffering we experience come from how we view our difficulties, not from the actual difficulties themselves. Using humor helps us put problems into perspective so they can be dealt with more powerfully—and so we can get on with life. I'm not saying that humor should be used in place of grief or tears; still, there are times when humor arises naturally out of misfortune or tragedy, and it can give a person power in an otherwise powerless situation. In addition to defusing tension and easing grief, there are many doctors, clinicians, and other really smart people who have all found the reason that laughter and humor make us feel good. Laughter affects us physiologically by decreasing "stress" hormones and activating the immune system; it kills off cells infected by viruses and causes a "eustress state" (similar to a "runner's high") that produces healthy or positive emotions. Now you have good reason to take advantage of one of the Diva's favorite expression, "If it feels good, do it!"

Allen Klein, author of *The Healing Power of Humor*, created a technique to demonstrate how humor can make painful moments laughable through the use of exaggeration. When our upsets are all-consuming and we can't see anything else, sometimes the only way to see the absurdity of a situation is to describe it in such overinflated terms that we begin to laugh. Then, instead of being the central figure in our own tragedies, we feel less confined and are less directly involved in our suffering. We have created a Diva exercise to help demonstrate this point.

Select a few Diva sisters from your Diva Emergency List (from Week 14) and practice this ahead of time so that when you really need it, you'll already know what to do. Cast yourself in a soap opera, using real characters from your favorite show or one that you've made up. Assume the identity of one of the characters, create a desperate situation for yourself, and give an Emmy Award–winning performance. Make sure you go over the top to act out your drama and despair. When the real moment comes, call your Diva sister and give her a snapshot of what's happening that has you in the pit of despair. She will urge you on and coach you through the tantrum. Continue this exercise until you can see the ridiculous pity party you're throwing for yourself and can laugh it off.

Do you take the time to incorporate humor into your life? Do you practice laughing at and with yourself? Do you give yourself permission to laugh at ordinary, everyday circumstances? Do you have wrinkle lines between your eyebrows caused from furrowing your brows too much? Do you like mustard? Just kidding; I wanted to see if you were still paying attention. Start to notice specifically what makes you laugh, what tickles your funny bone. When the Diva laughs, she opens up and lightens up. When you're able to find humor and laugh at embarrassing or humiliating moments, it moves you one step closer to Divadom. One of the reasons I laugh so much is that I give myself permission to laugh at myself. I look at the things that happen to me and around me every day and I see what's funny about them. Just recently I went to an all-day meeting, and not until the end of the day when I was leaving did I realize that I had worn two completely different shoes. I thought it was so hilarious that I ran back into the meeting to show everybody. Instead of being embarrassed or humiliated, I laughed about it and so did they.

Create a "trigger" to turn yourself around when you become stressed. Everyone has at least one picture, cartoon, or joke that sets them giggling. For example, I keep in my office an ad for American Express from 1991—part of a campaign that featured various celebrities who had been card holders for impressively long amounts of time. This particular ad featured a spread; on one side is typed JOHN CLEESE. CARDMEMBER SINCE 1971. On the other side is a full-page photo of Mr. Cleese posing with a serious expression and wearing a red dress, red heels, a red purse, red gloves, pearls, and a huge red hat with feathers that covers blond locks; he's holding two tiny dogs. Don't you think that's funny? If not, no problem—I do, and it's my trigger, so go find your own and leave me to laugh at Ms. Cleese.

— Molly

Diva Do's for the Week:

1. Learn to laugh. Practice. If you don't know how to laugh, or if you find you're too serious too much of the time, take a class in improvisational humor. Hint: If you find that you become defensive or argumentative when people question your ability to laugh, that's a red flag for you to lighten up! And laugh every day—do what you must to make it happen, but just make it happen. Find humor in your everyday life, whether it's in things people say to you, things you read, or things you say and do. Take a time-out from your day for five to ten minutes. Even if you're by yourself this can be very effective. First, do a belly laugh; laugh from the deepest part of your tummy. Then smile as big as you can for five minutes, without stopping. Notice what happens.

2. Make a list in your Diva Diary of all of your favorite funny movies. Use this list as a reference for those times when you just have to find a way to lighten up. Some of my favorites are: *Blazing Saddles, A Bug's Life, This Is Spinal Tap, High Anxiety, Just Visiting, Parenthood, The Whole Nine Yards*, and any Monty Python movie.

Frivolous Diva Do:

GO TO YOUR LOCAL CARD OR BOOKSTORE *and read the funny cards until you find one that makes you laugh out loud. Instead of sending it to someone else, keep it for yourself. Place it on your desk or someplace where it can serve as a reminder for you to lighten up!*

Delightful Delusions

In order to be irreplaceable one must always be different.
—Coco Chanel

*I*f you could be someone else for a day, who would you be? A famous old-time movie star or a bookish academic? An Olympic ice skater, or the president of the United States? How would you behave if you were any of these people? When we pretend to be someone or something else, our inhibitions seem to melt away.

I'm writing this in late October, close to Halloween. How perfect! Halloween is the Diva-in-training's excuse to practice being her most outrageous self. Thinking back, that's what I've been on several occasions.

One year I went to a nightclub on Halloween with friends wearing my daughter's high school cheerleading uniform. It was great fun to take on the bubbly, friendly, perky personality of the cheerleader. Someone actually thought I was a recent graduate. (He was under the influence, I think.)

The next year a little more Diva was exposed. For a Halloween party, I was a boxer. I wore the tank top, short Dolphin shorts (remember those?), and had the requisite black eye and bloody nose. And I spoke with a deep voice. I went around flexing my muscles. At five foot one with a small frame it was quite a sight. I liked the feeling of being powerful and strong and talking tough, bragging that I could take on anyone.

Finally I was ready to let the full Diva out! This was the year I was a heavy-metal rocker for a Halloween party. I dressed in torn jeans, tight short top, fake tattoos, exaggerated makeup, and wild hair. Since I'm pretty conservative, going out like this made it okay for me to be more outrageous. I talked more, and louder; I was funnier; I danced every dance. I was open to meeting new people. In fact, there was an attractive man there dressed as Superman, in a tight bodysuit and short red shorts. *Wow!* I flirted like crazy, as any Diva would. We were attracted to one another, continued to see each other, and he later became my husband.

There are Divas and Divos who have devoted their entire careers to this alter ego persona, such as RuPaul and Dame Edna. But the ultimate Delightful Delusion is Elvira, Mistress of the Dark. She has made a huge career and marketing bonanza out of being someone else. With a wig, makeup, and a low-cut black dress, she takes on another persona. She even has a special custom car, the Elvira Macabre Mobile. She's well known for hosting scary movies on television, but she also has starred in feature films. Marketing includes making public appearances and having a Web site, her own line of accessories, and a fan club. In real life she is Cassandra Peterson, wife and mother.

We all have these different parts in us, and Halloween is a great time to explore living outside ourselves. Another Diva opportunity for self-expression is to have a theme party, any time of year. Choose a "come as you *aren't*" theme that has people with personalities you would like to try out, such as: My Favorite CEO, Outrageous Movie Characters, the Hairiest People in History, or Personas of High School (jock, nerd, cheerleader, teacher, principal, the rebel, and more). Make sure everyone knows the rule is to be that person throughout the party! By playing with delusions, you're trying on qualities you can bring into your life.

Here are some other ways Delightful Delusions can spring you into Divadom:

- You are in a management position, but have trouble managing effectively. Imagine that you're Andrea Jung, head of Avon, or Jeanie Buss, vice president of business operations for the Los Angeles Lakers. Pretending to be someone you see as powerful will help unlock your own Diva power. Feeling confident in your knowledge, experience, and strength will overshadow taking things personally and trying to be everybody's friend.

- You have lost some of your enthusiasm for life that the stereotypical cheerleader has. Now add some fun back: In the moment, make up your own little cheer with high kicks—I bet you'll start laughing! When life starts to overwhelm the Diva, she takes a break and plays a game with herself or others to get the balance back.

If you have suppressed that rebel in you almost to the point of extinction, release her! Because of my roles as mother, grandmother, business executive, and more mature person now, I thought I *had* to act more reserved. But I loved the outrageousness of the heavy-metal rocker, and I have a picture of me in that outfit that I'm keeping on my desk as a reminder. I know that I can incorporate, in my own way, some of her qualities without going over the edge. You won't see me in tattoos or short tops or torn jeans, but I will be more outgoing, add more makeup when I choose, add more flamboyant items to my wardrobe, and dance more (which I love) to bring out my total Divaness.

Let's not save our Delightful Delusions for only Halloween. Bring them on *now!*

$\mathcal{D}$IVA DO'S FOR THE WEEK:

1. This week, pick a day to be someone else. Dress as her, talk as her, act as her, be her (or him!). This could be anything you've thought about, from a gourmet cook to a successful author (my choice) to a movie star.

2. Join a community theater group or take an assertiveness training class.

3. Write in your Diva Diary how it felt and what parts you want to incorporate into your life as a Diva.

$\mathcal{F}$RIVOLOUS DIVA DO:

FOR THOSE OF US WHO *have always wanted large breasts, this week purchase the liquid-filled fakes, wear them, and enjoy the reactions (your own, as well as those of others!).*

Be Outrageous!

There is no woman bolder than I. I have the most reckless audacity!
—CATHERINE THE GREAT

The most outrageous thing I have ever done is to think I have never done anything outrageous!
—SUSAN REAMS (MOLLY'S MOM)

The word *outrageous* always used to scare me. I thought of it as borderline naughty or taboo. Outrageous people were not role models; they were dangerous, to be avoided or at least kept at a safe distance. They were the ones who had to be the centers of attention at all times. The people I knew and considered outrageous were way over the top, uncontrollable. If I were to catch their "disease," I might have to go into rehab indefinitely.

While I recognized that I had unique qualities, and I loved my uniqueness, I was very self-conscious about letting others see it. If I was going to be outrageous, I had to control when and where it could show up. I could share a little bit here in the form of one-liners or a little bit there with a funny accessory, like the giant solitaire diamond ring that I wore as a bracelet to a number of parties; but never did I dare to just *let it rip* all the time—what would the neighbors think?

But being outrageous is part of a Diva's persona. It's the part of the Diva mystique that allows her to fearlessly explore uncharted territory in her life, such as starting the business she's always dreamed of but never gave herself permission to try. Being outrageous is the thing that keeps a Diva from taking life too seriously. Divas say something irreverent instead of just thinking it, or wear an unusual article of clothing (maybe some faux leopard fur pants?) just because they love it. Take Lucille Ball, one of the most beloved comediennes of all time. Never before had a woman acted like she did on TV; now it's commonplace. She was a trailblazer who set the stage for women in television to allow themselves to be over the top. Martha Graham, the maven of modern dance, also carved a path for women in her field, especially since she found her destiny at the shockingly late age of twenty-two, a time when most dancers of the day were considered well past their prime. Bette Davis, Mae West, and Tina Turner are others who pioneered outrageousness in their fields. These women let nothing stand in their way as they blazed the trail to complete self-expression. In contrast to my more insecure days, I now admire people who can embrace this way of being; I'd rather call them unconventional than reckless.

Sometimes it takes outrageous failures to get to outrageous success. I recently learned that the average millionaire goes bankrupt 3.5 times in his or her career. I was actually relieved to hear that, because I find it hard to give myself permission to fail. But learning from our failures is what creates room for our success. One friend in particular comes to mind in this arena. My friend Chellie, a true Diva, is best described as someone who has seen and done it all; she has been to hell and back and now thrives from what she learned. She has experienced bankruptcy, spousal abuse, alcoholism, and near-death experiences, including being robbed at gunpoint. Instead of being a victim of her life's circumstances, though, she chose to be the one responsible for how her life turned out. Now Chellie embodies the word *outrageous*. She fears nothing. She lives a life that she loves, but she isn't afraid to admit that her life wasn't always so wonderful. She had plenty of experience that would cause most people to throw in the towel; but one day, while sitting in her rocking chair contemplating her relationship with an abusive husband, she realized that the victim stories were what kept her a victim. That single revelation enabled her to begin taking bold risks in the face of people telling her she was crazy or couldn't do it. She said to herself, *Chellie, you picked him, you can unpick him*. So she did, and she changed her life.

Attention all Divas: Are you sitting idly in the rocking chairs of your comfort zones wondering what's out there? I know I was. It was scarier for me to even contemplate taking a risk and finding out what was on the other side than to just trust that it would all work out and do it anyway. A Diva skips the drama in her head and jumps right into action—it makes life so much easier! Being outrageous isn't about being the funniest or the loudest or the craziest; it's about taking a risk in your life—no matter how big or small—and being willing to fail. It's about giving yourself permission to do something big just because you want to. I stepped out of my comfort zone one day several years ago, when a friend of mine challenged me to smile and say "Hello" to as many people as I could while walking down the street in downtown Chicago. I accepted her challenge, and the results were so powerful that it completely caught me off guard. Really. People were sometimes startled when I just smiled and said "Hello!" to them. Some people even looked at me as if I were crazy. But what was so surprising was that just as many people became instantly lit up and either smiled back or returned the greeting. It was almost as if I had shaken them out of their oblivion and brought them back into the world with everyone else. One man even turned around, struck up a conversation, and then asked me out on a date! One little word and one seemingly outrageous gesture made my whole day!

Now it's your turn. Take on being outrageous everywhere in your life, no matter what that looks like for you. Be unstoppable; be determined to have a great life—no matter what! There's a real rush you get when you do or say something you don't normally do. For example, stand up for yourself to your boss and your family; talk to people in an elevator (when you get in an elevator, turn around and face everybody and say, "Thank you all for coming; the reason I've called you all here today is . . ."). If it helps bolster your courage, wear an outfit from Week 27 out into the streets. Smile and say hello to people you pass in the street or in a store. Learn to love the things about yourself that currently embarrass you in front of others. Learn to have as much fun with a bunch of sixth-graders as you can with a group of adults; love that you have a unique sense of style. Go ahead Diva, be outrageous—you'll love it!

— Molly

𝒟IVA DO'S FOR THE WEEK:

1. This week choose someplace outrageous to visit; wear something outlandish to work, like a color you don't normally wear, a glittery top, or sparkly socks (my personal favorite); or say something over the top, unusual, or unexpected to your friends and family. You get to decide what your Diva definition of the word *outrageous* is, but if it's something that's easy or comfortable, then that's not it! It doesn't matter how big or small you play the game, just give yourself permission to play it. Then experiment with your new capacity to take life by the horns and write down in your Diva Diary what happened as a result. How did you feel? How did your friends react?

2. Get out your "bible," the Diva Diary, and make a list of people you consider outrageous. Write down the characteristics that make them seem outrageous to you. What celebrities or famous personalities do you admire? What characteristics do they have that are outrageous?

3. Choose one trait that you consider outrageous (unconventional, unusual, over the top, or what have you)—something that would require you to step outside your comfort zone. Take it on this week and notice what happens.

ℱRIVOLOUS DIVA DO:

BUY A GARTER BELT, *thigh-highs, fishnet or back-seam stockings . . . and wear them to the supermarket . . . or library!*

VIII

A Diva's Image

The Diva is just coming to life. Your blank canvas is waiting for you.
Paint your world with levity through color, makeup, and fashion
and be a babe-newborn!

Creating the Diva's Style

Life isn't about finding yourself. Life is about creating yourself.
—GEORGE BERNARD SHAW

Style is a mode of expression, a way of illustrating the defining characteristics of a particular person. It doesn't come from reading fashion magazines or buying trendy items each season. It comes from knowing who we are, being proud of it, and expressing it uniquely. Knowing what's important to us and what makes us feel powerful, alluring, playful, or mysterious leads a Diva to her own unique style. Audrey Hepburn, Madonna, and Coco Chanel are women we consider Diva Style Icons. They dress by their own definitions of fashion, not looking to trends or media to dictate what they choose to wear, and because of this have started huge fashion movements. By their example we see that there's no one overall or specific look for a Diva. Audrey retained the same simplistic, sophisticated style all her life, while from Madonna we can never expect the same look, let alone hair color, twice.

A couple of years ago I started noticing my own lack of style. In the past I had considered myself someone with unique taste, bordering perhaps on the wild side, yet somehow in recent years that part of me had disappeared. Looking at me in my simple, neat outfits, you'd never guess how bold and funky I could look—sadly, I just looked bland. This loss really bothered me, so I began to listen to what I was saying to myself each time I got dressed. I hoped to decipher the source of this disturbing lack of style. At that time (and now) I was both the CEO and designer for my apparel manufacturing company. In my mind these two "types" of people dress very differently, and I realized I was thinking I had to choose which *one* image I was going to relay to people. This caused a great deal of confusion because inside I didn't feel like either one and therefore had simply given up altogether on who the "real" me was. I was going by the belief that I had to choose only one look all the time! How boring! No wonder there was no creativity, freedom, or satisfaction in my life.

Magically, a new friend—appropriately named Eden—entered my life. Eden was outrageously expressed in her dress and seemed to actually take on different personas each time I saw her. She always seemed to be having a great time, and her wackiness was infectious. Because of my Diva commitment to having fun I dumped my old belief *one way for every day* and took on dressing in what had me feel fun, glamorous, sexy, comfortable, or wild—not worrying about the job, moment, or occasion. Now I'm a Creative Executive Officer who wears wide-leg trousers, cotton tees, rhinestone accessories, and carries a pink fur Barbie backpack instead of a briefcase! There are so many different things that I love to wear and now, as a Diva, I know that I can wear them all. How I mix them is what makes me, me!

The elements of fantasy and indulgence in all of the Diva's moods come alive in her dress. Divas celebrate their complexity and never limit themselves or define themselves by only one style all the time. To make creating your own styles easy and fun we've created five starting points. Like Barbie and her different looks (Malibu Barbie, Grand Entrance Barbie, Doctor Barbie, Cool Skating Barbie), the Diva has five core personas that she will mix and match at will to express her unique daily (and sometimes bi- or tridaily) moods. We call them the five core elements of Diva Style: The Power Diva, The Glamour Diva, The Fun Diva, The Rock Star Diva, and The Sexy Diva. Remember, Divas, we don't have to choose one; we embody all of these traits!

THE POWER DIVA

- **Key characteristics:** Strong, polished, tailored, serious, conservative, and assertive.
- **Diva Style Icons:** Coco Chanel, Katherine Hepburn, Marlene Dietrich, Susan Sarandon.

- **Designers of choice:** Armani, Ungaro, Donna Karan.
- **Items found in her wardrobe:** A fitted black tuxedo, men's tailored trousers, pointy mules, fitted button-down shirts, slingbacks or classic pumps, pearls, diamonds.
- **Signature outfit:** Black trouser suit or skirt with fitted black suit jacket, man's-style fitted white shirt, black slingbacks, and diamond or pearl stud earrings.

THE GLAMOUR DIVA

- **Key characteristics:** Mysterious, charming, elegant, intriguing, alluring, subtly sexy, sophisticated, and regal.
- **Diva Style Icons:** Audrey Hepburn, Charlize Theron, Halle Berry, Jackie Kennedy Onassis.
- **Designers of choice:** Givenchy, Halston, Randolph Duke, Valentino.
- **Items found in her wardrobe:** Vintage beaded dresses, big round sunglasses, fitted capris, silk blouses, a matte jersey floor-length gown, diamonds.
- **Signature outfit:** A flowing and feminine halter dress, defining the body, worn with open-toed, high-heel shoes with ankle strap.

THE FUN DIVA

- **Key characteristics:** Comfortable, cute, playful, flirty, colorful, and sparkly.
- **Diva Style Icons:** Cameron Diaz, Lucille Ball, Goldie Hawn, Sarah Jessica Parker.
- **Designers of choice:** Cynthia Rowley, Nanette Lepore, Betsey Johnson.
- **Items found in her wardrobe:** Cuffed jeans, sequin slippers, flip-flops, feminine girly blouses, fitted cotton tees and tanks, comfy wrap dresses, rhinestones, sequins.
- **Signature oufit:** Cuffed jeans, printed feminine blouse, and thongs or sequin slippers.

THE ROCK STAR DIVA

- **Key characteristics:** Follows no fashion rules but her own; outrageous, surprising, unexpected, exotic, charismatic.

- **Diva Style Icons:** Cher, Madonna, Cleopatra, Joan Jett.
- **Designers of choice:** Dolce and Gabbana, Jean Paul Gaultier.
- **Items found in her wardrobe:** Fringe pants, tight tees and tight jeans, fishnets, leather pants, metal accessories, bustiers.
- **Signature outfit:** Skintight leather pants and supertight mini tee with high-heel pointy-toe boots and some metal cuffs and a tattoo (or two).

THE SEXY DIVA

- **Key characteristics:** Passionate, bold, seductive, smoldering.
- **Diva Style Icons:** Marilyn Monroe, Jennifer Lopez, Sophia Loren, Kim Cattrall.
- **Designers of choice:** Gucci, Gucci, and more Gucci!
- **Items found in her wardrobe:** High strappy heels, tight dresses and pants, mini skirts, low-cut everything, low-neckline feminine dresses, stacked-heel sandals, diamonds.
- **Signature outfit:** Slinky black dress with side slit and superhigh strappy heels.

How we choose to wear each element or how we choose to mix these elements together is what makes up our individual style. Here are some hybrid ideas to call your own:

- **The Marilyn Joins the Supreme Court Diva** (The Power Diva + The Sexy Diva): Feminine smarts! Think Katherine Hepburn meets Marilyn Monroe in a perfectly tailored black man's trouser suit with a feminine silk halter top and a stacked-heel sandal.
- **The Auntie Mame at the Inaugural Ball Diva** (The Fun Diva + The Glamour Diva): *S-s-smokin'!* This gal might wear a cotton tank top with a taffeta ball skirt and thongs or slippers. Think Sharon Stone at the Academy Awards in her Gap mock turtleneck and long taffeta skirt. She caused such a stir that night and for weeks to come that she also fit the Rock Star Diva character with her unexpected choice of dress.
- **The Madonna Meets Elvis at Tiffany's Diva** (The Glamour Diva + The Rock

Star Diva): Think Las Vegas in the 1960s, Divas! Leather pants with a beaded tank, diamond choker, and tousled hair.

- **The Charlie's Angels Win the Nobel Prize Diva** (The Glamour Diva + The Sexy Diva + The Power Diva): Dressed to look *hot* and feminine yet still be able to kick some ass . . . picture Jill, Kelly, and Sabrina (Charlie's Angels) circa 1975—low-cut shirts with fitted vests and wide-leg flowing trousers. Oh, baby!
- **The Raquel Welch Rides a Harley Diva** (The Rock Star Diva + The Sexy Diva): Think Tina Turner! Low neck, fitted tops and short skirts worn with leather jackets and high heels . . . 'nough said!

Divas, no longer do you have to worry about how to keep up with the trends that are ever changing. A Diva knows her five elements and dresses according to them and by what characteristics of her personality she wants to elicit each morning, noon, and night.

Keep in mind the way we encourage individual expression is by experimenting. The next time you see someone wearing something that looks bizarre to you, instead of questioning or making fun, just know that he or she is working on creating a personal style and admire it!

As you start to play with your different facets of style expression, watch for the signs of sure Divadom. One sure sign that you've stumbled upon something true to one of your own Diva elements is the uncontrollable need for your hips to shimmy to and fro, overwhelmed with the need to dance and shake your booty right there on the spot. The other day while out shopping with my friend Eden, I put on a fringed belt. All of a sudden, in front of Eden, other shoppers, and the salesclerks, my hands were in the air and my hips were shaking back and forth. If this belt could bring out the white-man's-overbite-dance in the middle of the store, just think what it could do on the dance floor! I snapped it up—I knew I had hit the Diva Jackpot! It's playtime, people—and I'm fringed and dangerous!

—Carilyn

DIVA DO'S FOR THE WEEK:

1. Brainstorm your own fashion magazine. What would be on those pages? What styles would you feature? You can even have some fun and cut out images and mix and match them together or draw the pieces you feel are missing. Glue a picture of your head on top. The magazine could be titled *Me, The Diva Style Icon.* What outfits would you recommend for your own five elements of Diva style? How could you spice up your existing wardrobe? What stores would you suggest you shop at to find such goodies? Do a little research and use it as your personal style resource.

2. Take a risk and be glamorous in an unglamorous place: Wear black leather pants to the office! Wear diamonds on the weekend with your favorite white T-shirt!

FRIVOLOUS DIVA DO:

WEAR A CANDY NECKLACE *as a Diva accessory with your "power" suit!*

DIVA TRIVIA:

Can you guess which famous Diva said this . . . "Ever since that day when I was eleven years old and I wasn't allowed in the [tennis team] photo because I wasn't wearing a skirt, I knew I wanted to change the sport."
Answer: Billie Jean King

Who freed women from their stuffy Victorian-style notions in the twentieth century by designing comfortable and chic haute couture?
Answer: Coco Chanel

Color: The Magic Wand

Color speaks all languages.
— JOSEPH ADDISON; *THE SPECTATOR*, JUNE 27, 1712

I've always been fascinated by color. It can change moods, actions, and how others see us. In the hands of the Diva, it's a magic wand to create anything you desire. Different colors can make you hungry, call you to action, relax you, or excite you. Color is one of the great mysteries of the universe; a magnificent gift that allows us to create the palette of the world we see. For the Diva, there are two dimensions to the use of color: first, to influence how we feel in our Diva surroundings, and second, to help us present our image to the world. These factors are equally important to the Diva, for how we feel on the inside always translates to how we look on the outside.

When entering the fiftieth year of my life I made an alarming discovery—my world was beige. The best we can say about beige is that it's neutral and monotone. We don't leap out of bed and say, "Hooray, I'm going into my beige bathroom or putting on my beige blouse!" And yet my life was wall-to-wall beige. My apartment was off-white, with beige carpeting. I was surrounded by nondescript and that translated to my wardrobe—monotone white, black, and, of course, beige blouses. After I made the decision to commit to Divadom, the first thing I did was bring color to my world. I painted my living room a vibrant red and metallic gold. The space is glorious. It wasn't, however, what I had planned. I had planned on a very safe red and flat gold. Fortunately for me, my friend Jonathan upped the ante and purchased colors with a life of their own. The entrance to my home speaks of the Diva I am, deep and compelling with a sparkle all my own. My image is present to the world before I even enter the room, and everyone comments that I am indeed a Diva.

Red is a comfort color for me going way back to my childhood. My mom once painted our living room red. It caused quite a stir in a quaint and sedate New England town and taught me an important lesson—go with your heart, no matter what. My mom spent years beaming in the reflection of that red room—she had only to enter it and she was transformed from a lonely housewife to a creative genius. Know what delights you and do it—that is the Way of the Diva.

Color can give or take away beauty, power, and peace. When we wear color that enhances our natural coloring, people tell us we look great. When we wear a color that doesn't complement our tones, we're told we look tired and sick.

In the hands of the Diva, color is a powerful and volatile weapon. Be deliberate in your choices and know your outcome before you proceed so that you can use color to your advantage. Color impacts all areas of your image, from your makeup to your clothes and accessories. Here's the secret Diva code to color. Use it wisely, and you will have tapped into one of Diva's most powerful and effective weapons!

- Create passion, warmth, strength, vitality, or power with red.
- Imbue joy, liveliness, enthusiasm, and hope with orange.
- Communicate intelligence, youthfulness, and radiance with yellow.
- Invoke sincerity, sensitivity, independence, and tradition with blue.
- Demonstrate versatility, balance, regeneration, or sympathy with green.
- Inspire wisdom, philosophy, sophistication, and contemplation with purple.
- Generate love, warmth, femininity, and girlish allure with pink.

There are some fundamental principles of color that we must understand to use it to our advantage, and I'm simplifying all the scientific goop to one simple principle—all colors fall into one of two groups: yellow based or blue based. The color of our skin also falls into two groups, yellow or blue. To figure out your skin tones, you'll need the help of your Diva friends—we'll show you how in Diva Do 1. For now, there's just one critical factor to understand. Our eyes interpret color through a filter, and we see the opposite tones of the color presented. If you wear yellow-based colors, your eyes and everyone who sees you sees blue. If you wear blue-based colors, everyone sees yellow. Armed with this knowledge, these color principles become our secret weapon to looking more youthful, sexier, or more powerful. Here's how.

Every Diva has set of shadows in the lines and wrinkles on her face. If your skin has a yellow cast and you wear a yellow base color, it causes a blue filter in the eyes of those who see you (remember, it's the opposite), and that blue filter makes your shadows and wrinkles stand out. When this happens you look older, tired, or ill because the contours and lines in your face are exaggerated. If you were to wear blue-based colors, it would cause a yellow filter in the eyes of those who see you and your lines and wrinkles would disappear. Presto! Change-o! You're more youthful and vibrant looking. This same process works for those with a blue skin tone, only you'd want to wear yellow-based colors to generate a youthful look.

Have a color party with your friends. Have them bring separates in solid colors of blue, red, green, and yellow from their wardrobe. You want to end up with a mix of yellow-based and blue-based colors to complement each Diva's skin tone. For example, if you have a yellow-based skin tone, a yellow-based red will look a little washed out on you, while a blue-based red will look rich and dark. It's the same for all colors across the board. Wrap the solid color around your neck with a white wall as a background. Natural light works best to get the full impact of the differences. In a couple of tries you'll know if you're on the yellow team or the blue team. Then just choose your favorite colors with the appropriate tone for you, which is the opposite of whatever you are.

Did you ever wonder why queens are adorned with deep red robes? The color gives them power. Each of us can be like the queen, with our own signature color that whispers to us and shouts to the world—*I have arrived*. It's your secret reminder to live a life that is grander than one you could have ever imagined. When you choose your color, imbue it with all your secret Diva charms, wishes, and dreams. Look out world, here you come!

– *Maureen*

*D*IVA DO'S FOR THE WEEK:

1. Call your friends and have a color consult party. Have everyone bring lengths of fabric, towels, scarves, or anything that's a pure solid color. You can also buy colored tissue paper or sheets of felt. Have your friends bring over their wardrobes. To determine your colors, have a friend drape the color around your neck, near your face. Do your eyes look small, and does your skin look sickly? If so, that's not your color. You can't do this for yourself because you can't see how the colors change the way you look. If possible, hire a color consultant. Negotiate a group price or attend a color class.

2. Get a color wheel. Try an art store or the Internet. The wheel represents the tricks color plays on our eyes. For example, the color opposite the (warm) red is blue (cool). You'll be playing the opposite game this week. Warm colors, reds, yellows, oranges, project a cool filter; cool colors, blues, project a warm filter.

3. Start to train yourself in the world of color. Pay attention to the colors around you. Does a warm orange rug bring you comfort? Does an electric blue poster energize you? Write down your reactions in your Diva Diary.

4. Find your signature Diva color. Keep it around when you need a Diva boost. Remember, you always look fabulous in your signature color.

*F*RIVOLOUS DIVA DO:

WEAR PINK TODAY AND COUNT *the number of people who notice you. Since pink is girlish, wearing it brings out favorable reactions from both men and women.*

*D*IVA TRIVIA:

Why are fast-food restaurant logos and colors often red and yellow?

Answer: Red makes you hungry and calls you to action (buy more fries), and yellow makes you want to get going. Fast food—get it and get out!

Playing the Field (of Hair and Makeup, That Is!)

I'm not offended by all the dumb blonde jokes because I know I'm not dumb . . .
and I also know that I'm not blond.
—DOLLY PARTON

False eyelashes, wigs, acrylic nails, beauty marks, blond/brown/black/red hair, to tan or not, showering, shaving, waxing, tweezing: All these wonderful choices the Diva encounters are a large part of the fun of being a woman! We get to play dress-up *forever*—always trying new colors, new applications, new packaging, and new hairstyles. Yet it's so rare that we revel in this freedom. We tend to think of these processes as "maintenance" instead of associating them with luxury and pleasure. The time has come to girly up our outer core and indulge in the joys that come with playing the field!

I love constantly changing my hair. It's actually one of my signatures. My friends know to expect a different look every three or four months—and I'd do it more often if my hair would grow faster! I've often dreamed of being the Barbie from my childhood who could turn her hair from brown to blond with a simple twist of the head. Or better yet, I'd be the doll that could grow hair simply by pulling on it. What a concept! I would cut it, then pull it, color it, cut it, pull it, cut it, pull it, color, cut, pull, cut, pull . . . you get the picture.

When I became pregnant I found out I had to wait until my second trimester to color or bleach my hair. It seemed like an eternity. I had such a difficult time feeling like a Diva. My hair was long, and I had chosen to keep it that way because "men like long hair" even though it was drab and boring . . . ugh! My body was already changing, and the hormonal chemistry was messing with my ability to remember how to write my name, let alone how to style my hair. This experience sent me into a wild depression. I felt unsexy, unhip, and destined to be stricken with "Frazzled Mom Syndrome," (FMS) with the outdated hairdo, a passé wardrobe, no makeup technique, and no sex appeal. I needed help.

The day my first three months were up, I made an appointment with my longtime Diva hairstylist, Maria. I had a tall order: "Diva-ize me!" Within three hours, my life as I knew it was transformed. It may sound unbelievable, but as we saw in Week 3, Defining the Diva in You, we all now know it's possible. She cut off my long hair (perhaps a symbolic release from something to which I wasn't committed—something that wasn't the "real" me) and gave me a sexy short 'do with great color and highlights. (I know that some of the pregnancy books say that the desire to cut hair is inevitable during pregnancy; they advise avoiding it at all costs, because it's an irrational desire we'll regret when hormones return to normal. I disagree. As long as you have a hairstylist you trust not to automatically give you a typical FMS hairdo simply because you're pregnant, I say do it! And if you don't trust your stylist, it may be time to leave. Although a Diva appreciates loyalty, she also believes variety is the spice of life. So allow yourself to try new things *and* new stylists. Don't be afraid to look elsewhere. It can be one of the best ways to reinvent yourself.) Please know this whole FMS thing is not an insult to moms. Not every mom has FMS. But once a woman becomes a mother, there is a tendency to put herself last behind her children, husband, house, and career, and that can't help but show up in her image, personality, and happiness. If this has happened to you, please remember that FMS can be reversed if you make time to let your Diva out of captivity.

Here's how I fought back. After the hair miracle that Maria gave me I realized my makeup was in dire need of reinvention also. After all, I had to take action to keep my Diva alive . . . but where to begin? There are so many new do's and don'ts, rules and regulations to beauty and hair, it's enough to drive anyone mad. The Diva Solution? Ignore them and follow your own! A great way, I learned, is to start with the five core elements of Diva Style (from Week 29). So with my hair done, I randomly chose which makeup counters to go to. I found myself at the Stila counter at Nordstrom and asked for a "Fun Diva" (youthful, daytime, playful, and girly) makeover. The next day I went to the Bobbi Brown counter and asked for a "Glamour Diva" (circa-1950 or -1960 movie starlet) makeover. I continued until I had covered the five Diva elements. I was taught how to apply each product using the appropriate applicator and purchased only my favorite item at each visit (which I spaced out so I didn't send my bank account into Anti-Diva hell). Each makeup artist gave me a list of the products used on me; I used this list to check off what I had purchased plus what I already had at home and made a wish list for the rest to purchase along my journey.

Before you hit the makeup counters it would be beneficial to know what you already have buried in that catchall makeup drawer of yours (we know the truth, Divas!). To make this fun, share it with your friends. Hold a Diva Five Element Hair and Makeup Party. Have each of you throw all your makeup in a plastic bin and bring the bin, a box of Ziploc bags, and some magazines to the party. The game: to go through the five core elements of Diva Style and help each other decide which makeup products go in which Diva element bag—and to clip a few hairstyles to throw in each bag as well. The goal is to have all makeup and hair ideas organized into each of the five core Diva elements to make it easier, faster, and more fun to perform the toilette each day. Here are some ideas to get you started:

- **The Power Diva:** An understated but natural feminine look using warm neutrals, and medium-shade eye shadows and lipsticks.
- **The Glamour Diva:** Ultrafeminine starlet-style maquillage: false eyelashes, eyebrow pencil or brush and powder for both brows and beauty marks, red lipstick, thickening mascara, pale or no eye shadow, black liquid eyeliner.
- **The Fun Diva:** Mascara, glittery colored eye shadow, pink shades for blush and lips, scented and/or flavored lip gloss, roll-on body glitter.
- **The Rock Star Diva:** The "next morning" look with smudgy eyes and pale or simply glossed lips.

- **The Sexy Diva:** Smoky eyes using dark-colored powders with high-sheen superglossy lips worn on top of either nude or red lipstick.

  Tip: It may make sense to duplicate certain items to have in each bag, like mascara. Then, when you get ready in the morning, you don't have to sift through other bags to find what you need. And when you travel, all you need to bring is the appropriate bag (as well as the Bag of Tricks, below) instead of the entire makeup drawer!

A true Diva also needs her own bag of tricks . . . a secret arsenal of powerful tools she uses to pony up her sex appeal or hide last night's dance-party hangover . . .

- **The Diva's Bag of Tricks:** Concealer, eyelash thickener or conditioner, lip plumper, eyebrow brush, moisturizer with sun protection, tweezers, eyebrow trimming scissors, eyelash curler, self-tanner, cleavage-enhancing body oil with glitter preferred, Preparation H ointment (to abolish the Anti-Diva's eye bags). And don't forget as you're organizing, you don't need to keep everything!

- **The Diva's Trash Bag:** Caked makeup, clumpy mascara, bright blue eye shadow, and anything else you haven't used in a year!

The best part about playing the field of hair and makeup is the experimentation—it's the getting there more than the being there that's so thrilling. Soak up all the knowledge you can from different hair and makeup stylists. Let each makeup artist tell you about his or her own products and what makes them so fabulous. Learn any secrets of illusion or makeup application you can, and don't be afraid to mix brands to suit your own makeup needs. They can also show you how to apply false eyelashes—full or partial—so bring a set and some glue and have some fun! Play around with different products and their manufacturers. Spend time alone and with friends trying new hairstyles and ways to apply makeup. To the Diva, looking good with hair and makeup isn't maintenance or necessity; it's fun and a simple luxury of being a woman. In addition to adding beauty, it adds youth, joy, and playfulness to her allure. So dabble around, try new things, have fun, and truly indulge in the fabulousness of playing the field!

—Carilyn

Diva Do's for the Week:

1. Schedule an appointment with a fabulous hairdresser (go to someone who doesn't know you and ask for a new Divaesque hairdo). Find a new hairstyle that makes you feel groovy, baby, yeah! Or bring the photos you clipped at your party for The Sexy Diva and ask the stylist to show you how to create that look for yourself!

2. If you don't already have these items and you have some money to spend, go to a drugstore and invest in hot rollers, a crimping iron, a curling iron, and/or a straightening iron (my favorite). Spend at least thirty minutes this week playing with your new tools. Find an additional way to wear your hair. Straighten it. Curl it. Crimp it. Experiment . . . be adventurous . . . go wild! Wear it up, down, and all around! Wear a different hairstyle each day this week.

3. If the hairdo you crave is impossible for you based on what you've got, buy a wig! Wigs are our secret to instant transformation, and the perfect vehicle for a Diva Delightful Delusion. They are used to unlock our hidden inhibitions and become the Diva of our dreams. I felt like a supermodel one night out in Las Vegas with my tush-length, shiny, straight auburn wig, cowboy hat, and heels! Owwwooouuu!

4. Take a couple of trips to the department and/or specialty stores. Schedule makeovers at different makeup counters. Try a look you've never tried before. At one counter, ask for a Fun Diva look. At another, a Glamour Diva look. And at yet another, get the most wild makeover they can give you for your Rock Star Diva! Have some fun! Invite a friend who is also on her Diva journey— encourage each other to try new things.

5. Have an in-home beauty party hosted by Mary Kay Cosmetics! Invite your friends over and experiment with different Diva looks using all the Mary Kay products from the woman who gave women the opportunity to work at home with products they love.

6. Get your beauty sleep!

rivolous Diva Do:

WEAR AN OUTRAGEOUS WIG *to the supermarket where everybody knows you . . . we dare you!*

Diva Tip:

- To avoid FMS write down your Diva routine for your face and hair: what products you used where and how. Keep the slip in the bag with your makeup. When the Anti-Diva element begins to emerge, all you need to do is reach for the bag and get started.

Diva Charm School: Magnetism 101

She's got radiance, what she wears is incidental. Aura is everything,
the essence of the woman. If you've got aura, you just shine.
—DIANA VREELAND ON PRINCESS DIANA

*M*agnetism and charm—both highly elusive, intangible concepts, difficult to describe but recognizable when you see them, because everyone is drawn to those who possess them. Princesses Grace and Diana are well-known examples of women blessed with them—their magical aura preceded them wherever they went. Some people may come by these attributes naturally—but don't fret, Divas, they can also be learned. It's time to enter Diva Charm School. Take your seat up front so you don't miss anything. Get out your leopard notebook and your pink glitter pen. And let's begin. Welcome to Magnetism 101!

LESSON 1: THE DIVA'S COMPORTMENT

The way we carry ourselves says so much about us. A Diva glides confidently into a room, with the air of self-confidence radiating from her very presence making her even more attractive. How do you pull this off? Pretend you're wearing your tiara. Smile at each person. Make and hold good eye contact with your eyes open wide and alive. A Diva gestures gracefully with her well-manicured hands to enhance a story or show emotion. She keeps her arms open rather than crossed, letting people know she's approachable, available, and "open" to them.

LESSON 2: THE DIVA'S VOICE

A high-pitched, whiny voice can be irritating to listen to. Tape your voice—you may be surprised at what you hear. Listen for both pitch and inflection. Chances are, you may not like what you hear—and if you don't, others probably don't either. As a Diva you may want to lower your voice a little so it's more soothing, and add intonation if necessary rather than speaking monotone. Remember Marilyn Monroe and "Hot Lips" from M*A*S*H? They spoke slowly, softly, and "breathily." Practice speaking like this and put a new message on your answer machine in your sexy new Diva voice!

LESSON 3: THE DIVA'S GRACIOUSNESS

A Diva demonstrates good manners. She refrains from interrupting others when they are speaking, and is never rude to waiters. (Grandma Diva's main pet peeve.) As Diva's we respect all people, no matter what they do, because the Diva knows that all people have the right to feel great about themselves. A Diva puts everyone at ease when she introduces a new person into a conversation by adding a bit of information: "This is my dear friend Gloria, who just returned from Bali." A Diva also loves to compliment people. She lets them know what she finds attractive or special in them because she revels in others feeling great about themselves.

LESSON 4: THE DIVA'S THOUGHTFULNESS

A Diva remembers names and details of people's lives. *Tips:* After an introduction, say the person's name three times out loud during the conversation or use word association to help you. If you meet someone you already know and you can't remember his or her name, try a little flattery to smooth over the awkwardness: "I am so captivated by your good looks, your name escapes me." One of the Diva's most endearing qualities is her concern for others. People feel good about themselves when in her presence. She remembers events in her friends' lives and sends cards or calls. She appreciates what others do and remembers to thank them with words or small gifts. She will even take the time to send a handwritten note, an almost extinct practice. Divas know we all still love to receive personal mail. It's a simple way to brighten anyone's day. A helpful Diva hint is to keep some blank cards or postcards on hand (easily accessible) so you're ready to send one when the moment presents itself.

LESSON 5: THE DIVA'S MYSTERY

This is the most difficult to describe. I recommend watching Ingrid Bergman in the movie *Casablanca* to learn about the aura of mystery. It includes raising the curiosity level of others by doing or wearing something normally unexpected of you. People will wonder what's going on with you, what has happened or changed. Try being the best-dressed person anywhere you go, wearing your boa to a sports event or high heels to a backyard barbecue. You're doing something out of the ordinary, so you pique the interest of those around you. If you're on a first date, imagine yourself in a wide-brimmed hat bowed to one side (or better yet, actually wear one). During your conversation, cast your eyes down demurely and laugh softly at something your date says. Respond by showing him a unique part of yourself, such as a clever remark, quirky sense of humor, or your warmth by touching him gently on the arm. Imply in speaking that there's more to you, but you aren't ready to reveal it yet. A Diva doesn't give it all away. The element of mystery keeps them all coming back for more.

LESSON 6: THE DIVA'S CONVERSATION

A Diva strives for lively conversation and encourages everyone to participate. She knows it's not about where she is that's important, but instead, who she's with. She's very friendly and honest, willing to show her vulnerability and naïveté on a subject. The Diva's self-love runs so deep that she doesn't try to impress others or prove herself and can therefore celebrate other people by giving them the floor. She enjoys sprinkling conversations with humor, warmth, and playfulness. Shared laughter and experiences are very engaging because they make everyone feel good. The Diva is enthusiastic and curious about what others are saying. A Diva listens well and reflects other people's feelings back to them—and by doing so she lets them know she understands them. She is spontaneous, generous, and genuine in showing affection. In conversation a Diva makes people feel that they're the only ones in the world who matter.

Divas know they are special and unique. With these tools you can consistently create the intrigue of the Diva's Magnetic Aura. Call on the Diva Vibe at any time by visualizing yourself as a magnet. You are a charismatic, inspirational, and dynamic Diva! Now go out and charm the world.

Ri-i-i-i-ing! Class dismissed!

— Elena

*M*AGNETISM 101 HOMEWORK:

1. Talk to a stranger this week and practice your Diva Presence. If you're shy or have trouble with small talk, prepare yourself. Do a little reading; think of topics to bring up.

2. Plan a lunch with your friends and have everyone wear a hat. Practice being mysterious.

3. Buy a pack of notecards to keep in your desk so that you'll always have one to send when the situation demands.

*F*RIVOLOUS DIVA DO:

BUY A DOZEN MAGNETS. *Slip one into your own pocket and mysteriously slip them into the pockets of people you would like to meet. Watch the law of attraction in action!*

IX

$\mathcal{D}$IVA ELIXIRS

Ponce de León was searching for the fountain of youth. We believe he was mistaken to search outside himself, but then again Ponce was not a Diva, for the qualities of youthfulness live *within* us. These elixirs will give you access to bringing out the Diva whenever you've misplaced her.

Exercise—Not Taboo After All!

I don't work out. If God wanted us to bend over he'd put diamonds on the floor.
—JOAN RIVERS

*T*he urge to pass over this chapter may be strong. The Four Divas certainly know that! Hell, we canned this chapter in our first go-round 'cause nobody wanted to do it! But since then a transformation has taken place. Exercise, or Divacise as we have begun to call it, has become fun. How did this happen? Well, it was a journey all its own. And a long one at that! But if it can happen to us, it can happen to you. Read on . . .

For as long as I can remember, the only point of exercise, as far as I was concerned, was to change my physical appearance because it wasn't good enough as it was and because men like toned women (yuck!). To add to my negative self-image, it seemed like women were shrinking everywhere I looked—even the thinnest celebrities seemed to be abandoning their already perfect bodies for extra-slim versions! Viewing these women paralyzed me. I wanted to get fit, but exercise has always been a reminder of what's wrong with me, which is anything but a motivator. In fact, I've always rebelled against anything that's supposed to be "good for me." It's been a battle in my head for so long that I'm worn out just thinking about it! I want to be healthy. I want to look good, but most important I want to feel good about myself no matter how I look and I want to enjoy myself no matter what I do. It always seemed there was something else more important to do: work, clean, shower, tidy, feed my family, walk the dog, de-lint my belly button, contemplate the phenomenon of earwax . . . so many diversions and responsibilities.

What I realized was exercise was last on my list, which really meant *I* was last on my list. Exercise is one of the main ways we can break the rule of having to put others first. It's a bold statement we make to ourselves: *I am important*. My Diva commitment changed my perspective: As I started to become more fit, life became more joyous, my head cleared, my confidence rose, and my energy level began to soar. It also gives us a great sense of accomplishment and the satisfaction of completion each time we do it. I realized this awful act we call exercise was actually a direct connection to Divadom!

How did I begin my exercise turnaround? My first step was to enlist a friend to take this voyage with me. Because I Am Diva, and prefer variety and fun to monotony and stagnancy, the image of being a rat on a wheel (okay, I guess it's really called a treadmill) never appealed to me so I knew my place for exercise would not be the gym. Now, if the typical gym was anything like "Gymboree" where people are climbing over, crawling through, and dancing on top of brightly colored cushioned toys, it would be a different story. My friend Julee didn't even belong to a gym, so there was no threat of going to one. That forced us to get creative. We knew if we were going to stick to it, it would have to be fun. We both love dancing, so we got the community paper and saw what was being offered. Out first Divacise adventure began with hip-hop dance. We were the two oldest gals in the group, but we were certainly the most childish! It was so much fun, and what a workout!

Those eight weeks were so exhilarating and enjoyable. Julee would come over to my house, and we'd practice the routines together. Since our men never liked watching us practice, we often preformed to my daughter, Remy (who, at six months, really didn't have a choice), and my dog, Roxy. The instructor, Charletta, told me I had funk and was impressed with my moves. What a compliment! Charletta's class also helped with my confidence performing in front of people, because each week we would perform in a group as well as alone to the rest of the class. I was petrified at first but then remembered my Diva traits and let myself be vulnerable and have fun expressing myself. It was my real-life chance to be rock star! Woo-hoo!

To our astonishment Julee and I were enjoying ourselves, getting in shape, and keeping in touch with each other. It was our time to catch up and have some girl talk. Which got me to thinking . . . maybe, to the Diva, this exercise stuff is really about being with friends, and becoming trim and fit is simply a side effect. It also proved that exercise isn't limited to how many minutes I spend on a treadmill or how many push-ups I can or cannot do. To the Diva, exercise is time spent having fun using her body. It's also an opportunity to learn something new. What ways do you like to use your body? Get creative: dance, martial arts, handball, hula-hooping, hopscotch, one-on-one basketball, double Dutch jump rope, unicycle riding, roller skating, Pogo Stick hopping. Just beginning? How about a wild game of jacks? Use that arm . . . up down, up down, up down!

Dance is something I'm very passionate about and have been for as long as I can remember. And since starting these classes with Julee, I've found a new venue for dancing that's always open—my bedroom! My commitment in life is to really enjoy every minute, and dancing into shape is my exercise of choice (that and an invigorating game of hopscotch with the neighbors). I've often locked myself in my bedroom, turned on the 1980s music channel, and danced like crazy until I fell to the bed in exhaustion. My husband wants to get in on the fun and has recently proposed that we have a dance-a-thon one night a week at home (what we've now termed *Sunday Night Double D.*—for Diva and Divo—*Dance Party*). How awesome is that? We can inspire each other, and I get to share my greatest passion with my greatest friend! It can't get better than that.

Let's face it, Divas, exercise may not initially sound like a Diva's way to pass time, but as we look closer we see it's the key to unlocking the confidence that comes with being a Diva. It brings us enjoyment because it's a way for us to catch up with our Diva sisters. It clears our head for imagination and creativity to flow freely. It gives us energy to fulfill our many passions. It's an outlet for our creative expression. To the Diva, exercise is one of the great elixirs of life. *So get off your Diva Butt and do it!*

—Carilyn

*D*IVA DO'S FOR THE WEEK:

1. Spend some time looking at why you do or don't exercise. We want to get rid of all the disempowering reasons like mine—having to "fix" myself because I didn't measure up to the supermodel ideal.

2. Buy a hula-hoop (Toys "R" Us sometimes has them for $3.99!) and hula for twenty minutes a day while you watch your favorite movie or gyrate to your favorite tunes!

3. Sign up for a dance class that sounds interesting to you in your community or at a dance studio. Maybe your gym even offers some. Or if structured dance doesn't sound interesting to you, just get yourself to a club or even your living room and dance freely. Make up your own moves. Dance doesn't have to look or be a certain way to get you outside yourself and feeling sexy. Immerse yourself in the culture of dance and ignite passion, sensuality, and sexuality! If you think you have no rhythm, not to worry. Americans have a dance for you. It's called line dancing. You don't need rhythm. You just need to know how to memorize steps. Line dancing has to be one of the most fun ways to dance, because once you learn the steps you get to dance with everyone on the dance floor. It's like community dancing—I love it! Most western clubs offer line dancing classes before the club opens. Check in your neighborhood for the place nearest you.

4. If a dance class isn't something you want to fit into your schedule, have some fun at home. Push some bottle caps onto the bottom of your sneakers and tap dance on the living room floor (if it's not carpeted) like you're Debbie Reynolds in *Singing in the Rain*!

5. Get rid of the scale. Replace it with a beautiful visual image of what your goals for exercise are. For example, on my fridge I have a collage of Janet Jackson's bod, fun photos of my friends, husband, and daughter, the beach, people dancing, and other things that make me want to get a move on!

*F*RIVOLOUS DIVA DO:

ENJOY THE DIZZINESS OF A CARTWHEEL, *somersault, or handstand.*

Songs in the Key of Life

After silence, that which comes nearest to expressing the inexpressible is music.
—ALDOUS HUXLEY

Have you ever watched little kids when they listen to music they really like? They get so excited as they sing and dance—they're completely uninhibited and seemingly unaware of anything going on around them. It's as if the sheer power of the melody—or, in some cases, the lack of melody!—makes the rest of the world go away, and they're left to express themselves however they choose as they move their little bodies to their own rhythm. Like my younger counterparts, there are few things in life about which I am more passionate and excited than music. It's a treasured elixir of the Divas and can solve just about any problem as well as soothe the soul. It lifts me up, mellows me out, and revitalizes me. Even if I don't know the words of a tune, even if the band sings in a foreign language—or just mumbles—I can appreciate the rhythm, the harmony, and the feel of the song.

No matter where you go in the world, people recognize music. Whether it's a Gregorian chant, Handel's *Messiah*, tribal drumbeats in Africa, or your favorite commercial, from the softest whisper to the fullest sound, music is universally understood. It's a melting pot of sounds, rhythms, beats, and melodies. You don't have to necessarily like everything you hear, but nothing beats music when it comes to manipulating the Diva's mood, perception, and emotion. This powerful force has been intertwined into cultures in many different forms, all the while maintaining its beauty and mystique. Consider for a moment what it is about certain songs that you enjoy; notice if you listen to happy music, sad songs, or angry tunes. How does music make you feel? Does it remind you of a certain time in your life? Every time I hear certain songs by REO Speedwagon, they remind me of my first boyfriend. The moment the song comes on the radio, it's like a throwback to high school and I can remember the sights, sounds, and smells of those days.

In addition to affecting behavior, the power of music can also be healing. Music can help alleviate pain, calm or relax you, counteract depression, and encourage movement as part of physical rehabilitation. Whenever I have a headache or just want to unwind, classical music such as Handel's *Messiah* tends to make me feel better. Since the World War I and II eras, music therapy has even developed as a profession. Michigan State University established the world's first music therapy degree program in 1944, and in 1950 the National Association for Music Therapy was founded to help ensure that practicing music therapists were also qualified to heal.

Even if you're not ready to go to that length to discover the power of music, every Diva knows that having an assortment of tunes to choose from on any given occasion is key to altering a mood. What songs light you up and get you going? What do you reach for when you're kicking back at the end of the week or to get you pumped up before you go out on a date? How about when you've just broken up with someone—what songs come to mind? You can make your own Diva mixed tapes (or CDs) to match different occasions or feelings. Make a tape, for example, that reminds you of your high school days or to honor a certain time period that you especially loved. Make another one that has your favorite dance tunes so you can disco your way through cleaning the house. Going back to Week 29, you can create your own Diva style through music. Make a Diva Power tape including songs by Madonna and Sheryl Crow; a Glamour tape might include Frank Sinatra or Nina Simone; a Diva Fun tape might include groups such as the Barenaked Ladies; Aerosmith and Bonnie Raitt are mandatory on the Diva Rock Star tape; and Barry White is sure to please on the Sexy tape.

If you're not prepared to be this creative, then compilation CDs are a great way to go. Many large stores like Tower Records will even let you listen to certain CDs before you buy them. Are you in a tumultuous relationship? Then go buy the CD for *West Side Story*. Some good drama that parallels your own is a great way to work through issues. Thinking of adopting children? Borrow the *Annie* CD from your local library and sing along with the lyrics. The next time you see a movie that really speaks to you, get the soundtrack and memorize the words. If you're having "one of those days," pick your favorite song from the soundtrack and sing it as loud as you can (your car is a great concert hall, if you don't have the space to belt it out wherever you are). One of the first albums I ever received was from the musical *Godspell.* To this day, whenever I hear a song from the album, my mood shifts and I am instantly inspired—it makes me want to break into dance!

Periodically I go on "music benders"—I have to have some new music and I have to have it now. I will come home with six to eight CDs, some brand-new bands, some oldies but goodies. My goal is to grow my collection to a thousand to fifteen hundred CDs—and to have them all alphabetized by category so that I can find certain songs to correspond to my mood. For example, I have my dance music organized together so that when I'm getting ready to go out on the weekend with my husband, I can get into the party mood by cranking up my favorite ABBA or Bee Gee's tunes; they're so happy and infectious that I can't help but smile and dance around the house. In fact, it works on the whole family! When I'm working but want some calming music in the background, I reach for the classical CDs to keep me inspired. And on Sunday morning, there's no better way to ease into the day than to listen to Steely Dan, Dire Straits, James Taylor, Stevie Wonder, Steve Winwood, or other classics from the 1970s.

No matter what your musical preference, opening yourself to the power of song can help transform a day of despair into Diva delight. So what are you waiting for? Turn it on!

— Molly

*D*IVA DO'S FOR THE WEEK:

1. Make plans to go to the local symphony—it's relaxing, enriching, and moving. During the summer months, many cities and parks offer free concerts. Check with your local department of parks and recreation to get details of events in your area.

2. Buy a CD that someone in the store recommends; ask what the folks there like and why they like it. Take an informal poll in the store and go strictly on someone's recommendation.

3. Go global. If you haven't started to listen to world music, now's a good time to try. Many music stores have sections devoted to this—check it out. If you don't want to buy something, go to your local public library and check out their collection of music; you might be surprised at what you can find. Also check out the Internet; there are hundreds of options available to listen to stations or to create your own.

4. Play music with dinner. Mix it up and play a combination of Frank Sinatra, Nina Simone, classical, and the Three Tenors. Then, after dinner, liven things up and break out the disco or your favorite up-tempo tunes and dance.

5. Make up your own lyrics to a song; or, better yet, make up your own song. For the Super-Daring Diva Bonus Round, take singing lessons (or music lessons) and then sign up to sing at your favorite bar or establishment.

ℱRIVOLOUS DIVA DO:

SING OUT LOUD *in a public place, like at a mall, or on a bus, or—if you must—in your car, but keep the windows open!*

𝒟IVA TRIVIA:

- Did you know that listening to seventeenth- and eighteenth-century baroque concertos is excellent for memory retention? The beat of this particular music has been shown to decrease blood pressure and heartbeat, moving you into a state of relaxed alertness.

The Scents of the Diva: Aromatherapy

A rose by any other name would smell as sweet.
—WILLIAM SHAKESPEARE, ROMEO AND JULIET

The art of being a Diva includes power over our universe. As we live the legend of the Diva, we must learn the tricks to invoking the emotions and reactions we want from our many fans, including our families. And women have always known how to influence men through the sense of smell. Elena shared advice on how we can seduce or create a permanent impression through perfume in Week 11. I want to speak about scents that are more powerful than any perfume—the aromas of natural herbs and spices. These are tools of seduction and self-enhancement no Diva should be without.

When I was growing up, dinner was a fixed time in our household. If we do anything often enough, it becomes a habit, and our bodies tune in. My poor mom, Drusilla Lyttle Posey Donnelly Crean, had programmed my dad and her four kids for dinner at six every evening. At six-o-five, if there was no dinner, there was hell to pay! One day Mom was busy refinishing a table in the backyard and she lost all track of time. If was five fifty-five and dinner was nowhere in sight. Being a Diva, she soon had everything under control. She threw some butter and onions into a skillet and within sixty seconds, the aroma of home cooking filled the house. Dad walked in the door, smiled, and said, "Smells good in here, what's for dinner?" Diva Dru smiled and said, "It's a surprise honey, just give me a few more minutes. Make yourself comfortable." And when he left the room we rolled on the floor in laughter. A Diva spell passed from one generation of Diva to the next.

There is nothing in the world as captivating as our sense of smell. Luckily, today we don't have to be tied to our kitchens to conjure up magic in our lives. Aromatherapy is a powerful tool of the Diva. We can conjure up comfort, peace, love, and satisfaction with a few drops of essential oil. Oils can control our appetite, ground our energy, quiet the kids, and smooth our frazzled nerves. Nature's plan is so fabulous we can create any mood or atmosphere that we desire with a moment's notice.

I love essential oils for the power they give me to change my state of mind. One of my favorite diet aids is peppermint essential oil. Inhaling this aroma for fifteen seconds gives a sense of fullness. This scent, or any that reminds us of food, tricks our brain into thinking that we've eaten until we're satisfied. So instead of reaching for a second helping, I reach for peppermint. In a few seconds I have that fabulous feeling of being satiated without overeating.

How can the Divas build their arsenal of these magical tools? A drop at a time, ladies. Here are some of the secret powers of these oils:

- **Orange:** Conjures up joy, peace, and happiness.
- **Bergamot:** Relieves anxiety, stress, and tension.
- **Rose:** Creates magnetic energy that attracts love and brings joy to the heart.
- **Lavender:** Calms and relaxes, allowing for concentration and focus.
- **Ginger:** Helps ease morning sickness.
- **Neroli:** Used by the Egyptians to heal the body, mind, and spirit.
- **Myrrh:** The oil of wealth, used as a trading commodity.
- **Clary sage:** Helps with PMS and menstrual cramps.
- **Ylang-ylang:** Relaxing, it restores confidence and self-love.
- **Spruce:** Believed to possess the frequency of prosperity.

These oils work wonders in a number of ways. And for the Diva, they are your secret weapon. Here's a brief review of how you can use them to your advantage.

1. **Old Habit:** Quietly enter the meeting room, take your seat, and wait your turn.

Diva Practice: Conjure up some Diva power. Mix a few drops of bergamot (for stress release) and ylang-ylang (for confidence) in a tablespoon of pure almond oil. Anoint and align yourself with a few drops at your shoulders and the base of your spine for power. Create a similar mixture with pure rose oil. A few drops on a tissue, tucked into your bra, will release a beautiful fragrance all day long, making you a magnet for love and admiration. Make a powerful entrance into the meeting one minute before it's set to begin. With your secret weapons, the meeting is all yours, Diva.

2. **Old Habit:** You're going to visit a relative or friend who in the past has made you crazy. You dread the trip, stay as short a time as possible, leave upset.

    Diva Practice: Prepare for the trip. Bring orange oil to create an environment of joy, peace, and happiness. A drop or two on a candle or lightbulb (put on when the bulb is cold) will diffuse the aroma throughout the room. As you prepare, inhale this magical scent and remember a time when you were both extremely happy and having fun with each other. Start the conversation with an acknowledgment of the joy that this person has brought into your life and how important he or she has been to you. Sit back and watch magic occur.

3. **Old Habit:** You're shopping for an important outfit. You start to stress about the cost before you even enter the shopping mall. You buy something you really don't love because it fits within your budget.

    Diva Practice: Intend abundance. Visualize yourself in the perfect outfit at your upcoming event. Put a few drops of myrrh oil on a tissue and inhale the oil of wealth from ancient times. Fill your mind with unlimited possibilities. Intend on finding the exact items you want on sale. Keep the myrrh with you all day so you'll remember how wealthy and abundant you already are.

Warning: As you begin to experiment with essential oils, be careful—pure oils are too strong to put on your skin directly. To create a massage oil, mix pure oils with a good carrier oil, such as almond, available in most health food stores. Pour some under hot running water for a great bath. Victoria Nichols, an alchemist with Victoria's Essentials in Albany, New York (www.true-aromatherapy.com), created a special oil for The Four Divas, called Diva. It's based on an ancient Egyptian formula that was used to honor Ra, the Sun God, to thank him for bringing the sun up each day. At the close of each day, indulge yourself in this delightful Diva Milk Bath as your thank-you to the universe for all that is good.

DIVA MILK BATH

Blend the following oils together:

2 drops cinnamon oil

7 drops rosewood oil

6 drops honey absolute

4 drops juniper oil

4 drops cardamom oil

4 drops myrrh oil

4 drops cypress oil

Mix the essential oil blend with one package of powdered milk. Pour under running bathwater for a delightful, soothing bath.

— Maureen

Diva Do's for the Week:

1. Go to your local health food stores and savor the array of essential oils. Smell each one and note how you feel. Write down the ones that you love and especially the ones that you hate. This is your body's way of telling you what you need. Research the properties of those oils on the Internet or at the library. Record the information in your Diva Diary. Recheck the oils in three months and see how you've changed. Buy your favorite as your personal scent.

2. Buy an aromatherapy candle that possesses a quality you want to enhance in your life. Burn it in your bedroom before you go to sleep.

3. Treat yourself to an aromatherapy massage this week, available at any spa. The massage therapist uses essential oils mixed with the normal massage oils. You will be so grateful to yourself. Write the experience in your Diva Diary.

Frivolous Diva Do:

GET A TOE RING OR ANKLE BRACELET *and anoint yourself with your favorite Diva essential oil body mixture. Feel your freedom grow.*

Diva Trivia:

- British studies report that 90 percent of satisfaction from eating occurs in our brains through the smells of the foods.

Houdiva: Escape to Serenity

. . . there was only one solution to my problem: I needed a ride on a carousel.
— Eda LeShan from It's Better to Be Over the Hill Than Under It

As we step into the glow of full Divaness, we see that there are unlimited possibilities in life, and it's so thrilling to have the restraints removed that we expect more from ourselves. We notice that we're saying "yes" to everything. "Yes" to our friends and family. "Yes" to the opportunities of traveling often. "Yes" to the new projects others are offering us.

Unfortunately, this perpetual yesness, even though it's "yes" to things we enjoy, can inevitably lead to Diva Burnout. What does Diva Burnout feel like? Well, for me, it's like a rubber band being stretched to its max . . . ready to snap. All patience is gone; I'm tense, oversensitive, and irritable; I can't imagine speaking to one more person, even if it is my best friend. I'm liable to yell at my sweet little dog and hide from my neighbors—and my husband can't do *anything* right.

What are the secrets to releasing the straitjackets of our minds, restoring our tranquility, and rejuvenating our Divaness? Houdini was the most internationally famous escape artist, the master of getting out of binds. In this spirit, Houdiva must master the elixirs of escape. Remember, rushing through life is selling the Diva short on her fabulousness. What I have learned on my path to Divaness is that there's time to enjoy everything, but everything has its time. We can do it all—but not all at once. Divadom lasts a lifetime, so use these secrets to slow down and enjoy the scrumptiousness of Diva's personal serenity. The following are mini escapes, done on the spur of the moment, taking from less than an hour to no more than three or four, meant to refresh and renew your spirits and restore your energy. Remember, you're releasing yourself from the handcuffs and need to say the magic words, "Abracadabra! Shazam!" to transport yourself . . .

- Jump in your car and drive into new neighborhoods, getting lost on purpose. Bask in the sunlight, take in your surroundings, and feel those binding thoughts leave your head.

- Do some gardening. Put your hands into the dirt. Feel it. Pull a few weeds. Admire the flowers and leave with a smile on your face.

- Visit an art gallery and drown yourself in creativity and beauty.

- Go fly a kite at the park. Visualize yourself soaring and seeing the city from the air.

- Find some water—whether it's an ocean, a lake, fountains, or a puddle. Stare at it or jump in. Water draws out the negative ions from your body; you're left with only the positive ions. It soothes and refreshes.

- Have a picnic in your backyard.

- Catch up on your beauty sleep. Go to bed early with a glass of wine and a romance novel.

- Jump in a mud puddle barefoot.

- Plan an outing with other moms. While the kids are in school sneak out to a musical matinee of *The Full Monty*.

- At work put a sign on your desk, GONE FISHING, and go out for lunch, or go to the park and eat, and take a walk.

- Have a Let-It-All-Hang-Out Party in which you break all the Diva rules—eat junk food, drink beer, burp and fart, wear grubby sweats (I know there's one pair you kept!), and tell dirty jokes.

- List all the things you have to be thankful for, and then meditate on them.

- Rent a bicycle and go for a ride.

- Visit a children's museum where exhibits are interactive and get lost in a child's world.

- Ride on a merry-go-round and feel the wind blow through your hair.
- Treat yourself to your favorite ice cream extravaganza!
- Dress up like the Diva you are and go bowling.
- Buy a big bottle of bubbles, blow as many as you can—chase them, run through them, pop them!
- Go to a karaoke bar and sing your heart out.
- Go out in the rain without an umbrella and twirl around—then take a warm soothing shower.
- Of course there's always shop, shop, shop. My favorite escape is to wander through the garden and home accessories, furniture, and antiques shops near my home. Being surrounded by lovely, interesting items is pleasing and soothes me. Sometimes I purchase something unique and am so excited to get it home and see it in place.
- Or you can always take the Diva Default—the bubble bath with candles and music.

The mini escape leads the Diva back to herself. These growing pains of her evolution just add to her charm. As Houdiva opens the locks and uses the secret powers to rejuvenate herself, she finds her way back to Divadom again and lives happily ever after.

— Elena

*D*IVA DO'S FOR THE WEEK:

1. Add your own Diva mini escapes to this list to keep with you and refer to when Diva Burnout strikes. Remember, the Diva Strikes Back!

2. Escape three times this week, just to prove you can.

RIVOLOUS DIVA DO:

ESCAPE FROM HOSTESSLAND *and lock yourself in the bathroom for two minutes (maybe with a trashy magazine) during dinner. Giggle to yourself at the sheer freedom a locked door creates!*

X

*S*ENSUALITY

Deep inside the Diva simmer the embers of her perpetual fire. Prepare
to fan them into glorious flames as we slink and soiree into sensuality!

Lingerie (I'm Too Sexy for My Clothes!)

I love thongs. The day they were invented, sunshine broke through the clouds.
— SANDRA BULLOCK

*H*ere's a personal question for you: What's your most favorite pair of underwear? C'mon, I know you have at least one; every woman does, whether it's a pair of "granny pants" that are supercomfortable or something really "hot" like a garter or teddy that makes you feel sexy and confident.

Arguably the most important part of a woman's wardrobe, lingerie has been around practically since Eve wore the fig leaf. It has served as a social indicator, icon, and turn-on, ranging from basic support to extreme seduction—but always a powerful symbol of the feminine mystique. Whether you view it as a simple essential or the most decadent luxury, lingerie is a delicious secret that a woman carries with her everywhere she goes, choosing to conceal it or reveal it at her whim. It can set the tone for her entire day, determining whether she wants to be understated, confident, comfortable, sexy . . . My underwear drawer is my secret access to Divadom. Whenever I need that Diva lift, whether it's for a big meeting, a special evening, or even nothing in particular, I reach for the undergarments that match the mood I want to create.

From the baggy trouserlike bloomers and complicated, industrial bra-like contraptions of several hundred years ago to the leave-almost-nothing-to-the-imagination Victoria's Secret models of today, women's underthings have undergone quite an evolution over the years. As far back as 2500 BCE women in Crete used a bra-like contraption that was designed to push their breasts up and out—literally baring their chests entirely. Hey, that sounds comfortable. Then, in the late 1500s, women used padding for the first time to create a fuller bustline by binding little pieces of silky cloth to their chests—the precursors to Wonderbras!

Divas over the years have learned that almost more important than how you look on the outside is how you pamper yourself on the inside. The whole Diva aura of sensuality flows from within; you can set the tone for the whole day based on what you first put on in the morning. When the Diva puts on a racy new set of bra and panties, she walks and acts differently than if she dons the supercomfortable undies she's had for years. If you have an important board meeting, you might not want to wear your vixen unmentionables, so instead wear a comfortable red set. As we learned from Maureen's chapter on color, red represents power, so why not give yourself an edge?

Okay, since we're on the topic, I might as well reveal my favorite article of daily clothing. I can't believe I'm about to dole out this tidbit of personal information to more than just my husband and close friends, but here goes nothing. I love thong underwear. In fact, I have worn nothing but (no pun intended!) since I met my husband. Years ago, when I lived in Chicago, I bought my first token thong and hated it. I tried it on again and again, sometimes even managing to wear it for a few hours, but could never get used to the fact that that thin strap of material was supposed to go, well, you know where, so it always felt uncomfortable. It was like purposely giving myself a wedgie. I really wanted to like thongs, though, because I had this fantasy of being transformed into a Victoria's Secret model by strutting around in a saucy little number. I was convinced not only that I'd look sexier, but that that tiny piece of fabric would cause me to develop an entirely new persona: sex kitten.

So when I met my husband, I finally decided to bite the bullet and wear my thong in front of him. He absolutely loved it! So began my quest for the perfect thong. Happily, I have found many. Much to my delight, Victoria's Secret makes a control-top thong. Kind of sounds like an oxymoron, doesn't it? And many maternity companies now make maternity thong underwear—I can't wait for that moment! I gradually started to swap out my "big-girl panties" for the much smaller and, I must admit, more comfortable thong (no more wrestling with wedgies!). Now my entire underwear drawer is devoted to thongs, with another devoted to bras. Although my collection is nothing to laugh at, it pales in comparison to that of my friend Margaret, who has an enormous collection and sorts them all by color and style! No wonder she receives four Victoria's Secret catalogs a week! Anyway, I can't imagine what took me so long to make the switch. To me, there is just something wonderful about wearing a conservative outfit and having a sexy little nothing on underneath. I get to start off each day as a sex kitten. It's like I have a secret that nobody else knows—well, except for my husband who is the beneficiary of these details . . . and now all of you.

Meow!

— *Molly*

*D*IVA DO'S FOR THE WEEK:

1. For those of you who might blush at the mere thought of wearing something racy, here's your week to tap into your inner sex kitten! Stop into your local lingerie store and pick up a little "something something" for yourself. Many stores have a wide selection of everything imaginable—from beautiful to bizarre. If you don't feel brave enough to be seen in public, there are dozens of online sites you can visit. Whatever you buy, give it a chance and wear it at least a few times before you decide whether or not you like it. Also, do some investigating: Thongs come in several varieties (basic thong, g-string, v-string), so go to a store and ask a professional about comfort, fit, and so on. Also, FYI, the latest fabric, microfibre, is very comfortable and might be a great starting point for those just entering into the market. And one more Diva note: Don't feel inhibited if you aren't sample size; many stores carry a great selection of all sizes!

2. Take a poll among your close female friends, colleagues, and relatives and find out what type of underwear they prefer. Now ask the men in your life what they'd like to see a woman wear. Based on the results of your survey, buy something for yourself that might surprise others. Have fun!

*F*RIVOLOUS DIVA DO:

NOW THAT YOU'RE ALL FIRED UP, *go visit your local fire station and make a donation as an homage to men in uniform—wearing your hottest little number underneath, of course!*

The Spell of High Heels

Put yourself on a pedestal! If you don't, why should anyone else?
—LIZA STEWART, WOMEN'S WEAR FASHION DIVA, ON THE IMPORTANCE OF HIGH HEELS

*A*h, the spell of high heels . . . did you know that our Divas in the past were punished for using witchcraft if they wore high heels to get a man? A seventeenth-century decree of the British Parliament states: "Any woman who, through the use of high heeled shoes or other devices, leads a subject of Her Majesty into marriage, shall be punished with the penalties of witchery." High-heel shoes as strong witchcraft—wow! Definitely a Diva tip to remember when dressing for a first date.

I always had a feeling high heels had magical powers. Each time I slipped my feet into them, my body started to tingle. My posture took on a more seductive shape. I couldn't help but sway my hips to my own beat as I walked. On any important date they were the most essential part of my ensemble. Each morning as I enter my closet, I am captivated as I stare down at my high-heel friends, fantasizing about the romantic days and sensual nights they might bring me. They enchant me with their feminine shapes; seduce me with the character and gait I know they give me whenever I wear them. I love them so much I've named them. Hey, men name their penises . . . I name my shoes! All the categories of my shoes have a name, and they all have a specific job they do for me. I wish every day could be a high-heel day, but since my daughter was born most of them remain there on the floor pushed aside as I reach for my flip-flops or athletic shoes, more appropriate to tend to my busy schedule.

As a Diva, most of my shoe collection is made up of what I consider "sitters": shoes that were made basically only for a woman to sit and enjoy a leisurely time. Even my boots weren't made for walkin'; they, too, are sitters. Sitters are the way-too-high-for-any-kind-of-movement shoes, but they make my legs look longer and sleeker and make me feel tall and bewitching. In sixteenth-century Europe they called this type of shoe "chopines." It was extremely fashionable to wear dangerously high shoes: The higher the heel, the wealthier and higher the social status of the wearer. But instead of just sitting all night in them, women would have their servants support them as they moved around socializing.

My "strutters" are just below the sitters in heel length and can be danced in, although some discomfort may occur, and whenever I walk in them I feel the *most* sensual and feminine. I can't help but sashay through the room when I wear them!

The cushioned but still cute and fashionable shoes with a low heel are my "shoppers." They're the ones best for a day at the mall. Next come the "sneakers," which include athletic shoes and any other quiet shoes that make it easy to sneak up on people. And last are my "slippers" for home lounging, getting the mail, and quick trips to the market.

The power that shoes of "sitter" and "strutter" status have over the Diva and her admirers is untamable. Fortunately, I have never been a practical or reasonable Diva, so buying shoes made mostly for sitting makes perfect sense to me. If I feel sexy, tall, and toned in a pair of shoes they must be mine! Yes, I did say "toned." A Diva knows when she wears high-heel shoes that her calf muscles are getting a workout, and the look of a flexed calf is very appealing to the Diva—not to mention the men she passes on the street!

Collecting awe-inspiring shoes has become a habit and a hobby. It has also become a way for me to transform from a hardworking, on-the-edge-of-having-a-breakdown mom to a seductive, flirtatious, sexy-as-hell Diva. Divas know allure comes from a fabulous presentation. One of the best tricks of high heels is the way they visually elongate the legs. It's an illusion that is yummy for the eyes as well as the body. High heels elevate not only a Diva's posture but her confidence as well. Height is power.

As you try new shoes be on the lookout for the "Diva Strut." You'll know you've hit pay dirt when you put those heels on and your hips begin to sway from side to side. It feels as if Marilyn has taken over your body . . . oozing sex appeal . . . feeling ultrafeminine . . . knowing you have the ability to melt any man at any moment . . . that's it, baby! Shimmy, shimmy coco pop, shimmy, shimmy bop! *Hot* weather today, *hot* weather tomorrow, *hot!* Every day you are *hot* in these shoes!

I realize there are women out there who never wear high heels for many reasons, but think twice before shunning them—these shoes transform us Divas into powerful, sexy, taller, and more sensual and confident beings, if only for the duration of an evening. The next time you think it'd be nice to have that special pair of shoes but wonder if the heel's too high, tell yourself you deserve a night or two of doing nothing but sitting (or lounging, for that matter) lookin' *hot* . . . and treat yourself!

—Carilyn

*D*IVA DO'S FOR THE WEEK:

1. Pull all your shoes out of your closet. Try on each pair. Categorize them as sitters, strutters, shoppers, sneakers, and slippers. Are you heavy on one category and not another? Create a list of shoes you may need to round out your "sensual shoe" collection.

2. Do all the shoes in each category express a part of the Diva in you? If not, I recommend you toss them. Just because a shoe is a "sneaker" doesn't mean it can't summon forth the Diva. I recently found a pair of vintage-style running shoes made by Asics in red and gold. They scream *Diva* to me!

3. Visit the mall or designer boutique. Try on shoes you'd normally pass by. Notice how different styles and heel heights make you feel.

4. Schedule some sitting and lounging time—time made strictly for you to be the tantalizing, fascinating, intriguing Diva you are. Allow yourself to get all dolled up and wear those earth-shattering heels! If you don't yet feel comfortable wearing them out of the house, then stay in and put on some sexy lingerie as if you're Mae West. Bake cookies in them. Lounge on the faux bearskin rug (don't have one? Get one!) while eating bon bons and reading a tabloid—be silly! By no means are high heels restricted to "serious" scenarios!

*F*RIVOLOUS DIVA DO:

CALL YOURSELF BY ANOTHER NAME TODAY, *all day. When you meet people, introduce yourself as this new persona. I always wanted to be called "Heather." Heather likes to be frivolous, laugh loud, and wear provocative, eye-catching shoes.*

The Art of the Plentiful Woman: Lessons in Sex Appeal

Too much of a good thing is wonderful.

—MAE WEST

*M*y personal opinion of life is this: On some level we are all Sybil, the woman with the multiple personalities. Now, granted, our "others" may not all require psychiatric care, but we now acknowledge their existence nonetheless. One of the beauties who lives in me is a plentiful woman, overflowing with copious curves and charms. I am in awe of women of plenteous measures, women like Queen Latifah and Star Jones. Imagine the power of the woman who named them, either their mother or themselves. You know instantly where they stand—they are a Queen and a Star. I love everything about these women; their beauty, the rich, deep color of their skin, their creativity with hair and nails, their "attitude," and most of all the way they love their bodies, regardless of size. These women know how to strut and style. I love the way they dance, sing, and carry themselves. I no longer need to sit back and envy their power; I Am Diva Maureen, an extraordinary woman with curves of my own.

On a recent shopping adventure, I had the thrill of my life. I picked out an outrageous outfit—at least for me. It's a brilliant purple silk jacket and a wild pink-and-purple-plaid shirt and pants in a size 18. It's an outfit that shouts, *Look out, world, here I am* from the Diva in me. I was afraid to even take it to the dressing room. There I was, looking big and fabulous at the same time—a feat I have never been able to pull off before. As I was standing at the register, there was a large, beautiful woman purchasing the same outfit. I started to jump up and down. "Isn't it fabulous!" we shouted at the same time. I knew, in that moment, that I'd arrived. Out of sheer will and determination, I had been blessed with the courage, style, and freedom of my role models.

Sex appeal is not reserved for the thin and wispy. It's not reserved for blondes, tall women, or women with perfect teeth, busts, or butts. Sex appeal lives deep within the soul of a woman. It lives where we conjure up the passion that makes men weak in the knees. It lives in how we carry ourselves, how we speak, how we touch, and how we listen. It lives in our hearts and in our kitchens. It lives in how we show each other that "You're important to me and I'm important to you." It is the very essence of the Diva.

There is someone for everyone. If we look to nature, everything comes in pairs. Each animal belongs to a particular species. A female hippo doesn't lie in the water saying, "I'm too fat"; nor does a giraffe say, "I'm too tall." Each of us is perfect just the way she is. Maybe I've just been a giraffe trying to date a hippo. Is there a species just for me? "Short, smart, fat, funny white woman, desiring to have the confidence and joie de vivre of bold women."

The problem is not really in finding my mate—it's identifying my species. That work comes from the inside out. I am not a pastel kind of woman. I'm a bold, brazen, hell-raising kind of woman. I have sexy bras, perfume that makes me feel special, and colors that are full of life. It hasn't always been this way. I wore black most of my life because it makes you look thinner. Then the Diva in me woke up and said, "God, who cares? Bring in some color, girl!" Do you have a lusty, sexy, bold, and beautiful woman living in you? I encourage you to start looking. Here is how I did it.

In the past I waited for some man to find me "good enough" to date. To change that pattern, I joined a dating service for "Large and Lovely" women and their admirers. I broke the rules and sent the same short, witty, and exciting message to sixty men to see if there were any who were "good enough" for me. I think there are!

Wardrobe: Instead of wearing baggy clothes in dark colors to hide my figure—which actually made me look *larger* than I am—today I wear formfitting clothes. Carilyn taught me how to look sexy and beautiful in knits that hug my curves and flowing fabrics that bring out my Diva. I love the way they feel on me. I also wear bold colors that complement my skin tones (Week 30).

This week let's all be Mae West—lusty, loud, sexy, and flamboyant. Focus on your favorite body parts—it doesn't matter if that's your eyes or your bosom. Don't walk, strut. Don't look, penetrate with those eyes of yours. Make someone weak in the knees by the very presence of your plentiful woman. The secret is adoring the wonderful woman that is you. Once you do that, Diva, the world will notice.

— *Maureen*

*D*IVA DO'S FOR THE WEEK:

1. Find Maya Angelou's poem "Phenomenal Woman." Write it in your Diva Diary; post it all around your private, sacred Diva spaces.

2. Pick out the woman who is for you a role model of sex appeal. In your Diva Diary, write down all of her fabulous qualities and all the reasons why she shouldn't have such strong charisma (too short, too heavy, too thin, whatever). Put in a picture if you have one.

3. Now look at yourself. Can you see that you possess some of these same qualities?

4. Make it a practice this week to expand your sex appeal from the inside out. Remember Mammy in *Gone with the Wind*? Wear a red petticoat that swishes when you walk. Ooh! Sexy lady.

5. Go dancing or see *Ain't Misbehaving* if it's anywhere near you.

6. Find anything with Nell Carter in it; Aretha Franklin and Patti LaBelle make great role models, too. Think of what they project: confidence, self-esteem, and self-love. Practice that this week. Love yourself just the way you are and the way you aren't.

*F*RIVOLOUS DIVA DO:

BRING SOME OLD-TIME GLAMOUR *to your life. Create a Diva lounging outfit, silk PJs, boa-trimmed robe with high-heel slippers, or leopard pants just for you.*

Sexy at Sixty

*Never let the spirt of the girl in you disappear. Make sure she has fun,
to really believe there is always something new to discover.*
— NORMA KAMALI

For my sixtieth birthday two dear girlfriends gave me a short black negligee trimmed in silver glitter. I was grateful, but resistant: Do I dare wear it? How will I look? Would I be "not acting my age"? First I tried it on when I was home alone. Not too bad. My husband is used to me in my flannel pajamas, but I decided to go for it! Well, I wore it with very good results. Enough said . . . except that it proves sexy and sixty aren't mutually exclusive! It's more about the way you live your life.

Being excited about life and always learning new things is what keeps us young at any age. As we grow older we can grow in new, interesting ways. It's important to continue to surprise ourselves. Keep or develop a sense of adventure. This is the time for the Diva to explore the things you always wanted to do, but didn't have time for, or go back to doing things you enjoyed when you were younger, but put aside. Anne Richards, former governor of Texas and Diva extraordinaire, learned how to ride a motorcycle in her sixtieth year. In Palm Springs, California, there's a group of women who put on a show titled *Fabulous Palm Springs Follies*. Yes, it's like the Ziegfeld Follies—fancy costumes, high kicks, and all—with one exception. The requirement to participate is you must be a *senior citizen*. This season they ranged from fifty-four to eighty-seven years old. Talk about Divas living outrageously!

Along with adventure, aging heralds the return of romance! One of the things I enjoyed about my husband when we were first dating is that he likes to hold hands. We still do—age is no deterrent here. Make romance a priority in your life. Kidnap your significant other for a special date. Call him at work and talk in a low sultry voice. Dress up in your most alluring Diva ensemble anytime. Take a romantic cruise. Light candles for dinner at home, or while reading or watching TV. Talk to each other. Flirt. Cuddle. Sleep naked. At least now you don't have to worry about children walking in on you!

If you're single, engage strangers in conversation, being fascinated with whatever they have to say. Be receptive to meeting people wherever you are, whether it's the car wash, the post office, or a restaurant. When the Diva feels confident and dynamic she is a magnet for others. Put on a large beautiful hat and take yourself to a polo match, pretending you're looking for a stallion to purchase.

We're all more in touch with our mortality at this age, so as Divas we must make each day count. Don't put things off. I wear my red, black, or purple underwear any day I want instead of saving it for a special night. Also, I'm more comfortable with wearing what I want, where I want, and not so hung up on *What will people think?* My mind is still young. I still think like I did years ago. It's just that my body doesn't always cooperate. I hate the fact that I don't have as much energy as I used to have, and the occasional aches and pains.

It's even more important for us older Divas to take care of our health, to feel and look our best. There is a mind–body connection, so I go for my physical checkups when I'm supposed to, including the Pap smear and the mammogram. I keep my dentist happy by going twice a year for cleanings. I try to eat healthy most of the time. And I've learned to embrace my sweet tooth that only chocolate can satisfy.

For the Diva, attitude is everything. Living in the present, keeping our vitality, and always wanting more pleasure from life keeps us fascinating. Tina Turner is the perfect role model. I went to see her perform and I could feel her energy from the audience. No one could sit still, and in no time we were up and dancing. She's a woman in her sixties who has overcome much, has great style, is sexy, and still takes risks. (And lives with a younger man.) You go, girl!

Another woman I discovered recently is Eda LeShan, an author who writes about aging in a captivating and humorous way. I recommend her books, including *It's Better to Be Over the Hill than Under It: Thoughts on Life over Sixty*; *The Wonderful Crisis of Middle Age: Some Personal Reflections*; and *Oh to Be 50 Again! On Being Too Old for a Mid Life Crisis*. She had always wanted to write screenplays—so in her seventies, she did. Never stop challenging yourself. Madeleine Albright hasn't. She came to the United States at eleven years old as a Czechoslovakian immigrant. She attended Wellesley College, followed by a master's degree and then a doctorate in political science from Columbia University. During this time she married and had three daughters. Then in 1982, when she was forty-five, her husband left her for another woman. She continued on and became a professor of international affairs at Georgetown University. In 1993 she became the U.S. ambassador to the United Nations—a first for a woman. Then at age sixty, in 1977, she was sworn in as the first female secretary of state. Always a Diva, she is outspoken, likes high heels and jewelry, and owns several cowboy hats (great for bad hair days!). She has a collection of brooches to fit any occasion, or to show what's on her mind. For her swearing-in ceremony she had a brooch made of an eagle in sparkly red, white, and blue, and she wears a hot-air balloon pin when she's happy. A Diva's innate curiosity about life and learning make her irresistible.

With our extended life spans we have to plan our lives over a much longer period of time with no guidelines or sense of direction. Now is the time for the Diva to pull out all the stops and go for it! I plan to travel more and drive a sports car! Have you always wanted to have your own business, write poetry, tour the country in an RV, learn Russian, hang glide, snow ski? You get the idea. My friend Betty, who's retired, goes to the gym, has lunch with friends, plays tennis and golf and bridge, sometimes all in one day! Make *your* want list and go full throttle in your new sports car. Think of what you have to offer the world! The world is waiting in excited anticipation!

Recently there was a meteor shower, something that wouldn't occur again for thirty years. The best time to see it was between one-thirty and three o'clock in the morning.

My husband set his alarm, got up, and went outside to see if the sky was clear and if the stars were shooting. Then he came and woke me up and we went out front in our bathrobes and watched for an hour. I loved it. Romance is alive and well at our house.

— *Elena*

𝒟IVA DO'S FOR THE WEEK:

1. Plan a surprise romantic event with a loved one.

2. Do something *bold!* Go for a sailplane ride!

3. Make an appointment for whatever checkups you need. Preventive medicine is the best protection.

ℱRIVOLOUS DIVA DO:

BE A MYSTERIOUS WOMAN *in red today—paint your nails red and wear red lipstick. Add a large hat with a feather. Or a red rose between your teeth!*

𝒟IVA TIP:

- If you schedule your gynecologist appointment and your mammogram appointment six months apart, you'll get two breast exams within one year. Breast cancer is on the rise, and this can help in early detection.

XI

*D*IVADOM! THE WORLD TOUR

Divas are not confined to palaces, stages, or countries. On the contrary,
Divas are in every nook and cranny, around the bend in the road, or on
the top of a mountain. Be on the lookout for these special women
wherever you go. You'll know them by the sparkle in their eye,
the laughter that surrounds them, and their brazen,
look-out-world-here-I-come attitude.

La Dolce Vita

Mangia! Mangia!
—MY MOTHER

Nothing succeeds like excess.
—OSCAR WILDE

*B*uongiorno, *bella Divas!* I open my arms to you. I squeeze you tightly and let you in on the secrets of Grandma Diva's Italian heritage. Yes, Grandma Diva is proud to say she is half Italian and Italy is her number one travel destination. Italian people are so passionate, talented, and inspiring. Our flair for drama and fun breeds countless Divas, from the ones the world knows—like Isabella and Sophia—to the ones we don't, like me and my expressive aunts. The most important thing for all Divas to know is that every one of us can experience life with the intense love for living and indulgence that Italian Divas are raised with! Italian women know the secrets to celebrating life, and they have a beautiful country in which to do it. Watching the parade of confident, creative, expressive Italian women throughout my life, and growing up in an Italian household, I can't wait to share with you the Italian way.

"In the beginning . . ."—starting from infancy, little Italian Divas are indulged and loved by an extended family that lives close by. They feel secure instantly because of this and grow up with a sense of belonging and knowledge of family history. Self-expression is encouraged and creativity is not suppressed; children are showered with affection—never worried whether a hug or a kiss is appropriate in public. I remember my uncles pinching and twisting my cheeks (now, Divas, I'm talking about the cheeks on my face) and my aunt crushing me to her ample bosom with her hugs. The time is now to indulge the little Italian Diva in each of us. Stand in front of your mirror and tell yourself how great you are. Wrap your arms around your body and give yourself a great big Italian-style hug. Then take a red lipstick and write on your mirror I LOVE YOU! and read it every day.

With the emphasis on how awesome life can be, instead of how many calories that lasagne has, the Italian Diva's life revolves around food, family, and conversation. Everything is done with gusto and without limits. Love and indulgence ooze everywhere and start in the home with Nonna (Grandmother Diva), who cooks with the same strong passion she has for life because it's for the people she loves, singing along with Italian opera on the radio. Welcome to Sunday dinner at the Della Portas: My mother and aunts are helping in the kitchen. There is lots of food in case someone should stop by (including the Italian army!). Italians have a very generous spirit. Nonna is treated with respect because she's the glue that holds the family together and passes down her wisdom (as well as the family recipes—if you're lucky!) to her daughters (Mama Diva) and granddaughters. We kids would sneak into the kitchen to dip a piece of bread into the pasta sauce, and then be chased out. Nonna reigns supreme in the kitchen. Everyone eats together leisurely, enjoying several courses with wine, engaged in animated conversation, sometimes all at the same time. If ever you're so lucky as to be a guest at an Italian dinner, listen to the enormous sounds coming from the table. You would think no one is listening. It's important not to be shy—you'll never be heard if you are. You just have to jump in if you have something to say. And believe me, everybody has something to say about everything! Conversation over food is most important; everything is discussed, and Italians are deeply involved in each other's lives. The women are very open with their emotions and may disagree strongly, but they get over it quickly. Devotion to family wins out.

If you have no family close by, create your own Italian family. Invite people over with their children (kids running around squealing is part of the picture) and share your life stories.

On our last Italy trip my husband and I visited my cousin Carlantonio, his wife, two daughters, and his mother (the Nonna), who all welcomed us with open arms even though this was our first meeting. They took us to the original family farm and original stone house where my grandfather was born. It was such a thrill to connect with my roots and experience that sense of belonging. I will never forget how comfortable I felt with them. As Divas we can welcome people into our own homes with the same warmth and concern for their comfort.

Our Italian Diva sisters have a love of life and enjoy life's pleasures to the fullest, both in their dress and with their friends. How they express themselves in dress is so important to them that they have a special name for it—*bella figura*, meaning "beautiful image" or "good impression." They are very stylish, desiring elegant clothes and quality leather shoes and purses and unique jewelry. These Divas *ooze* passion from every cell of their bodies, and it's expressed in their short skirts, high heels, and fitted clothes. It's in how they look at you, how they walk, in their gestures, and their elegant, sultry, total presence. I remember I was thrilled when my cousins passed down some of their clothes to me. Sophia Loren comes to mind as the epitome of mystery, glamour, and class. The best-known actress from Italy, she has maintained her beauty and stature as a star over the years.

Watching Italian Divas socializing with friends at outdoor cafés in the *piazzas* (public squares) makes you wonder what exciting experiences they are sharing. They are animated, with lots of laughter and affection. No Diva can help wanting to be a part of it.

How can we incorporate this into our lives, you ask? Here is the Italian Grandmother Diva's recipe for life:

- **1 cup of expression:** When asked your feelings on something, be honest—don't be concerned with what you think they want to hear. Show your range of emotions.
- **2 cups of affection:** Remember to let people know you care. Send flowers now, not after they're gone. Give big bear hugs, not wimpy weak ones—and give them often.
- **3 cups of family:** Plan leisurely family meals with no TV. Talk, discuss—each opinion is valuable. Set a pretty table with candles, flowers, and music. If you have no family, reach out and adopt one. Investigate your genealogy to give you that feeling of belonging.

- **2 pinches of passion:** Put on a short skirt, high heels, and fitted blouse. Strut around in front of a mirror. Then pick a subject you're passionate about (a relationship or a charity, for example) and enthusiastically talk about it, putting your whole heart and hands into it. Feel the aliveness!
- **4 pinches of creativity:** Make something! A collage is easy and attractive. Be clever and look around your house for items to use—from straws to rags, to buttons and ribbons and wrapping paper. No buying anything. Arrange it together with glue and hang it up as a reminder of your "Italian" legacy.

From a little girl to a Nonna, all phases of the Italian Diva woman are respected. As she ages her role is not diminished; she's instead honored for all she has to offer the family. I am proud of my Italian Diva heritage and like all Divas, I embrace the passion for food, family, and friends.

For those Divas who weren't born into Italian families, we can take what this marvelous culture offers us and incorporate it into our everyday lives. Every Diva can live *The Sweet Life*.

Ciao!

— Elena

$\mathcal{D}$IVA DO'S FOR THE WEEK:

1. Go out to an Italian restaurant with special friends or family and spend a leisurely time over dinner.

2. Call a relative you haven't spoken to in a while.

3. Rent an Italian movie with subtitles.

4. Purchase something made in Italy. They make the most beautiful ceramics, for instance.

$\mathcal{F}$RIVOLOUS DIVA DO:

PRETEND YOU SPEAK ITALIAN TODAY. *Say things like:* lasagne, bueno, bella, buongiorno.

Vive la Diva!

I don't want life to imitate art, I want life to be art.
—CARRIE FISHER

anderlust. Plain and simple, that's what I have. And my destination of choice is France. It always has been, ever since I took French lessons in the fifth grade. The language was so romantic and sounded wonderful. *Bonjour, ma petite chèrie! Je t'aime beaucoup!* See what I mean? I visited France for the first time when I was sixteen, and it was there that I observed the certain *je ne sais quoi* that makes French women such natural Divas.

For many years after this trip, I wondered what it was about the French style that seems so easy and effortless, and yet so put together and elegant. I resolved to unravel that mystery when I returned to France, this time as a student for a year. I was completely in awe of these *desmoiselles* (slang for "girls") whose style reflected a perfect combination of aloof and sophisticated. I studied and admired these women, some of whom became my friends. I noticed that their inimitable approach to style touches all aspects of their lives. To the French, life seems to be an art form, and this is readily apparent in their love of food and wine, their fine art and architecture, their hospitality, and, yes, their clothes, too.

Some of the French, particularly the Parisians, have a bad rap for being impolite. Our French sisters may be reserved, but I also found them to be extremely hospitable. It may take a while to get to know the French, but once you do, they are friends for life! It could even be said that being reserved is exactly what makes the French Divas more seductive and sought after; it adds to their air of allure and mystery. They aren't outwardly emotional—

except for the traditional public displays of affection when they greet each other with kisses on the cheeks; rather, they are private, intimate people.

The words that come to mind to describe our French Diva counterparts are *simplicity, refinement, graciousness,* and *class*. One of the best-known French Divas is the actress Catherine Deneuve, the quintessential image of classic French elegance and beauty. My French girlfriends seemed to exude the same kind of style and confidence as this Diva icon. I observed them, and even tried dressing like them to look French, but I never felt as put together as they looked; I felt more complicated. It was then that I started to understand the key to French women's style: simplicity with a soupçon of elegance.

The French have a saying: *"Moins on en dit, ça vaut mieux"* (the less said, the better). They seem to carry this into their style and their lives. For example, *les Divas françaises* buy far fewer clothes than we American Divas, who have become conditioned to acquire clothes for every different season and event. The French ladies have a knack for knowing how to do more with less; quality, not quantity, is the name of the game. Take clothing, for example—we American Divas may well believe in the basics of being well dressed, but we do not devote the time to selecting *the* perfect staples. The French, on the other hand, know that one perfect pair of black cigarette pants or one pristine white blouse trumps a closet crowded with near misses any day. They are accustomed to starting out with the basics, to which they add a special jacket or accessories, such as jewelry, shoes, scarves, belts, and bags that they use to update their personal style, season after season. Everything matches to create an effect that appears to have been effortlessly put together at the last minute with the very important notion that less is more. That is reflected too in their joie de vivre. The simple nature comes from within, and how they dress is merely a reflection of that.

Their joy of life is also expressed in the way the French entertain; from fine art to fabulous food and wines, the French ooze class, beauty, and style. It wasn't until I had lived in France for four months that I unlocked the keys to the kingdom and became part of the "inner circle" of an amazing group of friends centered on Vincent, Fritz, and Amelie Beux-Prere, two brothers and a sister. My whole experience of the French shifted the moment I established my friendships with this French Diva and her Divo brothers. After that, I was always included in every activity. The entire gang of about twelve people was so welcoming, always making me feel important and right at home, from creating an impromptu dinner party to having an afternoon aperitif at the local café or hanging out with *les Divas françaises* to discuss the finer points of relationships, politics, and life. Even several years after I had returned home from France, my friends still included me as part of their group. Each time we called each other, the first question they would ask me was, "When are you coming to stay with us?" I did return several years later with my mom, and the Beux-Preres welcomed us with a seven-course lunch, including champagne and several different wines, delicious cheeses, and exquisite homemade desserts. Even the grandparents were in attendance. A seven-course lunch, just because my mom and I were in town! They didn't speak much English and my mom was hardly conversant in French, so I was the translator. The language barrier didn't affect any of us, though, and their primary concern was our comfort and pleasure.

Here's what we can learn from our French Diva counterparts: Practice being gracious everywhere in your life. For example, be a gracious hostess: Have a dinner party and invite people who don't know each other; make a point of having your different groups of friends become friends with each other. For a Super Diva dinner party, make it a potluck; provide the entrée and ask everyone else to bring the other courses, along with the recipes so you can all share new culinary ideas with each other. Another lesson is to go out of your way to make someone else feel special. For example, whenever you have houseguests, create a little basket for them complete with little toiletries or fresh fruit and wine; put mints or chocolates on their pillows. These little touches are sure to make your guests feel at home. Finally, a tip for your next trip to the store: When you go shopping, be discerning—evaluate the crease of the pants or the sheen of the buttons when you buy something. Look for just one perfect staple item and forgo getting the whole outfit. The goal here, Divas, is to simplify our lives, inside and out. Taking on what our Diva sisters from overseas can teach us will help all of us to be more enriched, gratified, and satisfied. *Vive la simplicité!*

— *Molly*

𝒟IVA DO'S FOR THE WEEK:

1. Read *A Year in Provence* by Peter Mayle. It's a delightful, easy-to-read, and very amusing view of *la vie française*.

2. Create the ambience of a French bistro right in your own home. Buy a baguette, Brie or Boursin cheese, a simple bottle of table wine, and some *sables* (butter cookies), *tartes*, or other French pastries—*bon appétit!*

3. Own at least one silk scarf. Practice wearing and tying it different ways and with different clothes. Ooh la la!

4. Study your favorite foreign culture online.

𝓕RIVOLOUS DIVA DO:

GO AHEAD, SKIP THE SHOWER TODAY! *You can still dress the part of the Diva, with glitter and fabulous accessories.*

𝒟IVA TRIVIA:

- Catherine Deneuve was chosen as France's Marianne, it's symbol of national feminine beauty, in the 1980s, and was honored with having her likeness engraved on coins and stamps.

"Cuchi—Cuchi!"

Confidence is the sexiest thing a woman can have. It's much sexier than any body part.
—AIMEE MULLINS, PARALYMPIC ATHLETE

To tell a woman everything she may not do is to tell her what she can do.
—SPANISH PROVERB

*S*aucy, *sexy*, and *spicy* are three words I have heard repeatedly describe our Latin Diva sisters. They have such vitality, sensuality, and *attitude*. Remember Charo? I think her entire career was built on the talents of her hips and how fast she could shake 'em while she squealed "cuchi-cuchi." There is nobody like her . . . whoever heard of cuchi-cuchi anyway? I wanted to be this boldly wild yet cute and feminine woman named Charo so badly! *The Love Boat* was always more entertaining when she was guest-starring. She possessed a magnetism that intrigued people, and while I could barely understand a word she said, I knew she was extremely passionate about it and that she didn't care what anyone else thought. She is a one-of-a-kind Diva . . . and how! Rumor has it that she had a judge legally change her birth year! Gals, we can have what we desire!

Known as "the lady in the tutti-frutti hat," Carmen Miranda was another uniquely expressed Latin woman with a great accent and talent for the unusual. Another inimitable Diva, she took on the traditional look of the Bahian market women who wore baskets of fruit, veggies, and sundries on their heads and made it her signature.

These Latin women have boldly gone where no woman has gone before. Ingenuity, a willingness to do anything, and assertively going after what we want are special traits that all Divas can learn from our Latin sisters.

I sailed the Virgin Islands with my family one summer, and it was there I learned a huge lesson in being an honorary Latin Diva . . . ain't nuthin' but attitude, baby! As everyone else spent time relaxing on one of the islands, I had been spending my time trying to sit in the most flattering position for my fat pockets, wondering if my try-to-cover-the-ass-as-much-as-possible bikini bottom was doing its job. A minute later two Spanish women sizzled past me who were my size or more, each wearing a skimpy Brazilian-cut bikini. They captivated me. They were oozing sensuality. It seemed they didn't have a care in the world, let alone a care whether too much ass was showing. They giggled to each other as if sharing the best secret of all, knowing that wherever they were was the place to be (a true Diva trait)! That Brazilian bikini bottom, I noticed, actually looked quite flattering. I had an epiphany! Maybe more fabric meant more ass and less fabric meant less ass. (Except of course when it comes to the thong bikini. I'm a firm believer in leaving something to the imagination. Plus, I can't stand anything creeping up my rear!)

Why did I feel I should be wearing the cover-all-'cause-I'm-a-mom-with-baby-fat bikini instead of the look-at-me-and-my-sensuality Brazilian-style bikini? *I Am Diva*, after all! These anonymous women inspired me for life! If I say I'm sexy, then I *am* sexy and I am certainly entitled to wear an attitude-rich Brazilian-style bikini bottom! It may have been their carefree attitude that first intrigued me but it was the bikini that caught me. It seemed that Brazilian-cut bikini summed up everything I was looking for as a Diva: an attitude that says, "Wherever I am is the place to be. I love myself. I am scintillatingly sexy, magnetically compelling, and subtly strong. Watch out because I will rock your world! Sizzle, sizzle, sizzle."

We are often stuck viewing ourselves a certain way, doing things in a way we think is "appropriate." Charo, Carmen Miranda, and those two Brazilian bikini-wearing babes on the beach weren't afraid to stand out from the rest. They embraced and used what they had instead of pretending or yearning to be something they weren't.

This seductive nature, a confident attitude, and sexual energy is what we Divas call *machisma*: sensuality, sex appeal, ambition, ingenuity, outrageousness, and strength all at once. Take your pick, Divas . . . which way empowers you?

1. **"Appropriate"**: Sitting at home waiting for love to find you there on the couch.
   Machisma: Getting out of the house, going dancing, and asking that sexy guy in the corner to dance!

2. **"Appropriate"**: Suppressing your naturally loud and boisterous laugh.
   Machisma: Getting yourself hired as a professional laugher for television shows.

3. **"Appropriate"**: Wearing the largest cover-all-of-your-ass . . . ets-hiding-what-you-don't-want-others-to-see-while-pretending-to-feel-sexy bikini.
   Machisma: Strutting the Brazilian-cut bikini and the Brazilian bikini's high-sex-appeal attitude.

The time has come for us all to discard appropriateness and learn from our sizzling Spanish sisters. Let's put some fruit on our heads and shake our hips as wildly as we can in a teeny-tiny Brazilian bikini. Give yourself permission to be sexy no matter what (no excuses, girls . . . remember, it's all in the attitude)! Unleash the rhythm, unleash the fire, unleash the "cuchi-cuchi"!

— Carilyn

Diva Do's for the Week:

1. Take on the attitude this week of, "Wherever I am, that's the place to be!"
2. Buy a Brazilian bikini bottom. If you aren't yet ready to wear it, frame it and hang it on your wall as a call to Diva action that says, *I am sexy because I say so!*
3. Walk around with an apple on your head. Can you shake your hips while balancing the fruit? Practice until you can!
4. List three exceptionally silly or ridiculous things about yourself or something you did. Can you now see how they might actually have been charming or given you an idea for a signature "you-ism"?
5. Observe your world. Are there unusual things you can learn from, be inspired by, and mold into something representative of your Diva? Are there women you've seen on the streets or on the beaches who can inspire you to turn on the 'tude?
6. Talk one day this week with the thickest accent you can muster up.
7. Listen to "Pussy Control" by Prince or "U Can't Touch This" by M.C. Hammer and feel the instant rush of sexiness and power take over you!

Frivolous Diva Do:

"ACCIDENTALLY" FORGET TO WEAR *your panties today à la Carmen Miranda (who was allegedly photographed dancing wearing no underwear. Apparently it was not perceived as being "naughty" but as a freedom from restriction for her dance routines . . . sounds good to me!).*

Diva Trivia:

- How did Charo get her trademarked "cuchi-cuchi" while wiggling? She stole her moves from a dog from her childhood who wiggled when happy. His name was Cuchillo; his nickname, "Cuchi."

Rodeo Queens and Other Divas from Around the World

The soul should always stand ajar, ready to welcome the ecstatic experience.
—EMILY DICKINSON

Divas are women of glamour, class, and sophistication, so you might think that Divas can only be found in cosmopolitan cities. You'd be wrong. There is no corner on culture, economic level, or birthright. Divas are created out of sheer determination, guts, and will—not geographic location. There are precious lessons that we can learn from Divas in different cultures and from Divas who live in their own worlds. Some Divas stand alone at the start of an adventure, and some Divas thrive in specific communities. This week we're going to celebrate both of these expressions of Divaness from unexpected areas and in unexpected ways.

Rodeo Queens (and princesses) scream *Diva* from the top of their tiara-laden cowboy hats to the tips of their shiny boots. I was introduced to these Divas by my friend Linda through Lisa Eisner's photographic essay on this delightful cut of western life in her book *Rodeo Girls*. These women are Divas to a T. In fact, Carilyn is an honorary Rodeo Queen for her love of her leopard cowboy hat and outrageous belt buckles. I just experience Rodeo Queen envy for the sparkle of the purple sequined shirts, flashing smiles of giddy joy, and the most beautiful, ornately designed silver and gold belt buckles.

These girls rock with their self-expression and unique style. But it's not enough to admire other Divas; the trick is to emulate the qualities and traits that speak to us. This is what we can learn from the Rodeo Queens:

Lesson 1: In a very strongly male-dominated environment, the women created a vehicle of self-expression that made their activity the center of attention. Who can resist a woman exuding confidence and self-expression?

Lesson 2: It's not necessary to expose your breasts or legs to have fun, be glamorous, and celebrate your beauty. You can do it all dressed up in the right outfit.

Lesson 3: We don't have to limit ourselves to certain times and places to wear exciting clothes and accessories. These Divas are decked out in sequins in the middle of the day without a black-tie event on the horizon. I'm buying myself a sequined shirt and wearing it anytime I want.

In another part of the world, far from Western influences, lives a tribe of women who rule their world. An article from *Marie Claire* introduces us to the Mosuo tribe of China. These women live in a matriarchal society that oozes *Diva*. Tribal members do not marry, and there is no violence in their culture. They have no word for "divorce," for "adultery," for "incest," or for any of the heinous acts that are far too common in the United States. Men live with their sisters and the tribe raises the children. Every woman aged seventeen to seventy-three has her own room, and each night the women gather in a circle for an evening dance. They choose their partner for the night, and the men follow them back for the pleasure of the Dame. The next morning, the men leave and the women run the affairs of the tribe. What can we learn from these role models?

Lesson 4: Divas thrive in groups. Divas support each other to grow. You are a Diva.

Can you remember a time when you were filled with self-doubt and a friend stood by you and showed you the lie you were telling yourself? Remember when you experienced the thrill of being with a group of women; where you were totally safe to be yourself? to be smart and funny and pretty and silly at the same time, and it was all okay? The safest times I have ever felt have been in the company of another woman, maybe my mom, or my sister, or a dear friend. Where I could just be Maureen, and that was good enough. Nowhere to go and nothing to prove. That is the power of women in pairs or quads or groups. Because when one of us loses our way, there is always a Diva close at hand who remembers who we truly are—a glorious daughter of Eve, Diana, and Venus.

There are countless communities of Divas around the world, and all of them share a common bond with us. One is in your neighborhood, for Divas can be found where love resides. Haven't you noticed them at the PTO meetings, or volunteering at the school carnival? They are present in the hospital, caring for the ill, or in the market by the produce. Divas can be seen at lunch, laughing with their friends and visiting the elderly at a nursing home. They also lead by example, and a few of them shine the way for the rest of us to follow. These Divas are involved in a life bigger than their own concerns. They rise above life's circumstances to shine wherever they are planted. Here are some great Divas to emulate.

I once knew a young Diva named Katie Brant. Katie was a vivacious, beautiful, smart, and loving Diva who was stricken with brain cancer very young in life. For years she battled this disease, undergoing surgery after surgery to extend her life. Throughout it all, Katie epitomized a teaching from Eleanor Roosevelt: "You have to accept whatever comes and the only important thing is that you meet it with courage and with the best you have to give." No matter what life brought her, Katie faced it and brought fun, joy, and laughter everywhere she went. Near the end of her life, she forged a path for others and created Katie's Kids for the Cure, a nonprofit organization (www.katieskids.org) to find a cure for brain tumors in children. Although she passed on from this plane of existence at twenty-six, Katie has galvanized a legacy to move with her spirit. Katie is a Diva and brought out the Diva in everyone she touched. For me, she is my role model of how we can each make a difference for someone else, no matter what we face.

Sometimes we can become overwhelmed by the circumstances in our own lives, let alone what's going on in the world. The secret of the Diva is that the mere *act* of reaching outside the safety net of our lives makes all the difference in the world. Jody

Williams brought the world's attention to the cruelty of land mines. This Nobel Prize laureate changed the world with *first*, an idea, to ban land mines around the world, and *second*, an action, to form with others and create the International Campaign to Ban Landmines (ICBL). Mother Teresa changed the world with *first*, an idea, that people should have dignity in death, and *second*, an action—she created her Diva community, the Sisters of Charity.

What is it that you want to change in *your world*, right now, today? That's where we want to start. Is there one family you can help? Is there a child or an elder who needs some attention? Do pollutants threaten your environment? All it takes is two steps: *first* an idea, and *second* an action. Goethe said, "Whatever you can do or dream you can do, begin it! Boldness has genius, power, and magic in it. Begin it now!" Form a Diva pact with someone and launch your future, right now in this moment. Remember, it only takes one Diva to make all our dreams come true and that Diva is you.

— Maureen

DIVA DO'S FOR THE WEEK:

1. In your Diva Diary, create a page for your legacy. What is the gift you bring to the world?

2. Make a date with a friend to share your legacy. Have her bring hers and together create a Diva pact.

3. Observe "Divas" in your world. Write down your observations in your Diva Diary.

FRIVOLOUS DIVA DO:

EMULATE A DIVA WHO CHANGED THE WORLD TODAY. *Honor her in your own way, like wearing a white-and-blue headband for Mother Teresa, or a tiara for Princess Diana, or making a donation to the ICBL in honor of Jody Williams and her courage.*

DIVA TRIVIA:

In which Pacific culture are girls and women of rank treated almost as "Gods"?
Answer: Samoa and Tonga.

In which Asian culture are women known as shamans and priestesses, and samurai were annoyed because they had to present their credentials to women?
Answer: In the Ryukyu kingdom in Japan.

How many Divas does it take to change a lightbulb?
Answer: Are you kidding? We don't change lightbulbs!

XII

*L*UXURY

One of the benefits of being a Diva is that you no longer question
your right to indulge. In fact, it has become your mantra!
Those treasures that were once unthinkable now become possible
with a little planning, creativity, and ingenuity.

Diamonds, Multifaceted Like the Diva

I never worry about diets. The only carrots that interest me are the number you get in a diamond.
—MAE WEST

For much of my life, I felt like I was a diamond in the rough. I so wanted to sparkle, but I felt that my weight hid my true beauty. My mother had always called me a late bloomer, but at age fifty-one, I thought that I would never bloom. I was wrong. It is never too late to bloom or sparkle. It all depends on your point of view. Let's take Barbie for instance. I love Barbie. I have always loved Barbie. I will always love Barbie. For the first half century of my life, I envied Barbie's ridiculous proportions and her fabulous diamonds. When I shifted my paradigm, I realized I will never (nor will any living human woman) actually have them. But, as a Big Girl, aka Big Beautiful Woman (BBW), while I might not have her teeny waist, I will always have her beautiful breasts (see Week 9) and can acquire her magnificent diamonds. Which brings us back to the subject at hand.

Among The Four Divas, I am the only one who is diamondless. I think it's perfect for me to write about my love affair with the fantasy of owning diamonds. I still lust after them. I love diamonds. I love everything about them—the sparkle, the colors, and the mystery. A woman who owns a diamond possesses a secret and few mere mortals are bold enough to ask the woman with a diamond—Where did you get your diamond?

My friend Marsha has a magnificent diamond ring. Ten big gems in a platinum band. Marsha is a Diva in charge of her life. The source of her beautiful diamonds, you may ask? Well, according to this Diva it's her "F— you" ring; a gift to herself after her divorce. Why am I still diamondless, you ask me? Me, the one who—at the mere hint of seeing a diamond, diamond commercial, or a sparkle—sings "Diamonds Are a Girl's Best Friend" from the fabulous movie *Gentlemen Prefer Blondes*? Because I believed stupid lie number one: that if a diamond had any true value it had to come to me via a man.

Now, I did receive a diamond from my former husband, but it fell prey to another belief I secretly held. For a diamond to represent someone's love, it had to be big. We were young, and my diamond was tiny. It turned out to have failed the true love test. For most of my life, I believed that when it comes to diamonds, bigger is better. Today I must recant that particular fantasy and replace it with my new belief: There is a perfect diamond for me and for you. Turn on your diamond radar and you will find it. Mine are diamond stud earrings, about three-quarters to one carat each. I have been envying those studs for years. Before you home in on your special diamonds, a few facts will increase your diamond comfort level.

Get to know the basics first: The famous four C's of diamond buying are color, clarity, cut, and carat—there are tons of books on diamonds to help you make your choice. My personal caveat: Avoid diamonds that have a crack or are cloudy. You want them sparkly and noticeable. When it comes to size, I am now a believer in the lessons from Goldilocks and the Three Bears. Not too big, not too small, just right. Now, if you're thinking, *I can't afford diamonds*, trust me, I have a plan for us. It's called the Diva's Pizza-for-Diamonds scheme. We can get great diamonds for around a thousand dollars.

Until I have diamonds I can call my own, I'm making pizza instead of buying. I get to pocket ten-dollars-plus whenever Alex asks for it. By putting ten dollars a week in my Diva Box I can have my fabulous diamond studs in two years; one if I'm more frugal. We can all have everything we want when we make it a priority. Nothing is more important than our happiness, and for me happiness is spelled d-i-a-m-o-n-d-s. What about you?

— Maureen

 Diva Diamond Practices for the Week:

1. Go diamond window-shopping. Touch them, try them on, fantasize about them.
2. Cut out pictures of diamonds you love for your Diva Diary.
3. Put ten dollars in your Diva Box to start your diamond fund.
4. Turn on your Diamond Radar. Ask every woman you meet with diamonds you love the three important questions: What size are they, do you love them, and where did you get them?
5. Design your diamond gift to yourself. Plan your date of purchase and dream diamonds.
6. For those of you lucky Divas with diamonds, keep them shining by using Miraglow (www.miraglow.com). You simply put your diamonds in a specially designed container in the dishwasher with their magic solution and your diamonds come out gorgeous, according to the other Divas.

Frivolous Diva Do:

CUT OUT A PICTURE OF A DIAMOND *from a magazine and tape it on your finger. Wear it all day.*

Tiara Time-Out!

It is a happy talent to know how to play.
—Ralph Waldo Emerson

Since we are in the section titled Luxury, there is nothing like canceling an entire workday and taking a *playday*, known from this day forward as a "Tiara Time-Out." Yes, this takes great Diva power, but it creates amazing results in unleashing Divaness. You have been progressing in your Diva growth and now, at Week 46, you can do this. You are going to call in to work and tell them you won't be in. I understand your hesitation. I have a very strong work ethic, so even when I take off I'm thinking about what might be happening at the office. But I'm getting better at this, and do enjoy a day of play. You can, too. This means no cell phones or pagers. It's important for your mental health to realize everything won't fall apart if you're not there. Squelch that Anti-Diva voice telling you, *"No! No!"*

I began one Tiara Time-Out by sleeping in. I then took Angel, my bichon frise (that's a dog), to the groomer so she could be pampered, too. My first stop was the plastic surgeon to collect info and costs on doing all sorts of things to my body and face. With all my brochures in hand I went to lunch with a dear girlfriend and we discussed face-lifts, liposuction, and going to China for a vacation and laughed a lot. I was pretty relaxed at this point.

Next I hit the mall to purchase treats. I found two tops in bright red and hot pink for my newly organized closet, since color makes me feel good. Last but not least, I went to my hairdresser and asked for a new style and color and left it up to her. I loved the new me! I went home tired but very happy! This day soothed the Diva soul and senses.

Another terrific Tiara Time-Out for the Diva is to have a masseuse come to the house. Invite some friends or that special someone plus wine, candles, music . . . When you have a massage, if there is a special part you like massaged (nothing X-rated), indulge yourself and spend the whole time on that spot. I love to have my feet massaged. So-o-o relaxing! Or just have a facial. Some places even have a scalp massage for relieving tension.

Another time, two of my Diva girlfriends and I hadn't spent an evening together in a while. So we decided to treat ourselves to dinner and the ballet—*Swan Lake*, with seats in second row center. Divas always splurge on good seats—it's worth it! We dressed up, enjoyed a great dinner, and arrived at the ballet early to people-watch. It's fascinating to observe people, who they're with, what they're wearing, and make up stories about their lives. Then it was heavenly enchantment to see the ballerinas up close in their gorgeous costumes and absorb the wonderful music. We floated home.

I'm getting into this. I visualize taking a Tiara Time-Out on a rainy day in front of the fireplace with a good book and hot chocolate. Then taking a little nap . . .

Or going to an afternoon matinee and then to the beach to watch the sunset . . .

For my sense of adventure, taking a biplane ride, donning leather jacket and scarf à la The Red Baron! Having the pilot do tricks, turns and dives . . . feeling the adrenaline rush . . . and maybe my lunch, too.

This was so much fun I asked the other Divas what their Tiara Time-Outs would be.

Diva Molly went for the fantasy Tiara Time-Out and said she would take the Concorde to Paris. She would stay at a French five-star hotel, order in her favorite champagne, then shop at French boutiques. Afterward she would visit the local boulangerie for a baguette and take home some French pastries. Back in her room she would have a massage while sampling the sweets.

Diva Carilyn had so many I'm only listing two. First is to go horseback riding with friends and later have some margaritas and dance all night to 1970s and '80s music. Second is to check into a suite at the Beverly Wilshire Hotel with a view of Beverly Hills; sleep in, then shop at Barney's, Neiman Marcus, Saks, and along Rodeo Drive;

ending the day with a facial and a massage, and then ordering a movie in the suite with room service.

Diva Maureen would stay in a fabulous hotel and have an all-day relaxation session at their spa—facial, massage, hair, makeup, and nails. Enjoy lunch by the pool and take a nap. Later she'd be picked up by a limo with champagne aboard and head to a Broadway play. She'd finish off the evening with a late supper. In the morning her Tiara Time-Out ends with breakfast by room service.

Pamper! Pamper! And pamper some more! *We love Tiara Time-Outs!*

— Elena

IVA DO'S FOR THE WEEK:

1. Go to your Diva Delight List and plan a playday.
2. Add to your list of things you want to do. You may be ready now for more adventuresome or outrageous activities, such as trying kayaking or hot-air ballooning!

FRIVOLOUS DIVA DO:

TAKE HULA LESSONS OR BELLY DANCING *lessons or rent a video that teaches you how . . . or at least pretend.*

"Welcome to Fantasy Island"

Never do anything yourself that others can do for you.
—AGATHA CHRISTIE

Now that you're living as the Diva you were born to be, it's time to have some fun being treated like her. The best place? A four- (or five-) star hotel, of course! They are the Diva's ultimate theme park; the playgrounds for her many facets to brilliantly shine. Here we can be anybody we want to be. It's a great place for your most outrageous Diva Delightful Delusion. Play, laugh, relax, and be pampered. Have the valet park your car and enter into Diva Wonderland. Have room service wait on you while you watch movies in bed. Order an in-room massage after a rough day of lounging by the pool. Have the complimentary car and driver take you to a fabulous dinner. Now, don't go freakin', Divas, this indulgence need not break the bank! There are deals to be had and Divas know all the secrets, from two-for-one specials to the importance of VIP friends!

These magnificent Diva field trips give all of us immediate access to living our own superstar fantasies. From an in-room massage to exceptional personal service, we are surrounded by the most luxurious of luxuries; it feels *mahvelous, dahling!* Four Seasons Hotels and Resorts is my Disneyland, my all-time playland getaway of getaways. My husband's good friend was the reservations manager there for a while (a VIP friend!) and told me their philosophy is to treat everyone equally. So I guess it's no coincidence that I feel like Madonna whenever I go there. In fact, they're so good at what they do, I often think *they* think I'm Madonna! When I was staying at their property in New York,

I called the concierge for baby shampoo to give Remy a bath. Before the woman realized housekeeping had some, she offered to run out and get me some. *Run out and get me some!* I couldn't believe it. This, I could get used to. I *must* be Madonna!

As soon as the valet checks my car, my confidence level begins to rise and my blood pumps Diva. Now, being comfortable with my Diva status, I don't feel I'm being judged or assessed on whether or not I *deserve* to be there. I feel they *know* I deserve to be there. I feel they know *all* of us deserve to be there. Just as we are all naturally Divas, we all deserve to be treated as such.

If you're not quite ready to dive right into this extravagance, you can get your feet wet by starting with an indulging whirlwind day. Plan any service like a massage or facial at a four- or five-star resort for about $110 and simply pay the extra $10 or $12 to enjoy the spa and hotel facilities for the entire day. So, for about $150 (massage and spa fee plus $15 tip and two $7.50 poolside piña coladas), we Divas can enjoy a massage, poolside service drinking piña coladas as we sunbathe, a relaxing Jacuzzi, a cleansing sauna, maybe even (dare I say it) a workout in the hotel gym, and shower to get ready for the mingling with the other Divas and Divos in the bar while all day enjoying the beauty of the grounds being treated like a queen. All this for the simple sacrifice of either one month of Caramel Frappuccinos, fifteen lunches, ten nights at the movies with popcorn, or five dinners out!

But *come on*, Divas, you *deserve* to be dripping in this euphoric self-indulgence as often as possible . . . come to think of it, why not just go there for absolutely no reason at all but to mingle with other inspiring Divas and Divos in the lounge? Bring twenty dollars for a couple of drinks and stay all day or all evening. Or turn on the Diva Magnetic Vibe and never have to take that twenty dollars out of your purse! Just enjoy the exceptional service the employees are trained to give. You may leave wondering, *Am I Madonna?*

The Diva knows that surrounding herself with this particular crowd of creative and powerfully successful people and extravagant settings calls her to be all that she can be (kind of like the army, except geared for princesses!). Experiencing this lifestyle has us strive for more out of life. It reminds *all* of us Divas not to settle for less than we're worth and to extend our worthiness beyond the limits we place on ourselves.

The staff at these fine hotels believes you belong there, whether you believe it or not. Trust them. It's our responsibility as Divas to recognize and accept the fact that we *do* deserve it. Repeat after me, Molly's famous mantra: *"I deserve to have it all now. I deserve to have it all now. I deserve to have it all now. And so it is!"*

— *Carilyn*

$\mathcal{D}$IVA DO'S FOR THE WEEK:

1. Plan a fantasy Diva night at a four-star hotel within the next six months for yourself or with some friends. Get there early enough to enjoy the facilities. Even if your room isn't ready you can still relax by the pool, drink at the bar, lounge in the lounge. Ask for a late checkout, too, so you can enjoy the luxuries of your room up to the last minute.

2. Dress as The Rock Star Diva and go for drinks at a four-star hotel. Be very aloof and keep your sunglasses on as if you don't want anyone to recognize you.

3. Spread your Divaness into the world by pampering your friends. When my husband and I were staying at the Four Seasons in London we arrived at our hotel after a fabulous shopping spree to find champagne and chocolate-covered strawberries in our room. It turns out our good friends Eric and Klara had called from California and surprised us with this fabulous Diva gift, with a note saying, "Enjoy your vacation." What class! I'll remember that forever. When you know your friends are traveling, find out what hotel they're staying in and order a special surprise for them.

$\mathcal{F}$RIVOLOUS DIVA DO:

SPEAK WITH YOUR BEST SEAN CONNERY ACCENT *and pretend to be James (Jane) Bond.*

"$\mathcal{S}$NEAKY" DIVA DO:

MAKE A NEW FRIEND—*preferably one who holds a nice position at a four- or five-star luxury hotel. They offer a friends-and-family rate as a perk to all their employees. Yea for friends!*

*D*IVA TIPS:

- Hotels located in big cities will usually have a better weekend rate since most of their business is with business travelers. Always ask for the best rate available. They won't offer it themselves but must tell you once you've asked for it.

- City hotels will have special promotions around the holidays. And spas will always have holiday specials or two-for-one deals—say, mother and daughter around Mother's Day or honeymooner specials for couples.

- Hotels like the Four Seasons have cars available to their guests as a service and a driver who will take them where they need to go for the mere cost of a tip! For example, at the Beverly Wilshire Hotel (a Four Seasons hotel) they have a Rolls-Royce and Mercedes Benz available to their guests (with driver, of course). I had never been in a Rolls, and decided it was time I had, so I asked the driver to take me for a tour of Beverly Hills. It was awesome! Kevin, Remy, and I toured the beautiful area, with narration by our fabulous driver, in a Rolls-Royce, all for the measly cost of a twenty-dollar tip! Always find out what the amenities are and have fun using them.

Extravagance

It's impossible to overdo luxury.
— FRENCH PROVERB

The Concorde, Beluga, Brioni, Alixandre, Butterfield & Robinson, Feadship, Ferretti, Krell—these are some of the finest names in the world, according to the *Robb Report,* the magazine that caters to those who "live the good life." But, to tell you the truth, I have no idea what half these companies are, let alone what they make! At least not yet. I have heard it said that greatness is not a matter of price, but of good taste. I am an arbiter of good taste just like the next Diva, even if I don't have a money tree out in my backyard or live like Thurston Howell and his wife, "Lovey," from *Gilligan's Island.* I'm learning that there's more than one way to have it all. I have redefined extravagance to fit my lifestyle and my reality so that it's not the amount of money I spend on something, or even the label on what I buy, but how my purchase makes me feel. Extravagance is more attitudinal than monetary. No matter where you are on the Diva's spending spectrum, it's possible to bathe in the lap of luxury without having to take a second mortgage on your house.

One recent New Year's Eve my husband and I had just moved into a new house. We were exhausted from moving boxes for two days, so spending a lot of money to attend a lavish black-tie party was not high on our list of things to do. Instead, we chose to have our own extravagant celebration at home. We visited our local grocery store and picked up some snacks and hors d'oeuvres, along with my favorite bottle of champagne and some Russian caviar. And as the clock struck midnight, we toasted each other in our pajamas.

As I learned, a Diva can experience extravagance without even leaving the comfort of her own home!

On another occasion several girlfriends of mine and I flew to Colorado and went to a real, live dude ranch for a weekend. We rode horses in the Rocky Mountains, did ranch-type stuff, and drank beer. It was so much fun to get away with the girls, and I felt like such a cowboy. I had never done anything like that before, and that in itself made the trip extravagant. Doing something unique and out of the ordinary can be just the thing to satisfy a Diva's urge for luxury.

It has been my experience that sometimes I felt like I was "Jane Liquid," with plenty of money to spare—but in reality, I knew I wasn't. And worse, when I felt like I had money to burn, I usually spent it like a true champ, only to wake up later with the Anti-Diva guilt trip and a negative bank account to match. So I created a Diva practice that allows me to feel extravagant without feeling guilty. I created the Money to Burn game consisting of two budgets for my family and me. One is a low-end budget, when we don't have a lot of money to spare or have a big payment or purchase coming up. By following this budget, we have few if any surprises and we can enjoy life more; we can still splurge, but we plan for it. The other is a high-end budget. This is the one where we have more room to be self-indulgent and plan for the bigger-ticket items. Before creating these budgets, I always felt like I had to exercise complete control over my finances, and that I had to deprive myself of certain little "presents"—getting regular manicures and haircuts, shopping at my favorite grocery store, even buying cosmetics. Extravagance was a concept that was simply out of my reach. But having these budgets now has given me the freedom to live abundantly every day. The Diva learns that extravagance does not equal being excessive. As I said before, it's all a state of mind, and for the Diva, that's what counts.

No matter which budget you're on, there are many ways to be extravagant without breaking the bank. It just takes a little creativity and planning. For example, I once took my husband on a surprise trip. We went to our favorite Italian restaurant near the beach, then drove to LAX (the Los Angeles airport) and parked directly under the flight path on one of the runways. We opened the doors of the car and cranked up the stereo, playing Frank Sinatra. The only people within sight were the taxicab drivers who were parked nearby and looked on as we danced and sang and watched the planes land. It was wonderful. Then we went to a nearby bed-and-breakfast for a complete getaway. It felt like being on a trip, even though we were just a few miles from home. Total cost: about $150. And he was completely surprised and loved it. On one of our high-end budget trips, my husband surprised me for our anniversary and planned a fabulous trip around California over four days (as you can tell, I love surprises). We flew by helicopter to Catalina Island for the morning, had a fabulous lunch, then flew up to San Francisco, stayed in the city, and went to one of the best restaurants for a four-course dinner. The next morning we drove up to the wine country and did everything from sight-seeing to wine tasting, playing tennis, taking spa treatments, eating out at fabulous restaurants, and eating in our room and watching movies. Then, to top it all off, we went on a sunrise hot-air balloon ride down the Napa Valley. Total cost: about twenty-five hundred dollars.

Now is the perfect time to create your own Diva extravagance list and keep it someplace where you can refer to it often . . . like in your Diva Diary, perhaps. What items are on your low-end budget (read *attainable*) list? Write everything down, including simple pleasures like getting your favorite ice cream cone once or twice a week or going to your favorite dive restaurant around the corner. Also include bigger-ticket items on your "I've got money to burn" list, like the new Divamobile you've got your eye on, or the trip you've been dreaming of taking. Just because the size of your bank account may not match the grandeur of your dreams and fantasies, don't let yourself be stopped from experiencing life's little luxuries.

— Molly

*D*IVA DO'S FOR THE WEEK:

1. Continue to collect and accumulate your spare change in your Diva Dollar Box; make a list of a few "extravagant" and creative ways to spend your stash, varying in price.

2. Go to Tiffany's and buy something. You can get many of their items for less than fifty dollars, and there's nothing like getting a gift in the "little blue box."

*F*RIVOLOUS DIVA DO'S:

GET YOURSELF A POSTER *of a beautifully tranquil tropical island. Attach it to a wall and lounge next to it in your pajamas with a glass of champagne. Oh, the joys of being a woman of luxury!*

OR TAKE FIFTEEN TO THIRTY MINUTES *and do absolutely nothing. Don't answer the phone; don't go online; don't watch TV; don't cook; don't read the paper . . . just relax and feel the weight of the world disappear. Aaahhh.*

XIII

*L*IVING DIVA

Now armed with a plethora of tips and tricks, you are invited to bring
any and all of your Diva experiences into your real life. As the journey
comes to a close, remember all the joy comes from living Diva!

Friends Are Forever

A friend is a present you give yourself.
—Robert Louis Stevenson

Remember as a little girl pricking your finger and rubbing blood with a friend and promising to be best friends forever? Where is she today?

I have always had friends and an active social life, but it wasn't until my divorce that I discovered the true value of female friendships. The support of the sisterhood and unconditional love helped me survive the emotional trauma. A Diva knows that friends are worth their weight in gold—and Divas know the value of gold!

In our hurried, pressured lives we seem to have less time for friends and entertaining, but the desire for connection is still there. It's easy for me to put off having people over by telling myself I need to do this first, or I should wait until the living room is painted . . . But in reality we are never caught up on the chores of life, especially paperwork. In the meantime, life is going by and we're missing out on some wonderful experiences. Divas get very creative in order to maintain cherished friendships. A dear friend of mine moved and changed employment so she's more than an hour away, but kept the same hairdresser, who is also mine. Some things we can't give up! So we schedule our hair appointments at the same time when it's possible, so we can visit and try to get together for dinner afterward. E-mail is the greatest invention for keeping in touch anywhere in the world—your words are with friends faster than you could say them, plus you can also send pictures. Potlucks are still a great, easy way to entertain, and now you can pick up any type of cuisine without having to cook—have an international feast! In lovely weather try meeting at a park or zoo or gardens; then there's no housecleaning to do. Tie a vacation in with a visit to a friend. Meet someone halfway at a restaurant or store, combining shopping with chatting. Have a coffee or snack, any time of day or evening, from early morning to midnight. Some bookstores are open late, too.

Friendships require nourishment to sustain them, much like a garden—but like a garden they can also offer comfort year after year. A Diva is mindful of this and therefore thoughtful and generous. She waters her friends with words of appreciation, kindness, and understanding. She feeds them with little gifts "just because"; she fertilizes them with dependability and humor. And shields them from bad weather and wind by her compassion, providing a safe haven. She does all this without a scorecard, with no expectation of reciprocity. In return the Diva enjoys friends who are loyal and trustworthy; they give us advice when we ask for it and point out something when we need to see it, but are never judgmental. They know all about us and still like us. True friends bring out the best in, and want the best for, each other.

Have you ever noticed how people come into our lives for different reasons, and stay for various amounts of time? They may be there just to fill a need we had at the time, or during a period of transition in our lives. Other friendships may last longer, or may give us more pleasure. As our Diva develops and we move on to new interests and start achieving our dreams, there may be a loss of some friends. It's important to appreciate them for what they are and not try to make them something else. Some friends come in and out of your life, like JoAnne, my friend of thirty years, but you stay connected and when you do talk, you just pick up where you left off. A true Diva makes room for all types of friends, knowing they will enrich her life forever.

In writing this book and being under the pressure of a deadline, you may be wondering if we're at each other's throats. Whoever heard of four women writing one book? Four women can't agree on anything! The truth is, we came together as acquaintances (except for Carilyn and me) and approached things differently. It was indeed a learning experience, but the commitment we had to our goal surpassed our Anti-

Divas. As our Diva selves became released, we became closer, more open and trusting, and therefore more supportive of each other, offering ideas, time, anecdotes, whatever was needed. It has really been a heartwarming experience. All of us know that we are truly there for each other and can share anything and be whoever it is we feel like being.

It is important as Divas to honor our precious relationships with our friends. Rumor has it that, in the midst of gossip, Maya Angelou will walk out of the room! That's a practice worth emulating. Friendships are a valued asset that strengthens the Diva—a safe house that must be protected. If there is a hurt, Divas discuss it rather than pretend it doesn't exist until it festers and bursts into resentment. It's important to *be* a good friend in order to *have* good friends, and that means to be available when necessary, be honest, and be open to listening. As a good Diva sister it's also important to encourage our friends to go after their dreams and allow them to change and try new things along their Diva evolution. A Diva is not threatened by the changes her friends make but instead rewarded by their successes and inspired by their happiness.

Friendships change as we grow older. One of my greatest surprises and pleasures is having the friendship of my two adult children. Who would have ever thought this was possible? After all those years of worrying, they have become such a source of comfort and joy. I can't even describe it. For my sixtieth birthday my son, daughter, and daughter-in-law gave me a surprise birthday dinner party at a local hotel. They planned it for months, sending out invitations, collecting anecdotes and photos. My son was the host, so charming and humorous. They did a slide show of my life with narration, with a special focus on my hairstyles and fashions. Hysterical! There were friends and family there I hadn't seen in a while. One was a dear friend from high school who contributed some good stories; another friend traveled from Charlotte, North Carolina. My brother did the videography. It was so entertaining, and one of the most meaningful events of my life.

It's true, friends make the world go 'round. A Diva cherishes the relationships she has with her friends.

— *Elena*

*D*IVA DO'S FOR THE WEEK:

1. Handwrite a note to at least one friend this week.

2. Call a friend you haven't seen in a while and plan something fun together, like dancing, an opera or art exhibit, a car race, or a leisurely lunch.

3. Our neighborhoods are also a good source for friendships for Divas. Do you know the folks next door? Knock on the door of a neighbor you don't know and introduce yourself.

4. Plan a neighborhood progressive dinner, or appetizer party.

5. Create a Diva Darlings Notebook. In it you will list your friends and all pertinent info. Not just birthdays and anniversaries, but what they like, what they mention they need (for gift ideas), and things that may be pending—a trip, surgery, a move—so you don't forget to contact them. Send a note or postcard just to say "I was thinking of you, and how important you are to me."

*F*RIVOLOUS DIVA DO:

SQUEEZE YOURSELF AND AT LEAST THREE FRIENDS *into a photo booth and have your picture taken. See what body parts of each of you, you can recognize.*

Travel, Diva — Style

Though we travel the world over to find the beautiful, we must carry it with us or we will not find it.
— Ralph Waldo Emerson

*C*lang, clash, rattle, bang. What you are hearing is the sound of all the chains we have anchored around our ankles, arms, legs, and necks when it comes to all the trips we're going to take someday. Someday we'll go to visit Stonehenge, or the Eiffel Tower, or the world's largest ball of string (that's mine). Someday Alex and I will go to every touristy place there is in the United States just to experience the thrill of Graceland and the Grand Ole Opry together. Why? Because it's there. I only hope that Patrick, now age twenty-two, will still want to go to Mount Rushmore with me when Someday comes. I suspect it will be with his wife and family in tow.

Here's an alarming factoid: The average family saves for more than two years to be able to take a week's vacation at the Disney Resorts. Two years for one week. Why do we have to trade two years of our precious life to enjoy the wonders of this world? For all of my adult life, my dad, Patrick Crean, ached to visit Ireland, his homeland. All four of his children wished with all of their hearts that we could give that gift to him and my mom, Drusilla. Somehow, it was always out of our grasp. He died never having returned to the land of his birth.

Which brings me back to chains. We have more excuses, misconceptions, and flawed thinking about the subject of travel than Old Marley has chains from his ill deeds in Charles Dickens's *A Christmas Carol*. No time. No money. Too much work. Well, the Diva in us knows differently. You can have the time of your life in four days on a shoestring budget and create an experience to last a lifetime. Let's look at how we chain ourselves, one by one:

1. **You can't take off time from work.**

   Diva Antidote: Rent *Ferris Bueller's Day Off*. The world will not come to an end if you take two days off, Friday and Monday. That plus the weekend gives you four days.

2. **You can't leave your baby, child, husband, teenager, dog, or cat.**

   Diva Antidote: Have a party with four of your Diva friends. Watch a video of *That Girl* or *Alice* or *Mary Tyler Moore* and remember what it's like to be single. Even the most married woman has the right to be "single" for four days. Read excerpts from the book *If I Had My Life to Live Over Again* until you can't stand it anymore. Pledge to each other that you will take care of each other's dependents while you're gone.

3. **You don't have a passport.**

   Diva Antidote: Get one. You don't need a destination to get a passport. Track down your birth certificate (call the department of vital statistics in the city of your birth), have a passport picture taken, and make an appointment at the post office.

When I lost (or found) my mind and ran away to California, the first thing I did was get a passport for the boys, Patrick and Alex, and me. Why? Because my whole life I'd wanted to travel around the world. I wanted to be prepared. When I was twenty-one I wanted to go to Australia with my best friend, Debbie. When we were ready to buy the tickets, life happened to her and we chickened out. We both regret that today.

One day I received a call from my friends in New York, Joyce Pike and Marie Maxwell. There was an opportunity to go to Dublin for four days to lead the first introduction to the Landmark Forum in Ireland. The cost, with airfare from New York, a bed-and-breakfast in Dublin, and a rental car would be $489 each. "Are you game?" they asked. "Of course," I said. "Count me in."

After I hung up the phone, I had a mini anxiety attack. Was I crazy? I couldn't go to Ireland: I didn't have the money, I didn't have the time, and I didn't have anyone to take care of my son. The only thing I did have was my passport. It was enough.

Things work out the way we want them to when we grab for all that life has to offer. I somehow found the money (by spending less, making payments on purchases), I decided I would live through the jet lag, and my dearest brother Patrick came to my home and took great care of Alex so I could go. My desire to travel was greater than my need for anything else. I made it my priority. It was the greatest, most thrilling weekend of my life. I was a world traveler, a woman with a stamp in her passport.

As I sat in a smoky pub in my father's homeland, I raised a pint of Guinness in his honor. "Thank you, Dad, for giving me the vision of a world not limited to one nation but one that encompasses all the wonders of the world. And most of all, thank you for the desire to see it all. We're home."

— Maureen

𝒟IVA DO'S FOR THE WEEK:

1. Chains, chains, chains. For this exercise you need to buy and blast Aretha Franklin's famous song "Chain of Fools." Take colored construction paper and cut it into six-inch strips of paper, two inches wide. Take a Diva glitter pen in your signature color and write your reasons for not traveling on them. Glue the ends of the strips together, adding one strip to the next to create a colorful chain. Put the chain in plain view where you will see it every day.

2. On a quiet weekend, surround yourself with travel magazines and a cup of tea. Cut out pictures of all the places that you want to visit. Put them in your Diva Diary. Mark the most special place on your list with glitter.

3. Get a passport. This is vital. Even if you think you'll never use it, be prepared.

4. Sign up on the Internet for all those travel deals offered by the airlines. When there's a special, you'll be prepared to take advantage of it.

5. Open a travel savings account. Put away five, ten, or twenty dollars a week. Give the passbook to your uncle, your mother, or your cousin twice removed if you have to, to keep from spending the money on anything other than travel.

6. Plan a trip to anywhere for a long weekend. As long as it's somewhere you've been longing to see.

𝒻RIVOLOUS DIVA DO:

NOW THAT YOU HAVE YOUR BIRTH CERTIFICATE *for your passport, go to www.astrology.com and have your astrological chart done for free.*

Leap First, Look Later: A Lesson in Spontaneity

The essence of pleasure is spontaneity.

—GERMAINE GREER

A few years ago I started to compile a Top Ten List of the coolest things I had ever done in my life. At the time I was discouraged about all the things I still hadn't accomplished. After all, I was well into my thirties and I still hadn't *done it all*. Rather than beat myself up for the missed opportunities that had passed me by, I decided that it was time to take a look at the cool things I have done, the places I have conquered. I'm fortunate to have been many places and seen many things, but one event that ranks at least in the top three was my cross-country trip in the summer of 1997—by myself. I had recently left a job (one in a long string of "left jobs"!) and was busy trying to figure out what I wanted to do when I grew up. I wanted to take some time for myself, and I consider myself to be a fairly spontaneous person, but to just drop everything on a whim and leave family, friends, and felines behind in Chicago seemed a little extreme. Friends and family told me, "You should take a week or two to relax, then focus on getting a job." There was so much of the United States that I had never seen before, and the thought of planning my own little trip, all by myself, sounded intriguing . . . but there were many reasons why this wasn't a good idea. OPPORTUNITY OF A LIFETIME kept flashing across my mind in big, neon lights. What if I do take this trip? What if I don't? Hmmm . . . decisions, decisions.

Have you ever heard the phrase *paralysis by analysis?* Sometimes I feel like the poster child for that sentiment. It sure doesn't do much for spontaneity. I have a thought about someplace I want to go or something I want to do, but then almost automatically the little Anti-Diva voice in my head says, *You can't/shouldn't do that, you don't have the money, you don't have the time, blah, blah, blah.* It's almost like my adult self is chastising my playful little kid self. This is where I tell my adult self to lighten up and let go; to stop thinking and step into Divadom!

So I plotted and planned my journey, then packed up my car and for six weeks, I drove around the country visiting new places, seeing old friends, and exploring the United States on my own personal adventure. Except for a few days traveling the West Coast with a girlfriend who loved my idea so much that she came out to join me, I drove solo for ten thousand miles. It was one of the most liberating experiences I've ever had! I spent hours each day driving and listening to songs that made me laugh, others that inspired me to sing like a rock star, and some that even caused me to cry. (Important Diva sidenote: Listening to any band live is great—after I've finished singing my heart out with the band and the audience applauds wildly, it makes me feel like I was on stage with them and that everyone is clapping and cheering for me! That's always a very Diva moment.) I brought 120 CDs on my "U.S. Tour" and listened to every single one of them. I also listened to various books on tape, and I experienced America in a completely unique way.

A true Diva knows the difference between being alone and spending time by herself—and this trip was what I needed to see that difference. I had spent lots of time by myself through the years, but really being on my own on this trip caused me to look at who I am and what I'm up to in life. I felt totally free, and with all the people I encountered, including strangers and friends in various places, I never once felt lonely during the entire adventure. I was completely thrilled to be on a solo trip on my own terms. This complete feeling of independence and gratification is something that every Diva should go through on a regular basis in her life. And you don't have to drive across the globe to experience it.

How much do you allow yourself to be truly spontaneous? Do you live for your daily routine or do you loathe having any routine at all? Take some time this week to notice your level of spontaneity. Do you have to plan to be spontaneous, or can you drop everything and go on a moment's notice? Determine which of these matches your style, then do the opposite this week. It may take some time and it may feel weird at first because we are creatures of habit (even if it includes not having a habit at all), so start small. For example, sleep on the opposite side of the bed for a week. Put your pants on with the other leg first. Go get a manicure or a drink with a friend on the spur of the moment. If you have a routine, break it; if you don't have a routine, create one. Just try it on for a few days . . . don't worry, Diva, you can always go back.

Here's an exercise in spontaneity: Mark a date on your calendar for six months from now . . . then forget about it. When that day arrives, do something spontaneous like go on a mini road trip or hop on a train and go somewhere you've never visited. Are you up to the challenge, my adventuresome Diva sisters? I bet you are!

Many of us find it hard to break out of our routines because of the "shoulds" and the expectations in life. This week give yourself permission to enjoy a few spontaneous adventures. Run outside in the rain in your "good clothes." Take a day off and go to an amusement park; ride on all the kiddie rides and take your hands off the bar on the roller coaster. Go pick flowers in the park and give them to a complete stranger. Adding a dose of spontaneity to the Diva's life can be thrilling, like driving a convertible sports car with the top down on a beautiful day with the wind flowing through your hair! It's liberating and invigorating. Go ahead, Diva, give yourself permission to live on the wild side. It might just give you a new sense of independence that you have never before felt.

– Molly

$\mathcal{D}$IVA DO'S FOR THE WEEK:

1. Plan three times this week to do something spontaneous that you wouldn't normally do. Afterward, jot down in your Diva Diary what it was like for you. Did it feel like hard work or was it liberating doing something familiar in a different way?

2. Plan unstructured time for yourself on a daily basis to do whatever you want in that time period. Get your nails done; go for a walk; read a book; write a book; meditate—whatever it is that's just for you.

3. Create your own Top Ten List of the coolest things you've ever done. Post it somewhere conspicuous, like in your office, on your refrigerator, wherever it will be a constant reminder of your accomplishments.

4. Make another Top Ten List of things you'd like to do in the future. Keep it in a visible place so you can cross out items as you accomplish them. Don't forget to include your date with spontaneity six months from now . . .

$\mathcal{F}$RIVOLOUS DIVA DO:

FIND A MAP OR BETTER YET, A GLOBE. *With your eyes closed, spin it and point to someplace. Open your eyes, and then spend at least fifteen minutes daydreaming about visiting that place. If you've already been there, either daydream about things you've never done in this place, or pick someplace new.*

Celebration!

The most important trait for any woman to develop is the trust in her own resolve. That innate strength is something all women should strive for and once obtained is owned for the duration of our lives.
—Jeanie Buss, executive vice president, business operations, Los Angeles Lakers

*C*elebrate *good times* ... The time has come to acknowledge and celebrate every minute detail that is you because *you make a difference!* You are (and always have been) a risk taker, colorful, glamorous, intelligent, powerful, strong, beautiful, frivolous, exciting, magnetic, dynamic, charming, unpredictable, unconventional, sexy, and brilliant. You are Diva!

Without acknowledgment and celebration, the Diva risks extinction. These two practices act as fuel for the Diva's fire to blaze on. Acknowledgment of all her accomplishments, big and small, reminds Diva how fabulous she is. Celebration of these acknowledgments is the way we bring fun to every moment of life. "Wait!". . . I can hear you already . . . "I can't really celebrate finishing this book because I didn't read it cover to cover . . . or I didn't do all the Diva Do's . . . et cetera." Stop it! And instead, acknowledge the practices you did do. Acknowledge the fact you bought the book. Acknowledge the fact that you took time for yourself to read any part of this book! Celebrate that you are a woman! Celebrate that you can read! Celebrate that you have friends! There are so many things to celebrate in life and things we do every day that we never acknowledge ourselves for. It's not only major things a Diva celebrates. I celebrate every day that I make it to the office in one piece by enjoying a Caramel Frappuccino. And after a hectic day of work my husband and I tell each other all our accomplishments throughout the day, acknowledge that we are still sane, and celebrate by playing music loud and having a

Double D. Dance Party. My glass is not only half full, it's filled with a rich, thick and creamy, scrumptious Oreo cookie milk shake . . . and my pie is a huge triple-decker devil's food chocolate cake with semisweet fudge frosting and chocolate sprinkles on top!

Get out that Polaroid shot from Week 2, Escaping the Dungeon. And let's have a good laugh. What comes to mind? What's different about you today? Have another Polaroid taken of you today, and vow to do it again another year from now. Don't freak out—this is not the Diva's way of watching herself age! Instead, it's a way for you to keep the Diva alive as time goes by; a way to check in with yourself and make sure you're still curious, adventurous, happy, playful, and passionate. Know that you have the powerful tools to access the Diva in you at all times and never forget to use your Diva sisters!

Always remember the fabulous Divas who have been there for you along the way. There is power in numbers, for it's through the eyes of another that we can see our own vision come true. In the Diva sisterhood lives your greatness and the fruition of any future you see. They are a source of great Diva power. Of course what we believe about ourselves is extremely important and what we choose to do makes a difference, but if it's to live in our own mind alone it will die a lonely death. Whenever two or more share a vision, the forces of the universe are engaged for success. So form a Diva pact with your Diva sisters to continue the fun, laughter, and success that each day as a Diva brings. The Sisterhood of Divas is unstoppable, highly contagious, and world altering . . . not to mention outrageously playful and fun! Each of us is both our own and the other's Fairy Godmother. Together we make miracles come true and watch as Divadom, the Worldwide Diva Movement, spreads to all corners of the earth and beyond! Diva is our innate nature. Remember it and pass it on.

The time is here to create your personal Diva Proclamation—your own Diva creed with words of Diva wisdom you vow to live by now and forever. Think of your own or borrow from the list below. Write them on posterboard in hot pink pen and place it where you will see it often:

- Divas live by their own set of rules.
- Nothing is too inconsequential or frivolous for the Diva.

- The Diva is persistent, devoted, and honest.
- The Diva is always curious, looking to expand her knowledge.
- Thrilled with life's magnificence, the Diva lives in the moment.
- You will never hear the Diva say, "I wish I'd done that," because she takes every opportunity.
- The Diva's precious time is never robbed by regrets.
- The Diva believes in, listens to, and honors herself.
- The Diva is trusting, vulnerable, and fearless.
- The Diva is without worry of what others think of her.
- The Diva loves to laugh and never suppresses her feelings.
- The Diva loves a challenge and is never stopped by its difficulty.
- Always in action, never hiding out, the Diva is attentive, determined, and passionate!
- The Diva is attracted to all that sparkles and shines; anything that makes her feel like a princess.
- Music is a driving force for the Diva and dance is one of her favorite activities, which she indulges in whenever the urge strikes her, no matter where she is.
- The Diva is happy with simple things.
- The Diva is accepting of her body just the way it is.
- The Diva is playful, humorous, and spirited.
- The Diva is comfortable with and never embarrassed of her scintillating sexuality.
- The Diva celebrates everyone's uniqueness.
- The Diva has a sisterhood of friends she confides in.
- The Diva acknowledges all of her accomplishments big and small.

In Divadom, as in Wonder Woman's home of Paradise Island, all of us are beautiful, intelligent, compelling, and powerful individuals. The time has come, Divas, to accept the Lifetime Achievement Award for your commitment to fun and the joy you bring to others by being the extraordinary Diva that you are! So take the trophy, thank the academy, and party till the sun comes up!

—Carilyn

$\mathcal{D}$IVA DO'S AND IDEAS FOR THE WEEK AND YOUR LIFE:

1. Make a list of the small treasures in your life and in life itself. When you feel less than Divalike, get out this list and bring back those simple memories that can light up your entire day.

2. Rent a convertible car for a day. Put the top down, turn the music up, and just drive!

3. Buy some rose petals from your local florist. Make a path out of them anywhere you walk often and walk across them . . . just like a queen—Queen Diva, that is!

4. Put on your favorite music, grab something that looks like a microphone, dance around the room as if you're performing onstage, and express your superstar Diva status.

5. Plan a trip to Las Vegas with the girls. Pay a visit to the Wig Warehouse. Spend the entire afternoon trying on wigs of all shapes, colors, and sizes. Buy your favorite one and get ready for a night on the town!

6. Buy stickers and stick them everywhere you want to smile.

7. Guiltlessly bake and eat brownies—be sure to lick the bowl! If you have a young child in the family, share it together. The guilt magically disappears and it becomes an act of innocence and fun.

8. Rent and watch one of your all-time favorite movies. If you have a VCR or DVD player in your bedroom, watch the movie in there and have a meal in bed.

9. Put little surprise gifts under your children's or husband's pillow.

10. Invite friends over and play fun games like Taboo or card games like Peanuts.

11. Eat with your hands (at Moroccan restaurants this is preferred). Enjoy the texture and feel of food with all your senses.

12. When people leave an impression on you, tell them.

13. When you feel like squealing, squeal.

14. When you feel like giggling, giggle.

15. When you feel like whistling, whistle.

16. When you feel like skipping, skip.

17. When you feel like laughing, laugh.

18. You are Diva, celebrate and *enjoy!*

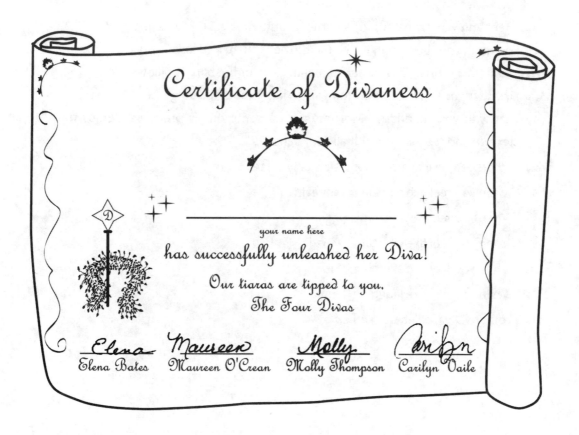

Certificate of Divaness

_____

your name here

has successfully unleashed her Diva!

Our tiaras are tipped to you.
The Four Divas

Elena
Elena Bates

Maureen
Maureen O'Crean

Molly
Molly Thompson

Carilyn
Carilyn Oaile

BIBLIOGRAPHY

We would like to thank these fabulous authors and their wonderful creations for the inspiration they brought us during the course of writing this book:

Austen, Hallie Iglehart. *The Heart of the Goddess*. Berkeley, California: Wingbow Press, 1990.

Ban Breathnach, Sarah. *Mrs. Sharp's Traditions*. New York: Scribner/Simple Abundance Press, 2001.

Bardey, Catherine. *Lingerie: A History and Celebration of Silks, Satins, Laces, Linens and Other Bare Essentials*. New York: Black Dog & Leventhal Publishers, Inc., 2001.

Baring, Anne, and Jules Cashford. *The Myth of the Goddess*. New York: Viking Arkana, 1991.

Bloomfield, Harold H., M.D. *Making Peace with Yourself*. New York: Ballantine Books, 1985.

Bolen, Jean Shinoda, M.D. *Goddesses in Every Woman: A New Psychology of Women*. New York: HarperPerennial, 1984.

Booth, Nancy M. *Perfumes, Splashes and Colognes*. Pownal, Vermont: Storey, 1997.

Bykofsky, Sheree. *500 Terrific Ideas for Organizing Everything*. New York: Galahad Books, 1997.

Cameron, Julia. *The Artist's Way*. New York: Jeremy P. Tarcher/Putnam, 1992.

Campbell, Chellie. *The Wealthy Spirit*. Naperville, Illinois: Sourcebooks, Inc., 2002.

Carlson, Richard, Ph.D. *Don't Sweat the Small Stuff . . . And It's All Small Stuff*. New York: Hyperion, 1997.

Christ, Carol P. *Rebirth of the Goddess*. New York: Addison-Wesley, 1997.

Culp, Stephanie. *How to Conquer Clutter*. Cincinnati: Writers Digest Books, 1990.

Dante, *Inferno*.

De Angelis, Barbara. *Passion*. New York: Delacorte Press, 1998.

DuBrin, Andrew J. *Personal Magnetism*. New York: American Management Association, 1997.

Eisner, Lisa. *Rodeo Girls*. Los Angeles: Greybull Press, 2001.

Elerding, Louise, and Evana Maggiore. *Formulas for Dressing the Whole Person: Creating Harmony and Balance in Your Wardrobe*. Woburn, Massachusetts: Mansion Publishing Ltd., 1999.

— — —. *Dressing the Whole Person: Nine Ways to Create Harmony and Balance in Your Wardrobe*. Woburn, Massachusetts: Mansion Publishing Ltd., 1998.

Felder, Deborah G. *The 100 Most Influential Women of All Time: A Ranking Past and Present*. New York: Carol Publishing Group (Citadel Press), 1996.

Flach, Frederic F. *Choices*. Philadelphia and New York: J. B. Lippincott Company, 1977.

Freeman, Arthur, and Rose DeWolf. *The 10 Dumbest Mistakes People Make and How to Avoid Them*. New York: HarperCollins, 1992.

Gurian, Michael. *Love's Journey*. Boston: Shambhala, 1995.

Irons, Diane. *The World's Best-Kept Beauty Secrets*. Naperville, Illinois: Sourcebooks, Inc., 1997.

Kingston, Karen. *Creating Sacred Space with Feng Shui*. New York: Broadway Books, 1997.

Klein, Allen. *The Healing Power of Humor*. New York: Penguin Putnam, Inc., 1989.

Kramer, Barbara. *Madeleine Albright.* Berkeley Heights, New Jersey: Enslow Publishers, 2000.

Krohn, Katherine E. *Marilyn Monroe: Norma Jeane's Dream.* Minneapolis: Lerner Publications Company, 1997.

Ladies' Home Journal. 100 Most Important Women of the 20th Century. Des Moines, Iowa: Meredith Books, 1998.

Landrum, Gene N. *Profiles of Female Genius.* Amherst, New York: Prometheus Books, 1994.

LeShan, Eda. *It's Better to Be Over the Hill than Under It: Thoughts on Life over Sixty.* New York: Newmarket Press, 1990.

———. *The Wonderful Crisis of Middle Age: Some Personal Reflections.* New York: McKay, 1973.

———. *Oh to Be 50 Again! On Being Too Old for a Mid Life Crisis.* New York: Times Books, 1986.

Loren, Sophia. *Women and Beauty.* New York: William Morrow & Co., Inc., 1984.

Miller, Ruth Wagner, and Sandy Parks. *Success Through Color Charisma.* Atlanta: Color Charisma Press, 1983.

Monaghan, Patricia. *The New Book of Goddesses and Heroines.* St. Paul: Llewellyn, 1997.

Monahan, Marta, with Jeff Andrus. *Strength of Character and Grace.* Los Angeles: Vittorio Media, Inc., 1999.

Morgenstern, Julie. *Organizing from the Inside Out.* New York: Henry Holt & Co., 1998.

Morris, Edwin T. *Fragrance: The Story of Perfume from Cleopatra to Chanel.* New York: Charles Scribner's Sons, 1984.

Newman, Cathy. *Perfume.* Washington, D.C.: National Geographic Society, 1998.

Niven, David, Ph.D. *The 100 Simple Secrets of Happy People.* San Francisco: HarperSanFrancisco, 2000.

Oakes, John. *The Book of Perfumes.* New York: HarperCollins, 1996.

Orman, Suze. *The 9 Steps to Financial Freedom.* New York: Three Rivers Press, 2000.

———. *The Courage to Be Rich.* New York: Riverhead Books, 1999.

Peck, M. Scott, M.D. *The Road Less Traveled.* New York: Simon & Schuster, 1978.

Perry, Joan, with Dolores Barclay. *A Girl Needs Cash.* New York: Random House, 1997.

Preston, James J. *Mother Worship.* Chapel Hill: University of North Carolina Press, 1982.

Reid, Lori. *Color Book.* London: Connections Book Publishing Ltd., 2001.

Rountree, Cathleen. *On Women Turning 60.* New York: Harmony Books, 1997.

Scarisbrick, Diana. *Tiara.* San Francisco: Chronicle Books, 2000.

Simpson, Liz. *Awakening Your Goddess.* New York: Barrons, 2001.

Stephens, Autumn. *Out of the Mouths of Babes: Quips and Quotes from Wildly Witty Women.* Berkeley, California: Conari Press, 2000.

Stuart, Anne, speech, *"Boas and the Blues,"* www.anne-stuart.com/page8.html.

Tartaglia, Louis A., M.D. *Flawless!* New York: William Morrow & Co., 1999.

Too, Lillian. *The Complete Illustrated Guide to Feng Shui*. Shaftesbury, Dorset: Element Books Limited, reprinted Barnes and Noble Books, 1996.

Travis, David. *The Land and People of Italy*. New York: HarperCollins Publishers, 1992.

Underhill, Paco. *Why We Buy: The Science of Shopping*. New York: Simon & Schuster, 1999.

Waldherr, Kris. *The Book of Goddesses*. Hillsboro, Oregon: Beyond Words, 1995.

Williamson, Marianne. *A Woman's Worth*. New York: Random House, Inc., 1993.

Winter, Jane Kohen. *Cultures of the World—Italy*. New York: Marshall Cavendish, 1995.

Winter, Ruth. *The Smell Book: Scents, Sex and Society*. New York: J. B. Lippincott Co., 1976.

Wright, Machaelle Small. *Behaving as if the God in All Life Mattered*. Warrenton, Virginia: Perelandra, Ltd., 1987.

MAGAZINE ARTICLES

Ceria, Melissa. "Buy Me a Dream," *Harper's Bazaar*, January 2002, 47–48

Jones, Ann. "Women of the World," *Marie Claire*, November 2001, 76–82.

Robb Report, various issues. Malibu, California: Robb Media, 2001, 2002.

Sarris, Andrew. "In a Class by Herself: Catherine Deneuve," *Town & Country*, January 2002.

INTERNET SOURCES

http://arts.endow.gov/artforms/Music/musictherapy.html, "The Music of Healing," article by Karen R. Nelson, 2001.

http://hometown.aol.com/Usmile2743/humor.humor_heals. html

http://members.aol.com/ ht_a/Usmile2743/humor.notSOfunny.html?mtbrand=AOL_US

http://www.psychjournal.com/newman.htm

http://www.tricolors.com

http://www.aloha.net/-mahalo/charo/

http://us.imdb.com/Name?Charo/

http://www.clubjosh.com/charo/

http://www.bombshells.org/gallery/miranda/

http://www.iamdanica.com

http://www.truecolor.com

http://www.miraglow.com

http://www.true.aromatherapy.com

MOVIE

The Wizard of Oz, Loew's Inc., 1939, renewed 1966, Metro-Goldwyn-Mayer.

The authors are grateful to the following publishers, individuals, and companies for permission to reprint excerpts from selected materials as noted below.

Bullock, Sandra. Copyright © May 2002 by *Marie Claire*. Reprinted with permission of *Marie Claire*.

Buss, Jeanie. Reprinted with permission of the author.

Cher. Copyright © October 1994 by Brant Publications. Used with permission of *Interview* magazine.

Frank, Paul. Reprinted with permission of Paul Frank Industries Inc.

Goldberg, Whoopi. Copyright © March 2000 by Meredith Corporation. All rights reserved. Used with the permission of *Ladies' Home Journal*.

Hopper, Admiral Grace. *LHJ's 100 Most Important Women of the 20th Century,* Copyright © March 1999 by Meredith Corporation. All rights reserved. Used with the permission of *Ladies' Home Journal*.

Kamali, Norma. As told to Lois Jay Johnson. Copyright © 2001 by Meredith Corporation. Used with permission of *More* magazine.

Lauder, Estee. Reprinted with permission of The Estee Lauder Company.

Parton, Dolly. Reprinted by permission of the author.

Reams, Susan. Reprinted by permission of the author.

Rivers, Joan. Reprinted by permission of the author.

Rowley, Cynthia. From an interview in *Marie Claire,* Copyright © 1999. Reprinted by permission of *Marie Claire*.

Sarandon, Susan. Copyright © February 2002 by Meredith Corporation. Used with permission of *More* magazine.

Starhawk. *Dreaming the Dark*. Copyright © 1982, 1988, 1997 by Miriam Simos. Reprinted by permission of Beacon Press, Boston.

Stewart, Liza. Reprinted by permission of the author.

Stuart, Anne. From her address, "Boa and the Blues." Reprinted by permission of the author.

The authors wish to thankfully acknowledge the following for their permission to quote their work: Suze Orman, Barbara de Angelis, Chellie Campbell, Sarah Ban Breathnach, and Simple Abundance Press.

*W*e would love to know about your adventures on your journey to Divadom. Continue the fun and share Diva secrets. Visit us at www.iamdiva.com or e-mail us at: thefourdivas@iamdiva.com. You can also reach us at:

The Four Divas
c/o I Am Diva
1960 Del Amo Blvd.
Suite A
Torrance, CA 90501